# Narrating the Organization

# New Practices of Inquiry

A Series Edited by

Deirdre N. McCloskey and John S. Nelson

BARBARA    CZARNIAWSKA

# Narrating the Organization
## Dramas of Institutional Identity

THE UNIVERSITY OF CHICAGO PRESS

Chicago and London

BARBARA CZARNIAWSKA holds the Chair in Management at the Gothenburg Research Institute, School of Economics and Commercial Law, Gothenburg University, Sweden.

The University of Chicago Press, Chicago 60637
The University of Chicago Press, Ltd., London
© 1997 by The University of Chicago
All rights reserved. Published 1997
Printed in the United States of America
06 05 04 03 02 01 00 99 98 97   1 2 3 4 5
ISBN: 0-226-13228-5 (cloth)
ISBN: 0-226-13229-3 (paper)

Library of Congress Cataloging-in-Publication Data

Czarniawska-Joerges, Barbara.
    Narrating the organization: dramas of institutional identity /
Barbara Czarniawska.
        p.    cm.—(New practices of inquiry)
    Includes bibliographical references and index.
    ISBN 0-226-13228-5 (cloth: alk. paper).—ISBN 0-226-13229-3
(paper: alk. paper)
    1. Organizational behavior.  2. Public administration.
3. Business anthropology.  4. Organizational behavior—Sweden—Case
Studies.  I. Title.  II. Series.
HD58.7.C93  1997
302.3'5—dc20                                            96-20954
                                                            CIP

⊗ The paper used in this publication meets the minimum requirements of the American National Standard for Information Sciences—Permanence of Paper for Printed Library Materials, ANSI Z39.48-1984.

# Contents

Acknowledgments   vii

Introduction, or Complex Phenomena
Need Complex Metaphors   1

PART ONE:  **From Narrative to Organization Studies**

ONE   The Narrative in Culture Studies   11

TWO   On Dramas and Autobiographies in the
Organizational Context   30

THREE   Interpretive Studies of Organizations:
The Logic of Inquiry   54

PART TWO:  **Tales from a Public Sector**

FOUR   Enacting Routines for Change   75

FIVE   Serials: Innovation and Repetition   100

SIX   Talking Numbers: Preferences and Traditions   122

SEVEN   A Quest for Identity   142

PART THREE:  **Interpretive Turbulence in
Organization Fields**

EIGHT   Paradoxical Material   167

NINE   Changing Devices   179

TEN   Constructing Narratives   195

Notes   207

References   213

Index   227

# Acknowledgments

This book has been made possible thanks to the financial support of the Swedish Council for the Humanities and Social Sciences Research and the institutional support of the School of Economics and Management at Lund University, Sweden. In terms of intellectual support, I have received both help and criticism (I imagine this makes it helpful criticism) from Deirdre N. McCloskey, Mary Jo Hatch, Bernward Joerges, Hans Lindqvist, Rolland Munro, and John Van Maanen. I am truly grateful to all of them, and still amazed at the amount of time and work they willed to my enterprise. I am grateful to Nancy Adler for help in struggling with my adopted language, and to Jessica Enevold for aiding me in the work of manuscript preparation.

The main ideas in the second part of chapter 2 were earlier sketched in "Autobiographical acts and organizational identities," in Stephen Linstead, Robert Grafton Small, and Paul Jefcutt, eds., *Understanding Management* (London: Sage, 1995). An earlier version of chapter 6 appeared in *Accounting, Management, and Organization Technologies* 2(4): 221–39 (1992), published by Elsevier Science Ltd. Permission from both publishers is gratefully acknowledged.

# Introduction, or Complex Phenomena Need Complex Metaphors

My purpose is to tell of bodies which have been transformed into shapes of different kinds. You heavenly powers, since you were responsible for those changes, as for all else, look favorably on my attempts, and spin an unbroken thread of verse. . . .

Ovid, *Metamorphoses*

## Transformations and Metamorphoses

Whichever way one looked among Western cultures at the beginning of the 1990s, one could see some sort of puzzling institutional transformation on the go. Things were bursting out of their labels, and words grew short of events. Frantic attempts at interpretation were multiplying. In the United States, industry was being reengineered as the latest installment in the drama of competition with Japan, while the education system was being reformed to meet the demand for political correctness—or to counteract the moral bankruptcy of the nation, depending on one's ideological persuasion. "Common" Europe was calling for many local transformations, which proved very tame, however, compared to the transformations desired or already visible in "not-yet-Common" Europe. In local contexts many transformations were engendered—in the welfare states by the legitimacy crisis for the social-democratic ideology, and in the postcommunist countries by the conversion of centrally planned economies into market economies. Peaceful economics was accompanied by war and destruction, for reasons nobody seems to understand although many try to explain.

Few would disagree that all this was taking place in societies that are organized, through and through. This was pointed out long ago by Dwight Waldo and has been powerfully restated by Charles Perrow. Even fewer, however, would be able to offer a convincing reading of all these developments by referring to organization theory. Knowledge about the actual functioning of formal organizations has been successfully blackboxed, in line with a conceptual tradition that has always seen them as "instruments." When it comes to social issues, researchers have explored problem families and the despair of fatal illness in great depth, but knowledge of everyday organizational life is largely limited to employees and, fragmentarily, to their families.

Why should this be so? There is no need to invoke conspiracy theory, but many factors contributing to this state of affairs do have a clear political character and are sometimes part of the political game within the discipline in question. Thus, economic organizations seem to be reserved for the scrutiny of economics, which, true to the science-fiction character of its models, has no time or patience for what actually goes on in the organizations in the field—or, one could say, in organization fields. Business administration, public administration, organizational psychology, and sociology are all too amorphous, as well as lacking any unequivocal legitimacy base of their own, to stand up to economics. When society (that is, the media) wants to know anything about business corporations, public administration, or even the finances of a new fundamentalist sect, economists are asked for their opinion, which promptly arrives—general, abstract, and hypothetical.

Nor are those involved in real-world organizations willing to reveal the everyday muddle to be found there. Instead, we get glossy (and glossing) annual reports, or stories of villains and heroes. Ordinary organization people get little attention, and when they do, as in William Hollingworth Whyte Jr.'s *Organization Man,* it is their lives in the suburbs that are the real focus of interest.

Artists find organizational life dull as a possible subject. Those who have had direct experience of real-life organizations—Italo Svevo, Franz Kafka, René-Victor Pilhes, or Joseph Heller—have written fascinating and insightful stories about them, but they are few. Thus, the most pervasive social phenomenon of contemporary Western societies remains unknown, glossed over, revealed in snatches, or disguised as something else: a romance, a spy story. After all, those genres have a more apt conceptual apparatus than social theory.

Viewed from within the dualistic frames of the nineteenth-century theories, the world seems to have become full of monsters. What Bruno Latour has called the proliferation of hybrids is taking place before our shocked eyes. Companies meddle in politics while public administration enters the market, the global seeks to control the local while the local constructs and subverts the global, and people go networking in virtual meeting rooms. Citizens become customers, employees become economic citizens, public becomes private, and private goes public as identities multiply.

All this seems to provoke a variety of reactions, from indignation to fear to celebration.

Whichever camp one chooses to join, one thing seems clear: the inherited vocabulary does not help us to understand the ongoing processes; the given devices cannot shape the ever richer material. Although this is happening in all disciplines, I shall concentrate on some difficulties—and opportunities—within my own discipline of organization studies.

## Inherited Devices

The mainstream conceptual apparatus of organization theory goes back to the 1960s and is metaphorically derived from open systems theory. Its main concepts are "organizations," separate units divided by "boundaries" from their "environments" and related to them by "adaptation." This conceptual move no doubt seemed very attractive at the time of its construction, providing a kind of middle space between mechanistic Taylorism and idealist administration theory. Alas, "what is a necessary step in the construction of knowledge at one moment, becomes an impediment at another" (Lewontin 1995, 131).

Lewontin is commenting here on another move to the same effect—that performed by Darwin. By introducing "organism," "environment," and "adaptation," Darwin sought to mechanize biology, at that time still all too prone to mystification and idealism. At present, however, this set of metaphors does not seem to be doing good work in either human biology or organization theory. The environment is not a preexisting set of problems to which an organism, or an organization, must find solutions; the problems were created by the organisms or organizations in the first place. The environment of organisms consists to a great extent of other organisms, and the environment of organizations consists to an even greater extent of other organizations. By the same token, the notion of adaptation is misleading when applied to understanding the relationship between an organism and its environment. Lewontin suggests "construction," while organization theorists like Karl Weick and Bo Hedberg talked of "enactment" in the same vein. Further, while it can be claimed that organisms have boundaries separating them from their environments, it is much more difficult to apply the notion of preexisting boundaries to organizations: mergers, acquisitions, transnationals, and networks make such an idea appear highly tenuous.

It therefore makes sense to ask, what is the use of the open systems metaphor? When the list of differences becomes longer than the list of similarities, when most of the related concepts (environment, adaptation, and even evolution; see Gould 1995) appear to be metaphorically deceptive, it seems obvious that what is needed is a new vocabulary.

Where can one turn in the search for such a new vocabulary, or at least for inspiration? The hermeneutical principle recommends explaining the less known with the help of the better known. This is why Darwin used economic metaphors for his theory of evolution, and this is what makes it so strange that the social sciences look for metaphors in biology. After all, as Rorty caustically pointed out, "if the body had been easier to understand, nobody would have thought that we had a mind" (1980, 239). I therefore suggest that we turn elsewhere in our search for metaphors. A great many vistas are open to us, of which I suggest three: anthropology, literary theory, and the institutional school within sociology.

## Anthropology as a Frame of Mind

The reason I suggest anthropology, and more specifically ethnographically oriented field studies, as an important asset in understanding institutional transformations has little to do with the traditional empiricism that claims the epistemological superiority of "sense data." As Rorty said, it is a mistake to think of other people's accounts of their actions or cultures as epistemically privileged in relation to the view of an observer. "But it is not a mistake to think of it as morally privileged. We have a duty to listen to his account, not because he has privileged access to his own motives but because he is a human being like ourselves" (Rorty 1982, 202). Anthropology is more a moral imperative than a methodological safeguard. Many social science studies can be seen as a monumental exercise in narcissism: the small world of the social sciences and its various preoccupations becomes magnified and projected on the screen of the global world. "The Other" remains but a deviant version of ourselves.

Within the academic discipline of anthropology, however, the study of the researcher's own country has been—and still is—felt to be a little suspect. Edmund Leach, in one of his last writings, warned, "at the cost of being accused of being old-fashioned," against anthropologists studying their own cultures, because their vision will be prejudiced by their life experience (1985, 10). One could say that this kind of influence is unavoidable, no matter where the field study is made, and it has become more common among anthropologists to account for their prejudices rather than to hide them. I have a feeling, though, that the multifarious arguments against studying "one's own culture" originated at a time when it seemed possible to speak of "one's culture" with the certainty of referring to a homogeneous and well-delineated way of life (if such a time ever existed). I, for one, would find it very difficult to establish what is my own culture, being a Polish-Swedish hybrid who communicates in English.

Once this perception is abandoned, it becomes clear that the differentiation, the mobility, and the dense communications in contemporary societies favor, rather than "cultures," more comprehensible social units such as "profession," "network of action," "lifestyle," or some other kind of "interpretive community." The Other does not always live in an exotic country, or even in an immigrant ghetto. And the purpose of studying other people is not to classify them, or to explain one's own remote origins, but "to enlarge the possibility of an intelligible discourse between people quite different from one another in interest, outlook, wealth, and power, and yet contained in a world where, tumbled as they are into endless connection, it is increasingly difficult to get out of each other's way" (Geertz 1988, 147).

Anthropology, thus understood, calls for a new set of strategies. Bruno Latour (1993b) speaks of *symmetrical anthropology*. To Latour's three laws of symmetry (same language for truth and errors, humans and nonhumans, Western and non-Western), I would like to add a fourth. Whereas the early anthropologists always studied people who were in a subordinate position (either being defined as "savage" or simply being dominated by a Western invasion), organization and management scholars study their equals, often their superiors. They study the ways in which things are done by people with the same education, coming from the same tradition, and advancing the same claims about knowledge validity as themselves. It is an anthropology of doppelgänger, which creates new perils but also new possibilities (as intuited by David Lodge in *Nice Work*). It requires the same vocabulary for anthropological and nonanthropological practice.

## Narrative Approaches to Institutions

One way of producing knowledge relevant to our times may lead to the adoption of a narrative approach to knowledge in, and about, organizations. Launched by Jean-François Lyotard, the notion of narrative knowledge comes close to the metaphor of the world-as-text; it alerts us to the ways in which the stories that rule our lives and our societies are constructed. Further, it can generate unusual insights by bringing organization studies closer to culture studies and literary theory.

The claim that the main source of knowledge in the practice of organizing is narrative is not likely to provoke much opposition. I suggest, however, that the next step should be taken. Acknowledging the existence and importance of narratives means that we need adequate devices for interpreting them, which leads us in turn to literary theory. Literary categories such as genres can serve as metaphors, or even analogies, for other kinds of institutions.

This book is an attempt to develop an interpretive device by combining insights from anthropology, literary theory, and institutionalism. The field material to which this device has been applied is extracted from my study of a transformation of the Swedish public sector, published under the title *Styrningens paradoxer* (The Paradoxes of Control, 1992b). This transformation could prove to be of global importance. On the one hand, the crisis is familiar to those countries that shared the same welfare philosophy and experienced similar problems, such as Germany and France, as well as to countries whose welfare ideology in its "privatized" version came to be a dominant influence in the 1980s, such as the United States and the United Kingdom. On the other hand, there are historical grounds for believing that Sweden could become a sort of research laboratory in matters of public administration, where new solutions are not so much "found" as constructed and tried out.

Here, I shall tackle this material with the help of an interpretive device constructed by drawing on narrative approaches as developed by authors such as Jerome Bruner, Alasdair MacIntyre, Walter Fisher, Donald Polkinghorne, and others, and combining them with the new institutionalist approaches as presented by Paul DiMaggio, James G. March, John W. Meyer, Johan Olsen, Walter Powell, and others.

The attraction of a narrative approach is that it pays attention to the *forms* in which knowledge is cast and the effects that these have on an audience, scientific or otherwise. The attraction of institutionalism lies for me in its central theme, namely, the origins and development of institutions, which is of crucial importance to an understanding of contemporary life. While the various competing individualist and rationalist perspectives have many uses, they fail to grasp the collective character of organizational life, which is the main concern of institutionalists. Further, these perspectives are unable or unwilling to provide insights into their own origins. Institutional analyses, in their emphasis on the specific temporal and spatial locations of institutions, are fully able to do so. And, it may be added, the new institutionalism happens to agree with (although it does not require) the constructionist view of the world that underlies my analysis.

The combination of narrative and institutionalist approaches can hardly be called new, however. Institutionalist sociology since its inception focused its attention on precisely the kind of transformations that interest me in this book, and made ample use of literary devices in doing so. It is enough to mention W. I. Thomas and Florian Znaniecki's reading of the letters of Polish immigrants and their life histories, William F. Whyte's *Street Corner Society*, or Robert E. Park's "sociological journalism" influenced by Burke's dramatistic analysis. In particular, the Chicago School tradition (for historical studies, see Stein 1960; Bulmer 1984; Lindner 1996) has produced works that perhaps became legendary too soon—that is, before their impact had been fully realized.

The affinity between institutionalism and literary theory does not go in one direction only. In the guise of genre theory, literary theory in fact offers an advanced theory of institutions. Commenting on the latest developments in literary theory—signalized, among other things, by exchanging the name "literary criticism" for "literary theory"—Elisabeth Bruss claimed that these were largely the result of an opening up of the discipline to social science concerns (Bruss 1982).

A conscious cross-borrowing of rhetorical figures and textual strategies that have enriched other disciplines can thus only benefit organization studies. I will be recalling similar genre blurring in several disciplines: economics, business and public administration, sociology, anthropology. All have built connections with literary theory: think of D. N. McCloskey's works in economics, Richard H. Brown's in sociology, Clifford Geertz's in anthropology. These authors testify to a "literary turn" that is replacing the "linguistic turn" in the social sciences. Suggesting that literary criticism can offer economics a model for self-understanding, McCloskey cogently explained the attraction of such a turn: "Literary criticism does not merely pass judgments of good or bad; in its more recent forms the question seems hardly to arise. Chiefly it is concerned with making readers see how poets and novelists accomplish their results" (1986, xix). In times of increasing specialization and difficulty in communications over disciplinary borders, such concerns can only be welcomed. This book seeks to apply them to organization studies.

Behind my present effort, and behind all my work, lies the idea of science not as an accumulating body of knowledge but as a conversation (Oakeshott 1959). I will return to this idea now and again in my text, but it also finds an expression on a formal level. If science is conversation, then scientific texts are voices in it. In order to follow the conversation, it is important to know who is talking to whom, who is answering whose questions. Therefore, all sources discussed in the text refer to the original edition. For direct quotes, I add the date of the particular edition used. I hope that this small innovation will help the reader to locate the time and the place where the voices were first heard.

# PART ONE

# From Narrative
# to Organization Studies

# The Narrative in Culture Studies

## Individual and Social Life as Narrative

The idea of social and individual life as a narrative can be found in many texts throughout history. In an essay from 1966, Roland Barthes proclaimed the social centrality of narrative:

> The narratives of the world are numberless. Narrative is first and foremost a prodigious variety of genres, themselves distributed amongst different substances. . . . Able to be carried by articulate language, spoken or written, fixed or moving images, gestures, and the ordered mixture of all these substances, narrative is present in myth, legend, fable, tale, novella, epic, history, tragedy, drama, comedy, mime, painting, . . . stained glass windows, cinema, comics, news item, conversation. Moreover, under this almost infinite diversity of forms, narrative is present in every age, in every place, in every society; it begins with the very history of mankind and there nowhere is nor has been a people without narrative. (Barthes 1966/1977, 79)

The structuralist analysis of the narrative that followed Barthes's manifesto in the 1970s did not prove immediately attractive to current social thinking. It was rather the poststructuralist extensions of and oppositions to structural analysis that reclaimed the narrative for general attention (Harari 1979), probably because the structuralists still cherished an ambition to tell grand stories and to compete with previous grand stories. The attraction of the narrative approach, as I shall present it here, lies in its pragmatism rather than in any lofty ideological premises. Narrative may not be the only way to approach contemporary organizations, but it does seem handy for the purpose.

One of the important attempts to extend the use of the notion of narrative beyond literature was formulated by Alasdair MacIntyre, a writer dedicated to issues of moral philosophy (1981). A reader might ask, is moral philosophy not a far cry from organization theory, even allowing for the issues of business ethics? A moral philosophy, as MacIntyre is the first to point out, assumes a sociology, or a theory of social life (and vice versa). Any contemporary sociology, on the other hand, must take organizations into account (Perrow 1991). Consequently, business management and public administration play an important role in MacIntyre's reasoning, which in turn makes his theory highly relevant to organization theory.

Let us then begin with the basic tenet of his theory: that social life is a narrative.

There are many possible ways of conceiving a human action. In many texts on management the term *action* is replaced by or used as an alternative for *behavior,* and *organizational behavior* is a term that is taken for granted, unproblematic even for otherwise critical authors and readers. Is there any reason to problematize the difference between action and behavior? There is, if we recall that the notion of "behavioral sciences" goes back to eighteenth-century empiricism, in which the "sense-datum" was proposed as the main unit of cognition and the main object of scientific study. Were we to describe our experience in terms of sensory description, however, "we would be confronted with not only uninterpreted, but an uninterpretable world" (MacIntyre 1981/1990, 79). Such a world would indeed be a world of behaviors, both meaningless and mechanical, because if sense-data were to become the basis for the formulation of laws, all reference to intentions, purposes, and reasons—all that which changes behavior into a human action—would have to be removed.[1]

We cannot understand human conduct if we ignore its intentions, and we cannot understand human intentions if we ignore the settings in which they make sense (Schütz 1973). Such settings may be institutions, sets of practices, or some other contexts created by humans—contexts that have a history, within which both particular deeds and whole histories of individual actors can be and have to be situated, in order to be intelligible. "Human beings can be held to account for that of which they are the authors; other beings cannot" (MacIntyre 1981/1990, 209).

Thus, assuming the centrality of human *action* in the sense of an intentional human act taking place between actors in a given social order (Harré 1982), we can further relate the concept of action to three relevant traditions of thought. One is literary hermeneutics as represented by Ricoeur (1981), who suggested that meaningful action is to be considered as a text, and vice versa. Meaningful action shares the constitutive features of the text: it becomes objectified by inscription, which frees it from its agent; it has relevance beyond its immediate context; and it can be read like an "open work." The theory of interpretation can thus be extended to the field of social sciences (ibid.).

The second important tradition is that of phenomenology, introduced into the social sciences by Alfred Schütz and his pupils, Peter Berger and Thomas Luckmann. Phenomenology's encounter with American pragmatism, which is the third tradition of importance here, produced two offshoots that are relevant in the present context. One is symbolic interactionism as represented by Herbert Blumer and Howard S. Becker, which has been transported into organization studies by John Van Maanen (see, e.g., 1982). Another is ethnomethodology as developed by Harold Garfinkel, Aaron Cicourel, and Harvey Sacks. Their inspiration was taken up with particular success by the British sociologist David Silverman (see, e.g., Silverman 1970; Silverman and Jones 1976; and Silverman and Torode 1980).

Ethnomethodology, despite its essentialist undertones,[2] is significant here because it introduces the notion of *accountability* as a central concept in the understanding of social action. Accountability is the main bond of human interactions, indeed the main social bond. Conduct can be treated as an action when it can be *accounted for* (a priori, simultaneously, or a posteriori; Harré 1982) in terms that are acceptable in a given social setting. We spend our lives planning, commenting upon, and justifying what we and other people do. Although some of this takes place in imaginary conversations conducted in our heads, most takes place in "real" conversations with other people.[3]

One criticism of ethnomethodological thinking is that it has difficulty in explaining the connections between various rules of accounting, which appear to be ascribed to specific situations. Latour (1994) claims that ethnomethodology can explain sociality but not society: there is nothing to fix various actions, to make situations repeatable. For him, technology is the fixing and connecting device, and in the present context it would be the reproduction technologies that permit the locating of present conversations in history, that is, in past conversations. By observing how conversations are repeated and how they change, we can classify them according to their genre, as in literary critique. In order to do this, we have to see conversations as dramatized stories, in which the participants are actors, authors, directors, and producers. In other words, *conversations in particular, and human actions in general, are enacted narratives.*

I will concentrate on the "enactedness" or dramatic character of organizational narratives in chapter 2. For the moment it is most important to note that the common way of understanding human action is by placing it in a narrative, that is, a narrative of an individual history, which in turn must be placed in a narrative of social history or in a history of the narrative.

This statement must be unpacked to reveal several substatements that in fact it entails. Regarding the first narrative, that of an individual history (and the topic of chapter 3), its importance is connected with the fact that in order to understand our own lives, we put them into narrative form; and we do the same when we try to understand the lives of other people. Thus, every action acquires meaning by acquiring a place in a narrative of life or, as it will be called in this book, in a narrative of identity. "Living is like writing a book" is a popular claim bordering on cliché.

This sounds as though we could tell stories as we please, and in so doing shape our lives as we see fit. This is actually a typical criticism of constructivism: that it conceives the world as a collection of subjectively spun stories. But we are never the sole authors of our own narratives; in every conversation a *positioning* takes place (Davies and Harré 1991), which is accepted, rejected, or improved upon by the partners in the conversation. When a new manager introduces herself to a group of subordinates, she tells them how she wants to be perceived. Their reactions will tell her how much of this has been accepted or rejected, what corrections have been made, and how the members of the group want to be perceived by their new boss. But the end of the introductory meeting does not end the positioning thus begun; this will continue as long as these people work together, and even longer in the history they will tell later.

What is more, other people or institutions sometimes concoct narratives for us, without including us in any conversation; this is what power is about. They decide on our jobs, where we should live, our identities. But even as puppets in a power game, we are still coauthors of history, that other enacted dramatic narrative in which we are also actors.

What is "history" in an age when history has come to an end (Fukuyama 1992), when the metanarratives are dead and have been abandoned (Lyotard 1979)? Answering Lyotard on behalf of the pragmatists, Rorty claims that "we want to drop *meta*narratives, but keep on recounting edifying first-order narratives" (Rorty 1992b, 60). History may be dead, but only if we were attached irreversibly to one specific version of it. Abandoning the modern metanarrative of emancipation does not mean giving up the longing for narratives that we happen to like, in a benign ethnocentrism that values our own way of life but relinquishes the idea of "modernizing" other people who are "underdeveloped," "premodern," or in some other way different from us. Responding to the condemnation of ethnocentrism in Geertz (1988), Rorty says dryly: "We would rather die than be ethnocentric, but ethnocentrism is precisely the conviction that one would rather die than share certain beliefs" (1991, 203). A quest for a good life extends to become a quest for a good society, excluding a missionary zeal that forces other people to adopt our point of view, but including a readiness to listen to other people and their narratives, so that, rather than dying before adopting any of them, we might include them in our own narrative if we happen to like them.

All this may sound like splitting hairs over abstract ideas, but it acquires a very concrete meaning in the context of "the modern crusades" (Kostera 1995) launched by Western business teachers in Eastern Europe. These countries have the right to follow their own quests, and to construct their own "edifying first-order narratives," for which Western narratives could provide inspiration but not a canon.

The question then arises about whether it is in fact possible to construct any shared concepts, whether it is possible to have a conversation, an exchange of narratives, without recourse to a metanarrative of some kind. In answering this, MacIntyre emphasizes the unpredictability of an enacted dramatic narrative of life and history.[4] Such constructing is never finished, and in the negotiation of meaning, the results are forever uncertain. The old metanarratives sinned in their ambition to end a conversation by trying to predict its outcome. If a canon is already known, there is nothing left to talk about.

The narrative structure of human life requires unpredictability, and this is, paradoxically, why the alleged failure of the social sciences is in fact their greatest achievement, namely, their failure to formulate laws and, consequently, to predict. This, according to MacIntyre, should be interpreted not as a defeat but as a triumph, as virtue rather than vice. He adds provocatively that the common claim that the human sciences are young in comparison with the natural sciences is clearly false, and they are in fact as old if not older. And the kind of explanations they offer fit perfectly the kind of phenomena they purport to explain.

Unpredictability[5] does not imply inexplicability. Explanations are possible because there is a certain teleology in all lived narratives. It is a kind of circular teleology that is not given a priori but is created by the narrative. A life is lived with a goal, but the most important aspect of life is the formu-

lation and reformulation of that goal. This circular teleology is what Mac-
Intyre calls a *narrative quest*. A virtuous life, according to him, is a life
dedicated to a quest for the good human life, where the construction of
a definition of a "good life" is a process that ends only when a life comes
to an end. Rather than being defined at the outset, a "good life" acquires
a performative definition through the living of it. A search looks for something that already exists (as in a "search for excellence"); a quest creates
its goal, rather than discovering it. This reasoning has an obvious relevance
in the context of organization theory, where so much attention has been
devoted to "organizational goals." Rationalists defend the notion, pragmatists declare it to be impractical. A narrative view gets rid of the problem
by reinstating the role of goals as both the results and the antecedents of
organizational action. Organizations, as we shall see later, can also be regarded as engaged in a quest for meaning in "their life," which will bestow
meaning on particular actions taken.

How can we relate individual narratives to societal ones? If we want
to understand a society, or some part of a society, we have to discover its
repertoire of legitimate stories and find out how this evolved—what I have
called a history of narratives. Thus, as MacIntyre points out, the chief
means of moral education in premodern societies was the telling of stories
in a genre fitting the kind of society whose story was being told. In the
process of education, or more generally of socialization, individuals were
helped to attribute meaning to their lives by relating these to the legitimate
narrative of the society to which they belonged.[6] Thus, the main narrative
of, and in, heroic societies was epic and saga, whereas the genre of city-
states was tragedy, both reflecting and expressing the prevalent stance toward human fate and human community.

Although neither of these cultures, the heroic societies or the Greek
city-states, was exactly unitary or consistent, MacIntyre nonetheless claims
that medieval cultures first encountered the problem of multiple narratives
on a global scale—with many ideals, many ways of life, many religions.
How, then, can anybody tell a particular story? To begin with, it is obvious
that every age hosts many competing narratives (indeed, periodization itself belongs to one story or another), and in principle one could choose
to relate such a story to any of them. On the other hand, it makes sense
for interpretive purposes to speak of a dominant or prevalent narrative
genre at any one time—what is called in science the mainstream. The novel,
for instance, is regarded as the most characteristic genre of modern times.
Kundera (1988) places Cervantes together with Descartes among the

founders of the Modern Era. Moreover, new genres emerge, such as biography and autobiography (both a consequence of the modern institution of personal identity), while others change their character so that we get "modern poetry," for instance. Thus, when we read Giambattista Vico, we know that we are reading a philosophical treatise, and that it is not a modern one. In this sense genres are like any other institutions, or maybe all institutions are like genres: "A literary institution must reflect and give focus to some consistent need and sense of possibility in the community it serves, but at the same time, a genre helps to define what is possible and to specify the appropriate means for meeting an expressive need" (Bruss 1976, 5).

If we add instrumental needs to expressive needs (or, better still, if we remove a divide between them), then organization theory and practice can be seen as special genres of narrative situated within other narratives of modern (or postmodern) society, so that organization studies can focus on how these narratives of theory and practice are constructed, used, and misused. But before moving on to organizations, let us extend our understanding of the concept of the narrative by examining its uses in the social sciences and humanities. We can start by looking at narrative as a *mode of knowing* and as a *mode of communication,* and go on to consider the role of narrative in the postmodern society and in organizations.

## The Narrative Mode of Knowing

> Knowledge is not the same as science, especially in its contemporary form.
>
> Lyotard, *The Postmodern Condition*

Lyotard contrasted the narrative form of knowledge that was typical of the nonmodern type of society with that modern invention—scientific knowledge. There is a peculiar relationship between the two: while science requires the narrative for its own legitimation (there has to be a story to tell why scientific knowledge is important at all), it repays the favor in poor coin. Not only does it refuse to perform the same service and to legitimate narrative knowledge (with the possible exception of structuralism and formalism in literary theory), but it fiercely denies narrative its legitimacy as a form of knowledge and, above all, demands that the question of knowledge status and legitimation remains taken for granted, unexamined. Paradoxically, however, as the grand narratives of legitimation lost their privileged status, narrative and science both came back into the light of scrutiny.

One of the authors to take up this scrutiny was Jerome Bruner, who compared the *narrative mode of knowing*[7] with the logo-scientific mode, also referred to as paradigmatic (Bruner 1986). The narrative mode of knowing consists in organizing experience with the help of a scheme assuming the intentionality of human action. Using the basic concepts of literary theory, Polkinghorne (1987) followed Bruner's lead in exploring the narrative, an attempt I will quote and will illustrate with organizational examples.

*Plot* is the basic means by which specific events, otherwise represented as lists or chronicles, are brought into one meaningful whole. "The company suffered unprecedented losses" and "the general manager was forced to resign" are two events that call for interpretation. "With the company suffering unprecedented losses, the general manager was forced to resign" is a narrative. The difference lies in the temporal ordering, and thus in a suggested connection between the two. As the example indicates, some kind of causality may be inferred, but it is crucial to see that narrative, unlike science, leaves *open* the nature of the connection.

If the reader recognizes this characteristic of the narrative as what has long been defined as "bad science," that is perfectly correct. The scientific knowledge, itself justified by the metanarrative of progress, immediately turned its back on its legitimating source, which it defined as non-knowledge (Lyotard 1979). But the flexibility of narrative makes it impervious to such a passing (two-hundred-year-long?) fit of temper. This flexibility means that the same set of events can be organized around different plots ("The general manager was forced to resign in spite of the fact that he offered to make good on the company's unprecedented losses"), whereby they acquire a different meaning. A cultural tradition, and a genre as a literary institution within it, is defined by a repertoire of plots constituting a given convention. Psychologist Jean Matter Mandler (1984), among others, applied the categorization of plots and types of stories to the stories of life.

Polkinghorne (1987) discusses also a special type of *explanation* that is possible within a narrative. His idea comes very close to Ricoeur's (1981) suggestion that "understanding" can be reconciled with "explanation" in an interpretation of a text (by combining hermeneutics and semiotics), in the same way as "motives" can be reconciled with "causes" in an interpretation of human action. Within the logo-scientific mode of knowing, an explanation is achieved by recognizing an event as an instance of a general law, or as belonging to a certain category. Within the narrative mode of knowing, an explanation consists in relating an event to a human project.

> When a human event is said not to make sense, it is usually not because a person is unable to place it in the proper category. The difficulty stems, instead, from a person's inability to integrate the event into a plot whereby it becomes understandable in the context of what has happened. . . . Thus, narratives *exhibit* an explanation instead of demonstrating it. (Polkinghorne 1987, 21)

The final relevant element in Polkinghorne's elaboration of the notion of narrative is his triple idea of *narrative presentation*. The adjective *narrative* can refer to three different presentations. One is a presentation directed toward oneself, a story we tell to ourselves to make sense of what we are doing ("I am now writing a book"). By definition, this—unlike the other two—is a presentation that cannot be witnessed by anybody and is thus of no interest to organization researchers. The second is the presentation of a story to others by telling, writing, or enacting it (sometimes stylized as the first type—I do not usually tell *myself* that I am writing a book). The third is reception—interpreting and understanding a story that is heard or read. Organization research concerns, and consists of, these last two.

While it may be clear that the narrative offers an alternative mode of knowing, the relative advantage of using this mode may remain obscure. Bruner (1990) points out that in narrative it is the *sequentiality* (temporal order of events) rather than the truth or falsity of story elements that determines the plot, and thus the power of the narrative as a story. A story that says, "The general manager was forced to resign, and then it rained for a week," that is, a story with an incomprehensible plot, will need some additional elements to make sense of it, even though the two events and their temporal connection may well be true and correct in themselves. Bruner calls this the narrative's *indifference to extralinguistic reality* (1990, 44), which is compensated for by an extreme sensibility to the reality of the *parole*. In other words, there are no structural differences between fictional and empirical narratives, and their respective attraction is not determined by their claim to be fact or fiction. It is situationally negotiated—or, rather, arrived at, since contingency plays as much a part in the process as aesthetics or politics. This trait is in fact noted by most of the analysts of the narrative, but is then put aside with some embarrassment, to be triumphantly dragged out again by the advocates of the logo-scientific mode of knowing. What kind of knowing is this, which does not allow for recognizing whether a story is true or invented?[8]

Bruner claims, however, that this peculiarity of narrative accounts for most of its power. This can be better understood in light of the role of narrative in what can be called "folk human sciences," people's nonscientific explanations and interpretations of life events. These explanations and interpretations are most crucial in establishing the connections between the exceptional and the ordinary. So-called folk psychology thrives on the ordinary, on what is "normal," usual, and expected, to which it attributes legitimacy and authority. At the same time, however, it has effective means at its disposal for rendering the unexpected intelligible, namely, the narrative. "The function of the story is to find an intentional state that mitigates or at least makes comprehensible a deviation from a canonical cultural pattern" (Bruner 1990, 49–50). This is possible because the power of the story depends not on its reference to some extralinguistic reality but on its openness for negotiating meaning.

As stories explaining deviations are socially sensitive, a form of story whose power does not reside in the difference between fact and fiction is convenient for such negotiations. One or many alternative narratives are always in the offing: "Forced by intrigues in the board, the general manager resigned. The result was such a collapse in morale among the staff that the company suffered unprecedented losses." The events acquire a meaning by the application of abduction, which introduces a hypothetical connection. Yet another story ("The general manager took all the customers with him, and as a result . . .") might offer a better or more convincing explanation, without ever challenging the truth or falsity of the story elements. We now have five versions of the story about the general manager and the losses, which are built around the same events. There is no way of deciding among them except by negotiation—between the author and the reader (whereby the author tries to get the upper hand but the reader has the last word) or, as in organizational life, between various readers. Stories, claims Bruner, are "especially viable instruments for social negotiation."

The "method of negotiating and renegotiating meanings by the mediation of narrative interpretation," it seems to Bruner, "is one of the crowning achievements of human development in the ontogenetic, cultural and phylogenetic sense of that expression" (1990, 67). The human species developed a "protolinguistic" readiness for the narrative organization of experience. This primitive disposition of the child is encouraged and elaborated in the course of life, exploiting the richness of the existing repertoire of stories and plots. Later it will enrich, challenge, and continue this repertoire.

The analogy between the socialization of a child and an organizational newcomer is obvious, but I want to carry the point even further. The main fount of organizational knowledge is the narrative. Although my whole book is dedicated to this point, there is still a "she who has a hammer sees a world of nails" argument against it. So allow me a self-reflective digression: how do academics learn their dual research-and-teaching profession? From the two-by-two variable models, or by asking their colleagues how they went about it? In all their different versions, organizational stories capture organizational life in a way that no compilation of facts ever can; this is because they are carriers of life itself, not just "reports" on it.

After more than twenty years of field organization research, I see with increasing clarity why analysts of the Modern Era suggested that science had replaced religion. Logo-scientific knowledge is granted to the members of the organization, be it a university, a company, or a local government, as grace is granted on Sundays in church. Awed and impressed, the actors "go home" and, dreaming the dreams of radical betterment, do as they did yesterday or as their best chum told them to. Intellectuals may live *off* scientific knowledge but not *by* it. Such "ignorance," fed by traditional habits of acquiring knowledge, costs us a great deal, but it may also have saved us from destruction by a modernism enjoying total success.

Throughout this book I shall try to maintain a value balance between opposites: routine and change, narrative and science. This is not a refusal to commit myself but an attempt to demonstrate that it is not one or the other part of these pairs of opposites but a balance between them that feeds the dynamics of organizational life. Thus, it should be seen not as a tipping of the balance but as a commonsensical observation, when I now point out that the major mode of communication, in purely statistical terms, is in fact narrative.

## Narrative as Communicating Mode

Like Molière's M. Jourdain, who discovered that he had been speaking prose all his life, Walter Fisher when reading MacIntyre's work suddenly understood that his own work in the area of communication had stemmed from a conception of human being as *Homo narrans* (Fisher 1984). From this emerged an attempt to combine the narrative and paradigmatic modes of knowing in what he calls a *narrative paradigm* of communication.

The narrative paradigm is based on a notion of *narrative rationality* (Fisher 1987), in contrast to the conventional model of formal rationality, whereby human communication is supposed to follow the rules of formal logic.[9] Fisher's redefined rationality involves the principles of *narrative probability* (a story's coherence and integrity) and *narrative fidelity* (a story's credibility established by the presence of "good reasons," i.e., "accurate assertions about social reality")(Fisher 1987). This redefinition of rationality, he claims, provides a radical democratic ground for a social-political critique, inasmuch as it assumes that everybody is capable of narrative rationality; unlike the traditional notion of rationality, it also allows for interpretation of public moral argument. Fisher demonstrates the use of his concepts in his analysis of the nuclear war controversy as a public moral argument (1984) and of the political rhetoric of Ronald Reagan (1987).

Fisher's claim that "all forms of human communication need to be seen fundamentally as stories" (1987, xiii) can be regarded as both narrower and more extensive than MacIntyre's conception of narrative. According to my reading of the latter, narrative is the main form of social life, the main device for making sense of social action. Thus, it either subsumes communication as a kind of action or makes it redundant (everything is "communication"). If, however, we insist on preserving the notion of communication to denote a special kind of social action, we will see that there are other forms of human communication than narrative—which Fisher himself enumerates—such as technical argument, poetic discourse, or such speech acts as those that Gumbrecht (1992) calls description and argumentation.

Some discourses or speech acts may aim at the destruction or at least the interruption of the narrative. The Dada movement in art can provide an extreme example of an experiment in human communication that opposed the storytelling mode, and yet we make sense of it by placing it in the narrative of modern art, or alternatively in the narrative of European history at the moment when post–World War I frustration was at its height (Berman 1992).

Fisher wants also to conduct a "criterial analysis" of narratives: it is not enough for him to see narrative as good or bad *for the purpose at hand,* to paraphrase Schütz. Consequently, he rejects pragmatism while sharing many of its ideas. His understanding of rationality is still geared to the *application of criteria* rather than the *achievement of consensus* (Rorty 1992b). This means that while espousing the narrative mode of knowing, Fisher does not want to abandon the paradigmatic, hence his expression "the narrative paradigm." There must be a priori criteria for what is good or bad in telling stories. This requirement recalls the argument in Habermas (1984) that there has to be a set of criteria for a good dialogue external to the dialogue itself. And Fisher does in fact acknowledge his debt to the German philosopher.

I am dwelling on this issue to emphasize that I adopt a Rortian or pragmatist view. Consequently, while sympathizing with many of Fisher's ideas, I do not espouse his overall purpose. "It is a corollary of the general pragmatist claim that there is no permanent ahistorical metaphysical framework into which everything can be fitted" (Rorty 1992b, 64). I do not accuse Fisher of planning to come up with such a framework, but his criteria certainly look as though they could be fitted into one. Pragmatically again, it is possible to envisage many situations in which the construction of such criteria might well serve a particular purpose. Once they have received a special status, however, they will end up as "principles" and "criteria" usually do: obstructing their own change or reform.

The notion of an "ideal speech situation," coined by Habermas (1984), achieved wide resonance in organization theory and practice, especially as a way of improving organizational communication (Gustavsen 1985). A similar success can be predicted for Fisher's ideas, which lend themselves well to consultancy purposes: with a list of "conditions for a good narrative," organizational communication can surely be improved. And yet understanding of organizational reality, such as informs this book, indicates that such an effort is impossible. "An ideal speech situation" and "a good narrative" are things that have to be locally negotiated and that are valid only for a given time and place. They are results, not preconditions, of organizational communication. Some claim that this phenomenon of the constant construction of society is in itself local and temporal, and belongs to late modernism or postmodernism.

## Narrative in the Postmodern Society

The relevance of narrative to an understanding of social processes can also, and more or less independently of the authors mentioned above, be traced back to Richard Harvey Brown's work on "poetics for sociology" (1977), inspired by the work of Bakhtin (1928). Although Brown presently acknowledges the influence of both MacIntyre and Fisher on his own interest in the role of narrative (1987), his article on "The Position of Narrative in Contemporary Society" appeared as early as 1980. Brown's main idea was that of *symbolic realism* (1977, 1987), which I find very attractive. It postulates that people are creators of their own worlds (in accord with Goodman 1978) while insisting on seeing every pragmatically constructed world as the real one, the one to act on.

Brown also points out the proximity between literary metaphors and the notion of institutions, emphasizing that institutions are not just patterns of actions. What keeps these patterns in place and makes their repetition possible are norms, justifications, rules of accounting—in other words, legitimate interpretations of why things should be done this or some other way. For all the importance of tacit knowledge, there would be no continuity and no civilization if people were not able to narrate their past, present, and future actions to each other. And this was, of course, what my interlocutors in my field study were doing all the time I was in contact with them. Faced with the task of accounting for their actions, they took for granted the need to justify themselves: how else would I know why they did what they did?

The taken-for-grantedness of institutionalized action sometimes leads to the mistaken conclusion that such action does not require to be justified or accounted for. Wrong! It may not invite problematization ("Really? How strange!"), but it assumes an institutionalized account, which in fact is an inseparable part of action itself. It is only the basis for justification ("this is how one acts in a democratic society") which is not questioned further, as it constitutes part of an institutionalized thought structure.

The uniqueness of Brown's way of espousing the narrative mode of knowing is that he does not lose sight of the question of power. This is important since there is much criticism of constructivist theories (to which the narrative approach belongs), allegedly unmasking their apologetic character. There is nothing inherent in the narrative approach to warrant such criticism. A narrative has a world-creating force, but worlds thus created can allow more freedom to some than to others. "The 'rationalization of production' or the 'competition for foreign markets' may narrow the freedom of workers" (Brown 1987, 135), as power is really the *power to define* (Brown 1989). Brown's approach is a disavowal of the conventional critical stance that sees managerial narratives as appertaining to "false consciousness" rather than "direct relations of reality as it is," and also a refusal to take any narrative for granted, if only because there are many competing ones. Organizations need a coherent narrative just as humans do, but there is a vast number of repertoires to reach for.

There is an apparent difference between MacIntyre and Fisher on the one hand and Brown on the other as regards the role of narrative in contemporary society. The first two celebrate narratives, whereas Brown sees them as an endangered species: "Narrative requires a political economy and collective psychology in which a sense of lived connection between personal character and public conduct prevails" (Brown 1987, 144). This condition, Brown claims, is rare in contemporary Western societies, where personal character has become separated from public conduct (see also Giddens 1991 on high modernity). The difference is misleading in that both MacIntyre and Fisher feel there is a need to celebrate narrative precisely because there is a rift between private and public discourse, because the language of virtues has become obsolete (MacIntyre 1981) and because a public moral argument has become an oxymoron in the light of emotive ethics (Fisher 1984, 1987). All three authors—and indeed most of the adherents of the narrative mode of knowing, whether or not they call themselves such—are vitally interested in constructing a public moral discourse that avoids nostalgic trips to the past (especially to totalitarian pasts), and does not stop at denouncing the postmodern fragmentation. They may differ in their view on the ultimate purpose (emancipation for Fisher and Brown, a quest for virtues for MacIntyre, and a fight against cruelty for Rorty), but there is always a moral vision to their theories.[10]

According to this formulation, the narrative approaches seem to be in conflict with the postmodern critique of the narrative. However, it was only the narratives of legitimation, the "metanarratives," that were exposed to the postmodern critique: "the little narrative remains the quintessential form of imaginative invention, most particularly in science" (Lyotard 1979/ 1986, 61). What we observe is a simultaneous "demise of the narrative" (Brown 1987) and a "return of the narrative" (Lyotard 1979), and each of these trends contains further paradoxically combined subtrends.

Thus, when Brown speaks of a "demise of the narrative," he means it literally up to a point: narrative as a literary genre is assigned little value in terms of contemporary aesthetic judgments, and as life imitates art and vice versa, this has an impact on social action. "Narrative is an iconic social representation of moral action, an expression and preparation, therefore, for the largest such representation—the democratic political community" (1987, 157). This is reflected in a linguistic tradition whereby what in English is called "the point of a story" may in other languages be called *moral* (Polish) or *sensmoral* (Swedish). No more, says Brown: the narrative has become an antinarrative because the self and the world are both unaccountable; living and telling have become opposites.

This is troubling only when two further assumptions are made. One is that narrative means the use of naive, unreflective realism or, worse, an authoritative realism that denies any other story. The other is that realism as such has little chance of survival in today's flood of language games. There are many counterexamples to the first assumption. Indeed, who else but Baudrillard offers us the most captivating narratives of current events?[11] As for the second, Tom Wolfe is not the only one who tries to convince us that realism is alive and well (Bradbury 1992). Among examples of the "return of the narrative," Lyotard (1979) counts all paralogical narratives such as Luhmann's systems theory and Feyerabend's antimethod.

In other words, talk of the demise of narrative actually smuggles in another story, although Brown is right in postulating that we need to find forms of narrative that fit our current requirements, including the awareness of the impossibility of a straightforward, authoritative narrative. He may also be right in pointing out that *irony* is a particularly appropriate form of public discourse, as it also "constitutes itself on the awareness of the impossibility of literally 'telling it like it is'" (Brown 1987, 171). Interestingly enough, although "narratives on organizations," that is, organization studies, are usually stylized in the "only true story" format, "narratives in organizations," tales told in the field, are manifold and often ironic.

## Narrative In and On Organizations

Narrative enters organizational studies in at least three forms: organizational research that is written in a storylike way ("tales from the field," to paraphrase the expression in Van Maanen 1988), organizational research that collects organizational stories ("tales of the field"), and organization research that conceptualizes organizational life as story making and organization theory as story reading (interpretive approaches).

### Narrating Organizations

The narrative form of organization studies is easiest to find in case studies: research cases, educational cases, and fictive cases, which all use chronology as the main organizing device. One recent example of such "tales from the field" is Robin Leidner's *Fast Food, Fast Talk* (1993). Leidner studied the process of service work with the help of two cases, McDonald's and Combined Insurance, and offered her readers two narratives, consequently elucidated along theoretical, not normative, lines, which is a common way of combining narrative with the logo-scientific mode of reporting.

Another interesting use of narrative can be found in the case teaching method which exploits, with full intention, the structure of narrative. Students are given the first element of the plot, while the third one is implied (a reverse of the first); their task is to fill in the second, that is, the action. The case concentrates on a detailed description of the original state, which must contain the cues for how to reverse it. The status of the case is halfway between fact and fiction; it is assumed that the case originated in actual research, but it is also taken for granted that the description is heavily stylized to satisfy the demands of the classroom.

Bearing this in mind, one finds it less surprising that even novels are used as cases in teaching management. Literary texts appear in the reading lists of management schools. *Harvard Business Review* encouraged its readers to "read fiction to the bottom line" in order to find managerial wisdom there (DeMott 1989), a suggestion that had been formulated long before by Dwight Waldo (1968). The title of an insightful article by Alvarez and Merchán (1992) summarizes these advantages very well: narrative fiction can play an important role in the development of imagination for action. Yet another possibility is to provide readers with close readings of novels from the standpoint of organization analysis (Czarniawska-Joerges and Guillet de Monthoux 1994). Although the students of organizations will no doubt profit enormously from reading novels themselves, there is an extension of the space of shared meanings that more focused readings can offer: the explicit connection between the narrative and the logo-scientific mode of knowing.

## Collecting Stories

Although the most common early references are Clark (1972) and Mitroff and Kilmann (1975), the institutionalization of the topic of organizational stories in organization theory can be safely located at some point in the early 1980s, as best exemplified in the works of Joanne Martin and her collaborators (e.g., Martin 1982; Martin, Hatch, and Sitkin 1983). Such organizational stories from the field were usually treated analytically by field researchers. Recently, however, they are increasingly retold in a slightly stylized way, in the belief that such stories can teach young students the practices of the field much more successfully than the scientific models. In this context, at least two examples, both of which focus on Anglo-Saxon organizations, are worth mentioning: Frost, Mitchell, and Nord (1978 and subsequent editions), and Sims, Gabriel, and Fineman (1993).

Boland and Tankasi (1995) point out that many well-known studies from the 1980s conceived organizational narratives as artifacts forever

petrified in the organizational reality, "out there" waiting to be "collected."
In time, however, the convention grew broader, as it began to include other
attempts, such as Boje's (1991), Boland's own efforts (1989, 1994), Forester's (1992), and Gabriel's (1995)—all of which accentuate the process of
storytelling as the never-ending construction of meaning in organizations.

### Organizing as Narration

It can be safely repeated after Fisher that narratives are a natural form of
organizational communication if the word *natural* is used to mean "unreflective, easily coming to mind." Fieldwork tends to reveal it in a somewhat
paradoxical way. Trained in "scientific" techniques of data collecting, I
tended to structure my interviews along usual analytical lines, my interest
in the narrative notwithstanding. "What are the most acute problems you
are experiencing today?" and "Can you compare your present situation
with that of two years ago?" are questions that will raise no eyebrows;
researchers ask people in the field to compare, to abstract, to generalize.
Some of my interlocutors would bravely engage in the logical exercise I demanded, but most would break through my structure, saying, "Let
me tell you first how all it started," or "You need some more background
first." Upon which they would engage in producing a rich narrative, which
might or might not be finally summarized along the lines I had suggested.
This used to bring me to the verge of panic—"How to bring them to the
point?"—whereas now I have at least learned that this *is* the point.

The next step is the researchers' interpretations. There is already a tradition of interpretive organization studies, mentioned by Burrell and Morgan (1979) and made distinct by Putnam and Pacanowsky (1983), Lincoln
(1985), and Jones, Moore, and Snyder (1988). Although the approach is
somewhat differently cut, most of the contributions in books dedicated
to organizational symbolism (Pondy et al. 1983; Turner 1990) are of an
interpretive persuasion. Some works, although clearly not all, in the organizational culture tradition lean toward the interpretive side (Frost et al.
1985; Frost et al. 1991).[12] An anthology dedicated to organizational artifacts (Gagliardi 1990) presented a whole array of interpretive approaches,
although it also hosted noninterpretive contributions. The point of all these
efforts, however, is to come up not with "improved" stories from the field
but rather with a kind of alternative or competitive stories in order to engage in a dialogue with the field. In such a dialogue, both genres—the one
of theory and the one of practice—can develop. What follows is my per-

sonal attempt at making such an interdisciplinary analysis of organizational life.

In interpreting my material from the public sector study, I focus mostly on two genres: *drama* and *autobiography*. The novel, a genre that certainly requires very serious attention, has been dealt with elsewhere (Czarniawska-Joerges and Guillet de Monthoux 1994). Other genres are mentioned insofar as they are relevant to the material in question, such as the numerical genre of economics ("true science"). Much attention is paid to rhetoric because differences in rhetoric help to differentiate among genres and because changes in rhetoric reflect change in a given genre. Special attention is also paid to the differences and similarities between the rhetoric of the field and that of the research community. Applying interpretive devices borrowed from literary studies to my organizational material, I hope to show how these can further our understanding of the complex and unpredictable—the major concern and interest of current organization studies.

Drama is an umbrella metaphor; it encompasses many smaller metaphors (enacted stories, serials, screenplays) appearing throughout the text. In contrast to this all-encompassing metaphor of drama as enacted narrative, the metaphor of autobiography might seem limited. But two devices are applied to different parts of material: drama to organizational life in general (a spacious device for a spacious material), and autobiography for capturing what was most poignant at the time and in the place where I made my study, the problems of organizational identity crises.

# On Dramas and Autobiographies in the Organizational Context

While written texts are very important to action and its meaning, it is equally important to preserve action's other aspects: the movement, the temporality, the improvisation. Hence the attraction of the drama metaphor. But isn't it a mixed metaphor? Aren't "dramas" and "narratives" different species?

As Fisher (1984) declared, the narrative paradigm has a close connection with "dramatism," that is, Burke's method of treating "language and thought primarily as modes of action" (Burke 1945/1969, xxii). Dramatism has a somewhat complex connection with the ways in which the theater metaphor is used in the social sciences. Some of Burke's devoted readers may claim that his theory of the relationship between language and action has little or nothing to do with theater,[1] that it is *dramatistic* and not dramaturgical. This is correct only if the theater metaphor is ascribed a very limited reading.

Lymann and Scott (1975) trace the theater metaphor in the social sciences back to Freud, Mead, and Goffman. Both Freud and Mead were fascinated by the idea of the self as composed of several "roles," first rehearsed in the "theater of the mind" and later performed in the "theater of life." Goffman (1959) de-psychologized the concept by contrasting various aspects of social life ("frontstage," "backstage"). His main interest, however, was the question of "transformed reality": how to tell "everyday life" from "fanciful realms," reality from "make-believe" (1974, 155). His answer agrees with that of Schütz (1973): one must speak of "multiple realities" or "different realms of reality," rather than insisting upon a contrast between "real" and "unreal." What appears as "untransformed reality" in one context is a transformed reality in another context—it is, after all, turtles all the way down. This is why "theater" is a good metaphor of life and not a contrasting notion.

Still, many if not most uses of the theatrical metaphor assume the basic notion of "authenticity" or a "true self" as opposed to theatrical behavior. As Davies and Harré (1991) pointed out, the very concept of the "role" emphasizes the static, formal, and ritualistic aspects of social life. Such uses of the theatrical metaphor do not tally with the notion of individual and social life as a narrative, or with the concept of the modern identity as an institution. The last two are closer to Burke's idea of people as symbol makers, symbol users, and symbol misusers.

As I see it, Burke's method is very similar to that proposed by the advocates of the narrative approach. Drama, in Burke's eyes, was a genre best suited to exploring the relationship between language and action that constitutes social life. And the dramatistic method does not exclude the theater metaphor, or vice versa, as many examples show. Geertz's use of the theater metaphor (1980b) followed a dynamic and symbolist interpretation of drama in the spirit of Burke. Goffman himself was inspired by Burke's dramatism and, especially in his later works, tried to recover the balance between the stability of "roles" and the uncertain dynamics of an unfolding narrative (Goffman 1981). Indeed, one could claim that the most fascinating part of Goffman's thought appears when he blurs the distinction between theater and everyday life, as in *Frame Analysis* (1974). Such metonymical rather than metaphorical treatment of theater fits very well with the spirit of Burkean dramatistic analysis.

In my present context, there is at least one aspect of the theater metaphor in a non-Burkean sense that I would like to preserve, namely, public visibility. This is connected with the specific character of the Swedish public administration, in which all proceedings are open to public inspection by law, but it has a wider bearing than this one: in Sweden, politicians and public sector executives, sometimes down to the lowest-level official, are constantly exposed to media scrutiny. Such contacts are more selectively regulated in the case of private companies, but it is increasingly so that they want more—albeit controlled—visibility, and at the same time mass media consider companies a more and more legitimate hunting ground, all of which contributes to closer contacts.

## The Paradoxicality of Leadership as Read in Dramatistic Terms

Throughout these pages the ideas of paradox, paradoxicality, paralogy, and even "deparadoxification" will play a very important role. An explication of them should be gradually built up through the text; by the end a performative definition should ensue. In order to avoid simple semantic misunderstandings, however, I can refer here to what Webster's calls "a shared meaning element" among synonyms of paradox: "something involving an inherent contradiction" (*Webster's New Collegiate Dictionary* 1981, 813).

## Paradoxes in Theater and in Organizations

Both domains, leadership and drama, are built around contradictory requirements that are fulfilled in successful performances. These requirements are schematized below with the help of Kenneth Burke's "dramatistic" model (Burke 1945). The two columns contain the requirements as regards agent, purpose, scene, agency, and act that, however incompatible, must be fulfilled in a single performance.

|  *Agent* | |
| --- | --- |
| Representing the interests of others, not one's own. | "Sincere" conduct (acting in accordance with one's own beliefs). |
| Types, not individualities. | Illusion of vitality (not stereotypes). |

|  *Purpose* | |
| --- | --- |
| Simple motives (easy to understand, constant, and coherent). | Coping with complex situations. |

|  *Scene* | |
| --- | --- |
| Consists of a static role structure ("friends" and "enemies," "bad guys" and "good guys," "progressives" and "conservatives," "cons" and "dupes"). | Constantly changing alliances, the need to compromise and cooperate. |

|  *Agency* | |
| --- | --- |
| Observing the well-known albeit unwritten rules, repeating successful tricks. | Constant improvisation, whereby the material is taken from whatever is currently of interest. |

|  *Act* | |
| --- | --- |
| Incessant action effect. | Constant talk, high mobility. |

An idea that aptly grasps the above combinations of opposite traits—of role (profession) and identity (personality), of talk and action, of spontaneity and rehearsed performance—is MacIntyre's concept of *character*. In fact, MacIntyre introduced his discussion of modern characters by alluding to a dramatic tradition[2] that "possesses a set of stock characters immediately recognizable to the audience" who "define the possibilities of plot and action" (MacIntyre 1981/1990, 27). What makes characters special is that they fuse a social role and a personality (the left and the right columns above), unlike other roles, which can sometimes be abandoned or subjected to distancing with the help of irony or doubt.

The Leader is an excellent example of a character. While dentists, for instance, can make jokes about their patients' teeth at a family dinner, sinning at worst against good manners, politicians may not ridicule their electors, nor may top executives poke fun at their companies even if caught unawares. Social roles are satisfactorily defined by the demands of the institution of which they form a part, and which may or may not specify certain personality requirements in those who are willing to assume the role. For the Leader this is not enough. The role and the personality must be fused; any crack will arouse indignation even though the fusion be perceived as paradoxical.

Every culture, MacIntyre continues, has its own specific stock of characters. The modern culture, he claims, came up with three such characters: the Rich Aesthete, the Manager, and the Therapist. While fully agreeing with this, I would like to add that every culture also inherits, and chooses from past repertoires, certain characters that did not originate in the particular culture but nevertheless fit it very well. The Leader, a clearly premodern character, acts hand-in-hand with the down-to-earth Manager in public administration organizations.

The drama metaphor has long been known to the political sciences. One could claim that ever since the days of the Athenian republic, democratic politics has always relied upon dramatic effects. Now, however, the public act has become an important part of all organizations; that we are now looking at the active production of special effects; and that the leading actors never stay onstage long enough for us to start believing in the seriousness of things. Anderson claims that we are witnessing "an increasing theatricality of politics, in which events are scripted and stage-managed for mass consumption and in which individuals and groups struggle for starring roles (or at least bit parts in the dramas of life). This theatricality is a natural—and inevitable—feature of our time" (1990, 5).

The fact that theatricality is increasing is a result of the present expansion of mass communications on a scale as yet unparalleled in the history of humankind. And theatricality is not only spreading, it is also becoming more visible because of the existence of media that not only display ongoing events but also favor the presentation of such events as are more visually attractive. This also seems to suggest that what cannot be dramatized is not important. This might explain why, when the dubious actions of organizational leaders are unveiled before a stunned audience, the accused leaders are apparently unable to understand why they are being criticized in the first place. They certainly had no intention of keeping their conduct secret; it just did not seem worth showing.

What traditional politicians may have difficulty in grasping, but what the officials I studied understand very well, is that in postmodern times the notion of "backstage" vanishes; even the production of spectacle is now open to inspection. We are used to seeing TV cameras on the TV screen, and the game of "is it true or just play-acting?" has become popular in all the cinematographic media. There are films about filmmaking and TV serials about TV serials, such as "Twin Peaks." In a biographical film about the pop singer Madonna, the camera shows Madonna being attended to by a throat doctor, while actor Warren Beatty sits in a corner watching. He says, "Don't you think it's rather silly to show people this? You can answer me off-camera." (Madonna shakes her head no.) "Sure," says Beatty, laughing, "what's the point of saying anything if it's not for camera?"

In his book *Immortality*, a powerful depiction of the postmodern condition, Milan Kundera includes a dream of a performance in which the actors take their bows while the applause can be heard from behind: the public was watching the performance backstage. There is a playful competition between the professionals and the semiotic reader/spectator (chapter 4), in which the former try to confuse the latter by blurring the border between frontstage and backstage, while the latter takes delight in seeing through the ruse.

Dramatization plays an important part in the shaping of preferences in a society. The drama metaphor can therefore be a useful aid to understanding how preferences are created, and such understanding can replace indignation, that most common of modern emotions (MacIntyre 1981). The metaphor can be used for *unmasking*, which can be seen not only as a moral activity but also as a sense-making operation that helps us to understand the world in which we live and which we create (Mitchell 1992). A dedication to the rituals and sanctity of democratic governance does not preclude the use of a drama metaphor in interpreting modern politics and the organizations created to carry it.

Yet most people react with a feeling of uneasiness when the dramatic aspects of organizational action are mentioned. They interpret the metaphor as meaning that it is "make-believe" and "not real," just as they marginalize narrative knowledge as "just storytelling." It is not, however, the stagy character of the performance that makes politics dramatic. It is its tendency to *dramatize* certain chosen problems in order to gain the attention of the public. The number of issues the spectators are able to identify and attend to seriously is limited, regardless of the degree of their sincere interest. The issues that become the topics of discovery and discussion are those presented in a dramatically appealing fashion.

As Goffman points out, a play is "not real" in the sense that the events portrayed therein do not actually take place; nobody dies, gets married, or goes bankrupt. But it is real in terms of the activities of its performance, rehearsals, and so on: no "fanciful realm" this, but straightforward organizing. And, Goffman adds, isn't it true that people in their everyday life spend much time daydreaming, planning, fantasizing? The characteristic trait of theater (and politics) is not that it is unreal but that "the unreality it presents is of a distinctly dramatic kind" (Goffman 1974, 552). Events must be selected and condensed, metonymic cues abound—in this way, a day's events all round the globe can be packed into a ten-minute news program.

"Dramatic" is therefore most emphatically not the same as "unreal." "Politics is the theater of reality," says Anderson (1990, 122). When drama is improvised on the political stage, there are people who succeed, suffer, fail, and die. Politics does not simulate reality but creates it; a successful "make-believe" makes people believe. Nor are politicians a deviant species. The main difference between them and "natural figures," as Goffman calls them, is that natural figures "do not have a cast of trained actors at their disposal or much time to polish a script, . . . merely their own amateur capacity at recounting events" (1974, 559). When they do the accounting, they dramatize it just like politicians do, only using somewhat different means.

In the context of public-sector organizations of interest here, politicians are perceived as the people who create the premises for reality in its many realms, who set the stage for others.

## Control and Leadership as Scene-Act Ratio

The observation that the performance of some characters sets the stage for others led to another use of the dramatistic analysis—in a series of studies of economic decline, which showed that such decline is accompanied by changes in the forms of organizational control (Czarniawska-Joerges 1989). Decline can be said to have occurred when a person or persons— an agency outside the organization, the leadership, or some other group within the organization—has provided a stage set called "decline," which then legitimates a certain type of performance, in which the role of the leader is both distinct and clearly prescribed according to the consistency required between the stage, the actor, and the act: "when the curtain rises to disclose a given stage-set, this stage-set contains, simultaneously, implicitly, all that the narrative is to draw out as a sequence, explicitly" (Burke 1945/1969, 7). In public administration the set is decided by politicians and top officials, and in corporations by top executives—or so they believe.

## The Drama

A successful dramatic performance by the leaders of crisis companies can be described in terms of the dramaturgical techniques listed by Merelman (1969).

A powerful *catharsis,* the relieving of emotional tensions, initiates the process of reversing the decline. The new leader paints a devastating picture of the current situation. The listeners are relieved to hear in public what they feared in private, and eagerly accept their part of the blame. The following *personification,* attribution of blame to specific persons, serves to assure them that they need not accept all of it. The members of management who have already left the company are cast as the villains and those who remained as fools, ready to expiate their failure by engaging in opportunities to become heroes. *Identification* follows. In one company I studied, the interviewed managers exhibited a whole range of emotions vis-à-vis the new leader, from unconditional love to deep admiration or at least grudgingly admitted respect. They were ready to identify with their new leader and to espouse his visions and ideals.

What is worth noting, though, is that appeals for identification formulated by the potential object of the identification are often based on logically contradictory if dramaturgically potent messages. One such typical message is that the leader represents a trend that is inevitable and a force that is infallible (in this case, the development of modern business); at the same time, however, leaders are bound to fail—and the cause to be lost—unless they are supported by their followers. Ambiguity, the necessary condition of symbolic performances, refutes logical interpretations of successful leadership (Edelman 1988).

Finally, there is a *suspense,* created by the contrast between a desired future and a threatening present. In the case I studied, excitingly staged meetings and conferences were frequently mounted to reveal the latest enticing visions of the future and to moderate the present threats, which never became concrete fears but never quite disappeared, either, so that a certain tension remained.

As an observer of this performance, I had to admire the leader's sense of organizational drama. At the same time, however, I could not quite suppress a feeling that although the audience was applauding and wanting to join in the act themselves, there was perhaps an element of manipulation in this smooth performance of ritualized dramas. But another study of a corporation in decline changed my mind on this point.

## Refusing to Perform

Analog was a multinational electronics company, and at the time of my study the electronic equipment market was failing. A general managerial meeting was called at Analog European Subsidiary (AES), opening with a videotaped speech by Analog's president. The gist of the speech was that the crisis could and must be turned into a positive event with the help of a critical examination of all practices and routines in a search for innovations and better solutions. The speech was received with understanding and acceptance; the shock came when one of the top executives of AES took the floor. According to an observer, he admitted that the leadership group did not have solutions to the present crisis and asked the line managers to help.

The reaction was one of perplexity and mistrust. The line managers did not know how to react to such an unusual appeal. A month or two later a big event took place, involving all employees (not only managers) in that part of AES that was headed by the same executive. The message, as registered by the same observer, was basically very similar. The audience was again utterly confused. They doubted the sincerity of the message: don't the people at the top always do what they want in the end? Eventually, the verdict became negative: this is not the way to behave in this situation! The scene-act ratio was not right.

The role of the leader thus proved to be well defined, although the definition was, as usual, revealed by transgression. What is more important to note is that it was not the leader who defined it that way. The reaction of Analog's staff shows that the followers or subordinates did as much as the leaders, when it came to setting the scene and selecting the appropriate performance (act).

What is an appropriate (consistent with the stage set) performance for a leader in this situation? Apparently, it should consist in resolving the paradox or "deparadoxification" (Luhmann 1991 and chapter 10 below), rather than presenting it openly. A "character" must achieve an impression of consistency, even applying methods that are inconsistent.

## Scripts and Performances

Leadership emerges from these examples as a stage performance, and the economic decline as the setting for a ritual drama in which leaders and followers have prescribed roles. In the first act the sky is getting dark, the tempest threatens, and the followers look to their leader. In the second act the leader performs. These two acts are immutable; the resolution comes in the third. One outcome could be that the leader fails, the subordinates take over to protect themselves from the storm, and they establish a republic. Another could be that the leader fails and a new leader comes to the rescue. The third is that the leader wins (the storm is over) and a great feast is prepared in honor of the hero. The experimental variant whereby the leaders looked to their followers when the storm mounted in the first act was refused by their fellow actors, at least in the Analog case. A ritual drama does not allow for such experiments.

Thus, a successful performance combines the theatrical tradition, whereby the audience participates and the actors improvise as the play proceeds, with a formalistic ritual drama, in which everyone knows the rules. Once the stage set is in place (the definition of the situation agreed upon), the leading actors act their parts, and the other members of the cast take their cues accordingly. The play proceeds along generally prescribed lines: the setting, with its suggestion of a continued diminution of resources (the decline), demands a certain performance; the actors playing the leaders will tighten their control, and the actors playing the followers will to some extent oppose this; if all is played well, the drama will soon end in a more positive spirit, especially if the right note has been struck and the audience applauds.

In unsuccessful performances, problems can arise while the stage is still being set. A difference of opinion—among the actors or between actors and audience—about which stage set is appropriate may ruin the performance from the start. Sometimes, however, an autocratic sponsor, director, or leading actor may prevail, forcing the others to accept one mode rather than another. And problems can, of course, occur in the performance itself, with some actors improvising in the style of the English pantomime and others in the spirit of a Greek tragedy. Some actors may refuse to play their roles properly. The audience may be in a charitable mood and support the troupe anyway, or they may boo and demand that the leading characters be replaced.

Whatever the details, the leaders' role is to provide the rest of the cast and the audience with the illusion of controllability. They are paid vast sums and granted numerous privileges not only because they may have to play the scapegoat someday (not all leaders are burned at the stake); no, they are rewarded because, thanks to them, we can stop fearing disorder. This is in fact why nobody hesitates to sack them when they fail; otherwise we would have to give up the illusion of controllability that we cherish even above freedom. The arbitrariness of life—especially organizational life—is too frightful to envisage. A leader who fails to provide the illusion, not by a poor performance (which is only human) but by showing us the illusion for what it is, by revealing the paradox rather than resolving it, cannot expect to be applauded. The illusion must be supported, whatever the cost. As MacIntyre observes, the effects of the modern project "have been to produce *not* scientifically managed social control, but a skillful dramatic imitation of such control. It is histrionic success which gives power and authority in our culture. The most effective bureaucrat is the best actor" (MacIntyre 1981/1990, 107).

## Control Philosophies

The above examples illustrate a resolution of the scene-act ratio in which the scene determines the act. It could be actually argued that there are alternative models of control, in which either the actor determines the scene and the action, or else action determines the other two. In every case, however, all three have to be consistent. The following table lists such control philosophies, changing Burke's terminology to better fit the usual terminology of organization theory: "act" translates as "action" and "agent" as "actor," but "scene" remains, although in the language of contemporary theater it should be rather called "stage set."

Environment as determining factor:
**scene—action—actor**

Agency as determining factor:
**actor—action—scene:**
entrepreneurship theory

**actor—scene—action:**
leadership theory

Constructionist model:
**action — scene**
**— actor —**

Control philosophies differ in their underlying belief about what is the determining factor. The modern project, materialist in character, assumes the priority of environmental factors. Once the stage is set in a certain manner, actors will adapt. This control philosophy was also prevalent in the Swedish public sector at the time of my study. Politicians were busy painting a picture of crisis, and, although ridiculed for doing so by the officials, they were also sharply criticized if they deviated from this role. In that sense, the two dramatistic aspects of their role were being combined. On the one hand, they were seen as comedians but were often admired for the professionalism of their performance. On the other hand, bearing tragic messages was expected of them by the officials and even by themselves. Tragedians and comedians at one and the same time; "clowns," it was sometimes said.

Attempts to change the control philosophy were treated with caution. What, after all, are the available alternatives? Leadership and entrepreneurship theories (in their conventional versions) choose to believe in individuals: actors create worlds, or at least their actions do. In constructionist perspective (which can be said to have been the ground of Burke's dramatistic analysis), actions create not only stage sets but also actors, who then try to act in accordance with the stage set and with what they perceive as their "character," although changes and deviations are possible. Although the action-scene-actor chain is circular in time (spiral, perhaps, as we never step into the same river twice), the focus on action allows for the inclusion of unintended consequences and random events (which account for most change) and relieves the tyranny of both structure (scene) and agency[3] (actor). But it excludes the possibility of control. "Our social order is in a very literal sense out of our, and indeed anyone's, control. No one is or could be in charge" (MacIntyre 1981/1990, 107).

This book is basically about how an illusion of control is maintained in a situation where no one is or could be in charge. A startling possibility—of an institutional change that might dispose of this illusion—is glimpsed here and there. But such a possibility would mean that organizations as we know them would acquire a completely new identity. How is this possible? When looking for answers, it is important to understand with what devices a public narrative about organizations is spun.

Assuming that organizations have identity, however, presupposes a whole chain of metaphors. The chain starts with an everyday juridical metaphor of the organization-as-person. How did it emerge, and why is it taken for granted? This leads us to the recently evolving definitions of individual identity, from the essence of the self to modern institution.

The modern institution of individual identity reveals historical links with the literary genre of autobiography. I wish to exonerate the organization-person analogy by substituting the rules of this genre for the "essentialist self" metaphor. The focus is on "organizational autobiographical acts": organizations' self-presentations as narratives. This way, the phenomenon that was often described both inside and outside organizations as an "organizational identity crisis" can be better understood.

## Organizations as Super-Persons

Despite the claim that machines and organisms are the most popular images of organization (Morgan 1986), there is another metaphor that is as popular but whose metaphorical character has been almost forgotten, so taken for granted has it become. This is the organization as super-person, as a single powerful decision maker, personified in a leader or leadership group, or expressed in the notion of the organization as a collective. The assumption of *Homo collectivus,* or Organization Man, can be seen lurking behind this conceptualization.

Accordingly, organizations are seen as consensus-based. With these two assumptions—of collectivity and consensus—in the background, an organization theory tells us how organizations learn, unlearn, produce strategies, and do all the things individuals usually do. Sometimes we are told that this is "just a metaphor," that organizations are not *really* individuals, but for all practical purposes they are *like* individuals. Here is an example:

> As an organization gets older, it learns more and more about coping with its environment and with its internal problems of communication and coordination. At least this is the normal pattern, and the normal organization tries to perpetuate the fruits of its learning by formalizing them. (Starbuck 1983, 480)

The constructionist view espoused in this book has trouble with the unreflective acceptance of such an anthropomorphic image of organizations. According to this view, organizations are not people at all (neither aggregates nor collectives nor super-persons); they are *nets of collective action* undertaken in an effort to shape the world and human lives (Czarniawska-Joerges 1992a). This definition tries to follow the ignored linguistic cue in the word itself (organiza*tion*), emphasizing that organization is an activity, and not the resulting "object." The constructionist view also relates to a certain understanding of human nature, namely, that "[t]here is nothing to people except what has been socialized into them—their ability to use language, and thereby to exchange beliefs and desires with other people" (Rorty 1989, 177).

When uttering words, people endow what they do (including using language) with meaning: they *account* for what they have done (justification), for what they are doing (monitoring), and for what they will do (planning). Thus, actions are constructed in conversations taking place between people, which give meaning to physical movements and all kinds of events.

This view does not allow us to dismiss the organization-as-superperson metaphor unexamined. If the everyday and theoretical languages insist on a certain usage, it is meaningless to claim that they "miss the point" or "use a wrong definition." It is not even certain whether a quotation from another author was at all necessary to illustrate this point: an organization that "does" or "does not do this and that" will probably pop up in the pages of this book as well. It is necessary to scrutinize the context of such usages in order to understand their genesis, and a promising route is by conceiving individuality itself as a modern institution.

## Modern Identity
### Individuality as an Institution

The most direct claim regarding the institutional character of individual identity that I have found is in Meyer (1986). In view of the extremely rich flora of definitions that *institution* seems to be attracting, I was curious to discover how it was understood in this context. Meyer, Boli, and Thomas (1987, 13) see "institutions as cultural rules giving collective meaning and value to particular entities and activities" but do not explain what the "cultural rules" are. March and Olsen, taking up the same thread, are nevertheless more concrete when they say: "Political institutions are collections of interrelated rules and routines that define appropriate actions in terms of relations between roles and situations" (1989, 160). One could then wonder whether such rules and routines are only the explicitly codified laws, statutes, and regulations, but I do not think March and Olsen intended to narrow their definition to such an extent. Already at this stage, the notion of the narrativity in social life proves helpful: the "cultural rules" or "rules and routines" can be interpreted as the "rules of narration" that are typical for a given time and place.

Another kind of problem produces another definition, namely, "institution [as] legitimized social grouping" (Douglas 1986, 46), which seems to be shared by MacIntyre (1981). According to this definition, organizations are also seen as groups of people, and are therefore an institution of a certain type. March and Olsen seem to lapse into the same definition when, two sentences after the definition quoted above, they say: "When individuals *enter* an institution, they try to discover, and are taught, the rules" (1989, 160, my italics).

In this text, an institution is a pattern of social action strengthened by a corresponding social norm. Berger and Luckmann's definition is therefore the most appropriate: "institutions posit that actions of type X will be performed by actors of type X" (1966, 72). A constructive reciprocity is assumed, that is, performance of an X type of action leads to the perception that a given actor belongs (or aspires to) type X, and vice versa. In other words, the intelligibility of action X is achieved by referring it to a type of narrative (a genre, maybe), where action X and actor X belong to one and the same plot. Thus, a manager working on an assembly line and a woman making strategic decisions in a corporation beg for some explanation, as such happenings violate the institutionalized order of things.[4]

In our case, actors are in fact "legitimized social groupings": work units, profit centers, departments, corporations, public administration organizations, associations of organizations, and all those whose interactions "constitute a recognized area of institutional life" (DiMaggio and Powell 1983, 148). Actors leave or are pushed out of a field, while new actors enter it (consider the powerful entry of environmentalists into political, industrial, and academic fields). Actions, despite the stability and repetitiveness that earn them the name of institutions, change in both their form and meaning; the narrative changes in every narration. Finally, the process itself is recursive, as Meyer, Boli, and Thomas (1987) point out: whereas actors perform actions, actions create actors, or rather their identities, within the context of a narrative, which in turn is created by actions and actors. In Burke's terms, the actor is redefined as a scene-act combination rather than as an agent. If this holds, then the notion of identity needs to be subjected to closer scrutiny.

The traditional school of thought, in both "folk" and scientific theories, claims that identity is to be found in the individuals themselves, in their genotype or in their "soul." To acquire an identity thus means finding one's true "Self" and exhibiting it.[5] This perspective has been severely criticized by the social environment school, which sees society as compelling individuals to play a limited repertoire of roles.

In scientific literature there is an equivalent to the "essential Self" definition, in which an organization's identity is equated with what its members believe to be its distinctive, central, and enduring characteristics (Albert and Whetten 1985; Dutton and Dukerich 1991; Alvesson and Björkman

1992). This kind of definition is then countered by an environmentalist one (e.g., Ashfort and Mael 1989).

This "nature or nurture" debate is circumvented in the constructionist way of thinking, whereby the creation of identity is seen as a two-way process—an idea that probably starts from George H. Mead's rejection of the "self-society" dualism (Baldwin 1986; Bruner 1990; Gergen 1991). Identity is created in the interactions between individuals in the social context. The individuals enter interactions complete with their genotype, but also with what the society inculcated in them: its rules, institutions, values, and, above all, its language. During this process, not only are individual identities created, but society is reproduced or changed. Thus, "Self . . . must be treated as a construction that, so to speak, proceeds from the outside in as well as from the inside out, from culture to mind as well as from mind to culture" (Bruner 1990, 108).

The human self, says Rorty (1991), is just a self-reweaving web of beliefs that are revealed as habits of action. This web is centerless and contingent, connecting the self "to those with similar tastes and similar identities" (p. 192). The Self is historical, and is both constituted by and constitutive of a community.

How is this possible? The idea of the reciprocity of the creators and their creations excludes the idea of either "a cultural dupe" or "a rational decision maker." The double role of the Self as creator and created is beautifully rendered in the notion of the Self as storyteller—"the Self telling stories that included a delineation of Self as a part of the story" (Bruner 1990, 109). While the Self is always busy making stories, the culture has quite a few ready-made to offer. We create ourselves projecting our identities against accessible plots, as it were, but every performance changes, augments, distorts, or enriches the existing repertoire.

The emerging picture of an individual interacting with a society runs into the same problems that have dogged role theory. After all, nobody has ever seen "a society." What we interact with is always other people, and society is performed by endless chains of conversations and physical actions, each irrevocably tied to the other. Thus, when I speak of conversations, not denying their physicality, I am assuming it.

Having made this caveat, it is safe to say that identities are performed in conversations. To be more exact, what we achieve in conversations is positioning vis-à-vis other people (Davies and Harré 1991), and against the background of a plot that is negotiated by those taking part in the conversation. Thus, the Self is produced, reproduced, and maintained in conversations, past and present. It is community-constituted, as Rorty says, in the sense of being created by those who take part in a conversation; it is historical because past conversations are evoked in the course of present ones.

The new general manager referred to in chapter 1 presented herself to her subordinates by evoking identities from the past; she then had to wait for the reactions of the present audience, and, regardless of whether the current encounter ends successfully from the point of view of the newcomer, it will be put to the test in the next encounter and in the next. Although this example exploits a particularly clear-cut situation—that of somebody facing a new community—the same process in a less dramatic version is repeated in every conversation that takes place. "Whatever's happened to X? Always so serene, she seems positively gloomy today." If the change can be explained away by specific causes, X will maintain her identity, but if not, then X's identity will become that of someone "who was always so serene but is now always gloomy." And, finally, if X is not willing or able to counteract the emerging image, she will be perceived as a gloomy person, in accordance with the institutionalized cues that tell us what a "gloomy person" is like.

This idea of the Self as socially constructed—in interactions between individuals within the social worlds relevant to them—usually raises the issue of sincerity. As Silver and Sabini convincingly show, however, "even sincerity can be seen as a match between feelings and avowals, requires rules, standards, and even manipulation—the constructed stuff" (1985, 199). What is more, sincerity in self-presentation belongs with other institutionalized attributes of the modern identity.

Which does not mean that the idea of individuality as an institution and the Self as an institutionalized myth meets with much applause. The Self is the Romantic response to the positivist system (on two rhetorics of modernity, see Brown 1989 and Gergen 1991). To admit that individuality is an institution is to give in to the system, to let it achieve the final colonization of the life-world (Schütz 1973; Habermas 1974).

The idea of the socially constructed Self that acknowledges its institutional origins reaches beyond those two kinds of rhetoric or, as Gergen would say, makes a patchwork of the two. It also facilitates noticing the analogy between the individual and the organization because the notion of accountability is still in place, only the rules of accounting seem to be different. Individuals and organizations narrate themselves to others, who react with approval or disapproval but who also reciprocate with their own life narratives.

## How Identities Are Constructed

Seeing individuality as an institution and identity as narrative provides us with a possible answer to why the image of organization as a super-person persists. In the first place, it is because the notion of an individual is an institutional myth developed within rational theories of choice, and thus close to the core of organizational analysis (Meyer, Boli, and Thomas 1987). Second, and as a result, organizations are anthropomorphized to reproduce the notion of accountability, which is central to modern culture (Douglas 1992). This linking notion is necessary to tie individuality as an institution to two other modern institutions: the state and the market. The invention of a "legal person," which makes organizations accountable both as citizens and as consumers and producers, constitutes a necessary link between the three and is then reflected in everyday language.

In other words, there is both an analogy and a connection between personal and organizational identity. The connection is that they are both subnarratives inside the modern narrative, which encompasses and requires individuals, markets, and states. The analogy lies in the fact that the rules for constructing personal and organizational identities are very much alike.

By assuming this, one problematizes the notion of organization as super-person by setting it in the context of modernity, while also preserving and exploiting the analogy between organizational and personal identities. The notion of individuality as a modern institution both depsychologizes the concept of "identity" and frees it from sociological determinism. In the narrative version, an identity is created not by any action but by a self-narrative (Bruner 1990). This notion goes back to Bakhtin's idea of a "dialogical self" (Kelly 1992), whereby the self is to be understood in relation to an audience, whose real or imaginary responses constantly shape self-presentations. The individual identity, a typical institution of high modernity (Giddens 1991), is thus to be found in an ability to account for one's actions in terms that will be accepted by the audience. Such anticipated account serves ex ante to establish which action is appropriate in a given situation (March and Olsen 1989). "A top executive like me does this and not that in a situation of a crisis."

But what terms are likely to be accepted by a given audience? We can speak of identity's "form" and "content," but as I have chosen to treat identity as a narrative, I shall borrow a terminology from the Russian formalists (Bakhtin 1928) and speak of "material" and "device" in place of "content" or "substance" and "form." The traditional "form and content" dichotomy unavoidably brings to mind an image of form as something external, holding the content within it ("a container"). This makes it seem perfectly possible to analyze form regardless of content and content regardless of form, and to meet any protests against such a procedure with incomprehension. Surely any text (or other work) has a content, a core, an inside (called *Inhalt* in German and *innehåll* in Swedish)? Surely any form, any shell, any vessel can contain many different contents?

This misapprehension causes a good deal of trouble in criticism, and even more when it is transferred to the analysis of identity as a narrative. The idea of an empty form that can be filled with practically any contents haunts individuals, educators, and public relations officers alike. In the "material" and "device" approach, this outer/inner dichotomy vanishes, and it is thus easier to see why one cannot be considered without the other, even though, of course, they are not one and the same. Discussing any material presumes a device, otherwise no discussion can take place, as there is no such thing as formless material.

In analyzing a text, we may choose a different device from the one used by its author; we may violate the convention within which the text was created, but then we are simply constructing a new text in which the original material and device become the material for the next analysis, as when Calás and Smircich (1991) analyzed the literature of leadership using "seduction" as a deconstructive device. By the same token, whenever we set out to analyze a device, it simply becomes a material to be elaborated with the use of a meta-device, as it were. These metaphors from the world of culture (work) rather than from nature make the essence of the operation more clear. Materials are usually denoted by innumerable nouns (wood, wool, concrete) that even grammatically call for a device to transform them into analyzable units. Devices are always made of some kind of material. This makes the distinction arbitrary and spurious, needing to be remade every time it is used according to the particular purpose at hand.

## The Material

What cultural material is accessible to construction of identity? It seems that the narrative of modern identity has to tell a tale of *self-respect, efficiency, autonomy* (internal locus of control in psychological terms), and *flexibility,* that is, the absence of a long-term commitment to one and the same object (Meyer 1986). This last is sometimes defined as distance, "the capacity to detach oneself from any particular standpoint or point of view, to step backwards, as it were, and view and judge that standpoint or point of view from the outside" (MacIntyre 1981/1990, 126). These qualities can be contrasted, for example, with the traditional Roman virtues such as *pietas* (reverence for the past), *gravitas* (bearing the sacred weight of the past), *dignitas* (a manner worthy of one's task and station), and *constantia* (faithfulness to tradition) (see Pitkin 1984). Whereas the modern identity conceives of Self as a project, the traditional identity compared the Self with the already existing social blueprint. "In the medieval era, before the Renaissance and thus the beginning of modernism, an individual was not an agency; just a part of a bigger social arrangement" (Pitkin 1984, 22).

Gergen (1991) introduces a notion of the "cultural location of self" by contrasting modern identity—individuality—with the different concepts of identity known to us from anthropological studies. The peculiarity of modern identity is that although it is formulated in and through interactions, the impression it aims to achieve is that it is individual, independent of other people's reactions. According to Vytautas Kavolis (quoted by R. H. Brown 1989, 165), perception of identity[6] requires three elements:

- an overall *coherence* between the individual's experience and the way this experience is expressed;
- a memory—on the part of the individual and of others—of a *continuity* in the course of the individual's life; and
- a conscious but not excessive[7] *commitment* to the manner in which the individual understands and deals with his/her "self."

If we compare the modern identity with the identity typical of heroic societies, for example, we notice that the former is plotted against the individual's own life history and not related to the community (MacIntyre 1981).

It is this material from which modern identity is shaped—its individual rather than community-based character and its orientation toward the future rather than the past—that makes autobiography the most appropriate genre analogy. As Lejeune put it, "autobiography is one of the most fascinating aspects of one of the great myths of modern occidental civilization, the myth of the *self*" (1989, 162). This is another way of saying that a literary genre evolved in connection with the emergence of a modern institutional order, which comprises the institution of individuality.

## The Devices

If it is useful to treat identity as a narrative, or, more properly speaking, as a continuous process of narration where both the narrator and the audience[8] are involved in formulating, editing, applauding, and refusing various elements of the ever-produced narrative, then the most appropriate literary *genre* (the set of devices and sometimes even the kind of material used) is that of autobiography. The analogy obviously lies in the fact that autobiography is a self-narrative of identity but also, less obviously but just as importantly, in autobiography's claim to factuality. Autobiography belongs to literature, but not to fiction.[9]

In fact, this analogy works both ways: Elisabeth W. Bruss (1976) presents autobiographies as an institutional way of creating personal identities, thus proposing to see text as action, much as I propose to see action as text:

> All reading (or writing) involves us in choice: we choose to pursue a style or a subject matter, to struggle with or against a design. We also choose, as passive as it all may seem, to take part in an interaction, and it is here that generic labels have their use. The genre does not tell us the style or the construction of a text as much as how we should expect to "take" that style or mode of construction—what force it should have for us. And this force is derived from a kind of action that text is taken to be. Surrounding any text are implicit contextual conditions, participants involved in transmitting and receiving it, and the nature of these implicit conditions and the roles of the participants affects the status of the information contained in the text. (Bruss 1976, 4)

Genre is a system of action that has become institutionalized and is recognizable by repetition;[10] its meaning stems from its place within the symbolic systems comprising literature and culture (and it is therefore diacritical, like that of all other signs). In the same way that we can characterize the modern identity only by contrasting it with nonmodern identities, so can autobiography as a genre acquire specificity by its deviation from other genres. Again, we detect an analogy and a connection. A societal institution, namely, individual identity, resembles and is also supported by a literary institution, namely, a genre called autobiography: "conceptions of individual identity are articulated, extended, and developed through an institution like autobiography" (Bruss 1976, 5). In constructing ourselves, we suffer from amateurishness; published autobiographies provide us with ready-made devices, legitimated by the success of their authors' lives.

Modern identity and autobiography emerged at about same time. Although what Bruss calls "autobiographical acts" existed as early as the sixteenth and seventeenth centuries, they were regarded as products on the same level as private letters or "memoirs," not as literature. "Biography" became a recognized term after 1680, but the category "autobiography" was not given a name until 1809 in England (Bruss 1976), after which the genre began to develop both in relation to other contemporary genres and in the ways it differed from them. On the one hand, for example, it borrowed the narrator-as-a-direct-observer from the realist novel (the firsthand experience); on the other, autobiography discovered that other modes of narration are available. This is because several textual strategies (sets of devices) are possible within one and the same genre (Harari 1979). They can be defined, for example, by the role assigned in the text to three types of personage that are characteristic of the genre: Author, Narrator, Character.

One typical strategy is to introduce an omnipresent Author, who claims responsibility for the acts reported in the text (and supposedly taking place outside the text in "reality") and for the text itself. This strategy is often adopted by the founders and the leaders of big corporations. The text and the world in the text have the same creator and, by the same token, create the Author's identity. It could be claimed that this is the purest form of autobiography-as-identity-creation, in which person, organization, and text all become one. But it is by no means the most popular one.

The introduction of a Narrator is a common device. Here is a person who is telling the story, but the author could equally well have been somebody else—although this might be the Narrator acting within the text in the role of Author. The distance thus created leaves more room for manipulation: the Narrator can praise the Author in a way the Author could not do herself, but can also distance herself if necessary. "The Self as narrator not only recounts, but justifies" (Bruner 1990, 121). In terms of organizational identity, this strategy opens up many possibilities. A Narrator could be a PR officer, for instance, who is telling a story of a mighty Author, a founder, perhaps, or a CEO. Or the Narrator might be the representative of a collective Author, perhaps an Organization, as in the examples that follow.

The strategy that is most complex and consequently leaves most scope for a skillful writer is one that introduces a Character. Here the possibilities of distancing, identification, and self-reflection are limitless. There is a hierarchy of knowledge: the Author knows most, and the Character least. In terms of freedom, the order is reversed: the Character can be wild, but the Author must be responsible. The Narrator, as the reflective one, always knows more than the Character but can be temporarily ignorant of the Author's knowledge ("At that point, I did not know that the marketing group had already formulated a plan" or even, ". . . that I will come across crucial information in the matter very soon").

The three can be one, but they can also separate or form dyadic alliances as needed. In *A Portrait of the Artist as a Young Man,* the mature James Joyce is the Narrator, the young James Joyce (Stephen Daedelus) is the Character, and James Joyce the Author comments on both of them. In such a triad, the Narrator is the rhetorician, the Character is the actor, and the Author assumes the moral blame or praise, depending on the doings of the other two. Gore Vidal often uses this strategy (e.g., in *Julian*). There is an old Narrator and a young Character, while Authorship is vested in Fate or some divinity, depending on the period of the story.[11] This sort of thing can lead to the most interesting complications, as illustrated by Umberto Eco in "A Portrait of the Elder as a Young Pliny" (1990).

In his old age, Pliny the Younger composes a letter to Tacitus, informing him of his wish to pass on the true story of the death of his uncle, the Roman general and scientist Pliny the Elder, during the eruption of Vesuvius in A. D. 79. He proceeds by introducing a Narrator, who is the young version of himself, telling a story in which both young Pliny the Younger and Pliny the Elder are Characters. A critical reader, or at least a reader instructed by Eco, soon notices that the Narrator has knowledge that, in fact, only the old Pliny the Younger as an Author could have produced — for example, what the deceased Pliny the Elder thought before dying.

So why not tell the story straight, as an old Author recounting from memory? Because then Tacitus might become suspicious about the authenticity of the story, believing it to be cooked up or invented by the Author (which, of course, it is!). Pliny the Younger thus initiates the textual strategy perfected by anthropologists and known as "being there" (Geertz 1988).

Such paradoxicality is not unusual: it reveals that Narrators are commonly Characters created by the Author and given special reflective status to increase their credibility. Pliny the Younger shifts himself about in time and place, thus producing two actors to alternate between.

These *actorial shifting operations* (Latour 1988b) are easier to perform in creating an organizational identity since such identities are assumed to have a collective character. Moreover, while the shifting of personal identity may infringe on the demands for coherence or continuity, or cast doubt on the claim to reality, the narration of organizational identities steers clear of all these dangers. Actors can be shifted between past, present, and future, and between any points in the global economy. There can be several different Authors (for example, top executives, or even a whole popular movement), the Narrators can distance themselves at will, and a variety of Characters can be called upon without the risk of producing a fragmented impression.

Which brings us to the point at which organizational identity and personal identity come closest to each other and are farthest apart: an organization cannot legitimately claim to be autistic or boast of defective "other-perception" ("nobody understands us," Bruss 1976). Organizational identity makes sense only in relation to the institutions of the market and the state, and one of them must "understand" it.

Similarly, there is a closeness between autobiography and organizational identity, which is absent in the case of personal identities. Autobiographies are always apologetic in character, even if the means of achieving an apologetic effect may be very complex and paradoxical. An autobiography can tell a story of wrongs and errors, but it must lead to an exemplary solution. Organizational identity must follow a straighter path. While individual people can spin tales of ill adjustment, neuroses, or plain misery, continuous success is a constant ingredient in the autobiographies of organizations. It is no good saying, "We used to be robber barons, but now we are community benefactors."

What happens if organizational autobiographical acts fail to arrive at a happy end? Several kinds of failure are possible. One occurs when particular autobiographies and organizational identities fail within the context of existing institutions, as, for example, when the public refused to accept the Exxon story of the oil disaster or Nestle's account of its powdered milk exports to Africa. But when failures become more frequent than successes, we may be dealing with the failure of an institution: "autobiography could simply become obsolete if its defining features, such as individual identity, cease to be important for a particular culture" (Bruss 1976, 15). A literary evolution consists of an audience demanding new works and new works demanding an audience. Does this not apply to institutional evolution in general?

An important caveat must be made here. The expression *organi-*

*zational autobiographies* could carry overtones of something final and closed, a "history of the company" perhaps, written every half-century or so. Such official autobiographies are no doubt important, but they could be more fruitfully compared to obituaries than autobiographies, which are "lives under construction." "'Identity' is a constant relationship between the one and the many" (Lejeune 1989, 34); it is constantly being constructed and reconstructed in actual conversations, and a published autobiography can be seen as a lengthy contribution to a conversation in which the responses are delayed, as the reactions of those who are unhappy with the positionings it describes often show.

The focus here is on what Bruss calls "autobiographical acts" and what Bruner describes as "an account of what one thinks one did in what settings in what ways for what felt reasons" (1990, 119); a remarkable sentence as it contains all five elements of Burke's model (agent, act, scene, agency, and purpose). One can paraphrase it as an account of what one thinks an "organization" did, when "one" is a narrator and "organization" is a character or an author. Such *organizational autobiographical acts* occur constantly in organizational life, but perhaps with special frequency and premeditation in times of challenge and turbulence.

# Interpretive Studies of Organizations: The Logic of Inquiry

The woods are full of eager interpreters.

Clifford Geertz, *Blurred Genres*

The woods may indeed be full, as Geertz says, but how to find a way out? The positivist frame of reference offers its adherents a clear and systematic structure concerning the "method of inquiry" and its outcome, the research report. Although most researchers working within this paradigm would readily agree that the progress of a project in practice may look quite different, and that creatively deviating report structures are not unknown, there is nevertheless a distinguishable pattern that has been imitated by generation after generation of scholars. Because of their relative novelty in the context of organization theory, interpretive studies present a fuzzy picture that sometimes leads to misunderstanding.

This situation has been aggravated, at least at the beginning, by the fact that the interpretive perspective was often defined by comparison with the positivist paradigm (see, e.g., Burrell and Morgan 1979; Putnam and Pacanowsky 1983) rather than on its own terms.[1] Although it was obvious that the new approach could not defend itself according to the criteria it was rejecting, the hermeneutic circle took its toll: in order to understand something new, the audience must be able to recognize it as to some extent familiar. Thus, the interpretive approach continued to refer to the set of positivist categories, creating as much confusion as comprehension. One of the sources of confusion was the adoption of the "paradigm" label, in hasty imitation of Kuhnian terminology. Kuhn, prompted by his critics and admirers who had counted up to twenty-two different uses of the word *paradigm* in his book from 1964, admitted the confusion and singled out three possible definitions of paradigm in a 1969 postscript. These were: a structure of a scientific community, a disciplinary matrix that this community shares, and shared examples—and he proposed to call a paradigm only the last one, in accordance with dictionary definitions (Kuhn 1996).

Now, is this not a typical academic debate, going against all the everyday and commonsensical uses of the word? Not if we accept Bruner's contrasting concepts of paradigmatic (that is, metaphorical) and narrative (that is, metonymical, syntagmatic) knowledge. The narrative knowledge is characterized by certain common traits (ordering in time, the structuring role of human purposes, and so on) but not by the existence of exemplars that are so typical of the paradigmatic knowledge (the syllogisms in formal logic are a good example of this; see Bruner 1990 and chapter 1 above). Interpretive studies represent an approach in the social sciences that comes closest to the narrative knowledge,[2] while positivism provides us with an example of paradigmatic knowledge. It is just this special character of narrative knowledge that makes it so difficult to describe the main features of the approach—a task that is particularly easy in the paradigmatic approaches.

## Choosing a Worldview
### Reality and Knowledge

"Reality is socially constructed"—this has become a declaration of faith among interpretively minded theorists. But is it, really? Common sense tells us, very convincingly, that even if we exclude metaphysical causes, there appear to be many co- constructors of our worlds—animated and nonanimated, sentient and not, viruses and machines. People are constantly constructing their worlds, but they are not alone in this endeavor. As pointed out by constructionists such as Latour (1993b) and Knorr Cetina (1994), there are not two worlds, one "physical" and one "social," nor should there be two sciences corresponding to them. The point of constructionism is that the world has no "essence" to be discovered. This stance does not dispute, however, that the *construction of meaning* is always social, as the tradition originating in Schütz (1953, 1973) and later developed by Berger and Luckmann (1966), Holzner (1968), and others has forcefully claimed.

This is not an idealist standpoint; it is grounded in a firm belief that an objective reality exists independently of human cognition. This belief, however, is not *testable* (Abelson 1986), or, rather, its testing can occur only in the realm between subjectivity and intersubjectivity. I can experience something as physically caused, for example, when I trip over a stool and feel pain, but I need another person to confirm that I tripped and that it was a stool I tripped over, and that the correct word to describe what I feel is *pain*.

> We need to make a distinction between the claim that the world is out there and the claim that truth is out there. To say that the world is out there, that it is not our creation, is to say, with

common sense, that most things in space and time are the effects of causes which do not include human mental states. To
say that truth is not out there is simply to say that where there
are no sentences there is no truth, that sentences are elements
of human languages, and that human languages are human creations. (Rorty 1989, 4–5)

Whether we claim to speak of a reality or a fantasy, the value of our utterance cannot be established by comparing it to its object, but only by comparing it to other utterances, as Goffman noted when he systematically
compared various forms of talk (1981). As the new pragmatists put it, the
correspondence theory of truth is untenable because the only thing with
which we can compare statements are other statements (Rorty 1980).

In this light, there are at least two possible criteria of what constitutes
"good knowledge": the pragmatic and the aesthetic. It is even possible to
claim that the latter are included in the former, and vice versa, if treated
broadly enough. Something "works" because it touches me, because it is
beautiful, because it is a powerful metaphor, but one also hears engineers
say of their machines, "Look how beautifully it works!" In such a perspective, good knowledge is what is judged by a relevant community (situated
in time and place) to be useful, moral, or beautiful. There are great advantages and great dangers associated with such communal definitions of
value, though.

The dangers are two: reification and group-think. Once you are "labeled," you can easily become "stigmatized": you *are* a positivist no matter
what you do; if you do something antipositivist, you may at best be called
inconsistent. Group-think ("we and our research") may seem cozy, but it
is also suffocating. It has been pointed out, by Orwell among others, that
there is no stricter control than that exercised by peers in a nonhierarchical
group linked together by strong emotional ties.

Why refer to a community at all, then, and why try to establish what
beliefs it shares? In Rorty's view, there are no a priori or universal criteria;
all there is is a *temporary and localized* agreement in a "scholar community" about what is "good," "functional," or "beautiful" (Rorty 1987,
1992b). By a "scholar community," he does not mean a concrete group of
people with names and geographical locations. By "temporary," he means
"as I write it or as you read it," and by "localized," he often means "in this
paragraph" or even "in this sentence." So in one paragraph he would say
"we fuzzies," meaning whoever does not care about formal methods, and
in another he would say "we social democrats," meaning whoever believes

that our society should minimize suffering; but it is quite clear that not all fuzzies are social democrats or vice versa. In Burke's terms, it is actions (acts) that constitute a community, not people (agents) or places (scenes). Thus, in this book, I try to use "we" in the sense of "everybody who reads this and agrees with it," which may vary from one paragraph to another.

## Language

What may have to be focused more directly within the broad framework constructed above is the status of language and, consequently, its role in the construction of both reality and knowledge.

For the sake of simplicity, the views on language can be shuffled into two groups. According to one, language is a medium between the knowing subject and the objective world; words have their referents in reality. Thus, their meaning comes from the fact that they stand for something else (in a softer version, they are conventionally attributed to something else), as illustrated below.

| Self | Language as Medium | | Reality |
| --- | --- | --- | --- |
| which "creates" meaning | "expresses" meanings | "reflects" facts | which is constituted by facts |

While many theoretical sources can be quoted for these ideas (for example, a popular version of the linguistic theory of Peirce), it can also be claimed that this is a common view of language that is held by organizational practitioners and by theoreticians.

In my study, however, I assumed that language is a set of symbols that acquire meaning by being related to other symbols (Saussure 1983). However, such couplings are local and temporary (although they can, of course, last for centuries). Thus, poststructuralists, who radicalized Saussure's view, spoke about the "free-floating signifiers" (Barthes 1975).

I do not intend to plunge deeper than necessary into the linguistic debate; my purpose is to relate it to the discussion of the worldview of interpretive studies. The view of the word, or the text, as independent of "reality out there" has serious consequences in that it refutes an—often implicit— ideal of organization studies as revealing the "reality" behind "appearances." The attempts to capture "the essence of reality" Rorty calls "metaphysics"—an interesting irony, as the positivist tradition was established as a revolt against metaphysics, only to join its foe in the end. This critique of metaphysics can be juxtaposed with Baudrillard's praise of "surface," as in the fictitious duologue that follows.

Metaphysics [is] a search for theories which will get at real essence. . . . The metaphysician prays, with Socrates, that the inner and the outer man will be as one—that irony will no longer be necessary. He is prone to believe, with Plato, that the parts of the soul and of the state correspond, and that distinguishing the essential from the accidental in the soul will help us distinguish justice from injustice in the state.

The metaphysicians attempt to rise above the plurality of *appearances*—in the hope that an unexpected unity will become evident—a unity which is a sign that something *real* has been glimpsed, something which stands *behind* the appearances and produces them. (Rorty 1989, 92)

Today, there are no more scenes, no more mirrors, but a screen and a network. No more transcendence or depth, but an immanent surface, where operations occur, a smooth and operative surface of communication. Just like television, this beautiful, prototypical object of the new era, the entire universe surrounding us and our bodies became a screen of control. (Baudrillard 1987, 12, translated by Richard Şotto)

The readers deterred by Baudrillard's French style will be pleased to know that a similar idea has been expressed in truly American style by William H. Whyte, Jr., who declared, ironically, that "Someday someone is going to create a stir by proposing a radical new tool for the study of people. It will be called the face-value technique. It will be based on a premise that people often do what they do for the reasons they think they do" (1956, 40).

The recommendation that we should study only appearances makes some people uneasy, probably because of its seemingly "idealist" and "antimaterialist" connotations. Hence the various attempts to reach *Beyond Objectivism and Relativism* (Bernstein 1983), of which I would like to name one, David Silverman and Brian Torode's *The Material Word* (1980). I found their approach, when applied to organizational tales, very useful (Czarniawska-Joerges 1994), as others have done before me (see Clegg 1987).

> As against the view of language as a reality *sui generis,* whether transparent or opaque, we insist that language necessarily refers, as appearance, to a reality other than itself. But, we propose, the way in which it does this is to refer to *other language.* Thus plurality is inseparable from language, and it is the play of reference from one language to another language that sug-

> gests the reference of language to a reality other than language.
> (Silverman and Torode 1980, 8)

I shall try to interpret what Silverman and Torode are saying by applying a line of reasoning inspired by Rorty (1980). The word *is* material; and any use of words assumes and refers to something other than itself. This, however, is purely a matter of belief: we know that there is "something other than text," only because our language tells us so. Nevertheless, we find it practical to act upon this belief. Everyday talk constantly refers to reality other than language while remaining oblivious to the fact that it actually refers to other texts. Social sciences, however, must not remain oblivious to that fact or try to blackbox it with the help of some ideology or other (such as positivism or materialism). The researcher's task, say Silverman and Torode, is to discover connections between the texts, which are often hidden. They call the device to be used *interruption:* the two authors suggest that we try to interrupt the smooth flow of the routinized tale, asking questions such as "How come?" "Why not the other way around?" or "Who says so?" or, in their own words, comparing what a text *says* with what it *does,* forcing the text to speak to other texts. It amounts to linguistic garfinkeling,[3] or a semiotic reading (see below in this chapter), in which the basis from which the questions are asked is not "reality" or "the truth," but another vocabulary. In fact, as we shall see, the actors in the field interrupt each other a lot.

Thus, Silverman and Torode's recommendation could be translated as meaning that "appearance," "reality," and "difference" are important elements of everyday texts, and must be seriously taken into account, which does not prevent us from debunking the "material/nonmaterial" dichotomy.

Nevertheless, there are still some hurdles ahead. If reality is composed of texts, what do we mean when we claim to be doing "field studies" and to have "study objects"? What do we expect to find "in the field"?

## Approaching the Field
### *Paying a Visit to the Other*

If all there is to be known are words, why should anybody bother to do field studies at all? After all, one can think up an organizational world; one can speculate about it, as both economics and fiction do. One can also read what other researchers have said about it and make a literary study of it—

unreflectively, as is most common, or reflectively, as in good literary criticism. Why, then, insist on the third possibility of going out into the "field," which although not always muddy and windy is certainly less comfortable—physically and psychologically—than our ivory tower? The answer, as is often the case, is hidden in the question.

The first two ways of approaching reality—by way of speculation or texts written by people like ourselves—represent an interesting but to some extent narcissistic exercise. Reality or, more precisely, the field is where the Other lives.[4] And even though anthropology in the past had obvious military and commercial uses, it was still largely inspired by this curiosity about the Other, *about people who construct their worlds differently from the way we construct ours.*

My purpose is not to romanticize field research. Anthropologically inspired studies, like the one that is the basis of this book, are fraught with difficulties.[5] A common enemy of field research within the researcher's own society is the taken-for-grantedness of meanings and their modes of construction. There is a good reason to suspect, though, that these meanings and modes usually accompany the anthropologist to exotic countries, as the controversy over Margaret Mead's studies has shown (Toulmin 1984). On the other hand, most researchers find professional practices other than their own almost as exotic as the mores of the Trobrianders (Sanday 1979). Desensitization or bias has to be compared with the clumsy ignorance of the outsider, which can be removed only by complete acculturation—if at all:

> Much nonsense has been written, by people who should know better, about the anthropologist "being accepted." It is sometimes suggested that an alien people will somehow come to view the visitor of distinct race and culture as in every way similar to the locals. This is, alas, unlikely. The best one can probably hope for is to be viewed as a harmless idiot who brings certain advantages to this village. (Barley 1986, 56)

Nigel Barley deserves to be a patron saint of ethnographic organization studies. He provoked as much controversy in anthropology in the United Kingdom as Carlos Castaneda did in the United States in 1968. Like Castaneda, he refused to make a clear distinction between "science" and "literature." His substantive program, though, was different. He demystified the anthropological procedure, revealing ethnographers as pathetic figures, dupes in alien cultures, whose heroism came from overcoming the hardship and absurdity of their situation, not from the superiority of their knowledge or their stance[6] (*The Innocent Anthropologist*, 1983; but see also 1986, 1988). Barley, against the judgment of his elders, also claimed that it made sense to study one's own culture, and received vindication in the form of a BBC series (*Native Land: The Bizarre Rituals and Curious Customs That Make the English English*, 1989).

Many of his observations apply not only to studies of villages but also to studies of corporations. In these, the natives may sometimes briefly nurse the illusion of sharing a common culture ("You, with your knowledge of economics, must surely see that . . ."). But these tender and ephemeral illusions do not remove the basic sense of alienation, which becomes obvious over any more prolonged period of contact. With luck, the visitor may be regarded as "an uninformed but well-intentioned researcher"—a euphemism for "a harmless idiot." In this particular case, my background—coming from another country and being a woman—automatically promoted me to such a convenient position.

Let us assume that the problem of "home-blindness," as it is sometimes called, has been successfully solved. Another problem immediately raises its ugly head: if we have to have dealings with people who are genuinely different from ourselves, how can we understand them? How can we communicate with the Other?

The best-known and most time-honored way is to learn the Other's language. But learning is never a one-way process; a teacher and a pupil engage in a dialogue that can become a power struggle. While the original balance is tipped toward the teacher, it need not remain so. Although colonizers often learned the language of the country they occupied, they were simultaneously imposing their own frame of reference (ideology, paradigms) on the natives. The reaction against colonialism generated a higher level of self-awareness among anthropologists. Geertz (1988) says, with a touch of irony, that sensitive ethnographers, who are aware of the problems, deny any possibility of communication; only by sharing the same experience in time and place can people overcome their mutual strangeness.

It is not necessary to adopt such an extreme stance; at any rate, the "sensitive anthropologist" is probably a product of Geertz's ironic imagination. In a more serious vein, other anthropologists tried to solve the puzzle, for example, in cybernetic terms, such as MacKay (1964), who maintained that communication between two alien systems is possible only when the systems together engage in the creation of a third common language, originally alien to them both. Along the same lines but at a more mundane level, the constructivists posit a solution that has been known for centuries: pidgin, spoken by those who travel between cultures (Fuller 1996), a linguistic hybrid.

Marianella Sclavi (1989), following ideas in Bakhtin/Medvedev (1928), claims that what is needed is an attitude of *outsidedness*,[7] which offers different grounds for communication from the much romanticized empathy. It aims at understanding not by identification ("they are like us") but by the recognition of differences —"we are different from them, and they are different from us; by exploring these differences we will understand ourselves better." In an interview given shortly before his death in 1975, Bakhtin put it as follows:

> In order to understand, it is immensely important for the person who understands to be *located outside* the object of his or her creative understanding—in time, in space, in culture. For one cannot ever really see one's own exterior and comprehend it as a whole, and no mirrors or photographs can help; our real exterior can be seen and understood only by other people, because they are located outside us in space, and because they are *others*. (Kelly 1993, 61)

Lest my plea be understood as a call for exoticism, it is worth mentioning that the model of the extopic attitude that Sclavi follows in her own research is Truman Capote's "A Day's Work,"[8] in which the writer follows the whole working day of Mary Sanchez, a cleaning woman who is everything he is not: woman, Hispanic, large, working-class, heterosexual. Such an attitude involves not romanticizing but a respect for strangers; instead of "taming" them to become "like us," we assume that there will be differences; this in turn we see as a source of knowledge, not least about ourselves. This is very important and also very difficult to live up to in business and public administration, where researchers often behave as though they were practitioners, giving advice, establishing the "best practice," and in general meddling with realities.

One way of avoiding this involves more (although not self-indulgent) self-reflection. The interpretive anthropologists such as Marcus and Fischer (1986) suggest that the researcher should operate on two levels at the same time, recounting the tales of "other worlds" while also reflecting on the status of these tales. The researcher nevertheless always produces a meta-account (even though the totalizing effect can be reduced to editing or making a collage of field accounts), and should therefore also reflect upon its status. The second and fourth steps (interrupting tales of the field and one's own tale from the field) represent the reflective procedures that have recently been attracting more attention than before. Such reflection can be assisted by taking a look at the "procedures of the field," at how the texts of organization studies are produced in the first place.

## Most Frequent Choices

A troublesome convention in these matters insists on a separation at this point between "quantitative" and "qualitative" methods, with the second belonging "obviously" in the realm of the interpretive paradigm. The opposite procedure is to claim that the interpretive approach can use quantitative techniques (and why not?), and that meanings can be counted (but what for?). The point is not to demonstrate that interpretation may be a variation of the positivist paradigm. The difference is in perceiving the language of numbers as "natural" (and therefore standing unequivocally for the referents in reality), and in treating it as conventional, along with literary language. From this last perspective, the choice between numbers and words is a communicative choice, no less, no more.

As people in organizations use words rather than numbers for communication (unlike, let us say, statisticians, although even they probably use more words than numbers), the so-called qualitative methods are in fact used more often. But this does not make them automatically relevant or suitable.

Two other traits can be seen as common to many interpretive studies. One is the emphasis on processes rather than structures. It is the process of construction that is interesting rather than the constructs themselves— a point that escapes many researchers, who, after solemnly stating that "reality is socially constructed" and quoting their Berger and Luckmann, proceed to study the reified results of a construction process that is never revealed. The second is a consequence of the first, and it amounts to a preference for historically situated studies rather than cross-section or synchronic ones. Meaning emerges over time and changes over time; further, in present conversations we evoke others from the past, not because they are fixed in the past and can be found there like flies in amber, but because the "making of history" is in itself historical. But this does not mean that interpretive studies must be plotted against long periods of time. There are no strict rules in the interpretive approach, not because it is "fuzzy" (it is fuzzy because of it), but because it is aware of the temporality and local nature of rules.

Let me then speak of what is. In field organization studies, in my own time and reference group, two types are the most frequent: case studies and window studies.

*Case studies* have a long tradition and have sources and prototypes in history, medicine, and law. Basically a historical approach, it suffered a horrible fate at the hands of Robert Yin, who monopolized the method only to spend his energy on twisting it into a resemblance of positivist legitimacy. Just take a glance at the definition:

> A case study is an empirical inquiry that:
>
> - investigates a contemporary phenomenon within its real-life context; when
> - the boundaries between phenomenon and context are not clearly evident; and in which
> - multiple sources of evidence are used. (Yin 1984, 23)

Now, bear with me (and Yin) for a short moment while I try to make a close reading of this definition. We can agree that a case study is an empirical inquiry, noting in passing that the notion of an empirical inquiry is rather imprecise. It may contain anything from a field study to the statistical analysis of secondhand data to a content analysis of literature. But Yin continues to narrow the definition down. The second element in the definition is reached by exclusion: neither historical studies nor studies of out-of-context phenomena are case studies. Regarding the first, it is hard to see the grounds for such an exclusion; one wonders what Chandler (1977, 1990) would have to say about it. Regarding the second, the study of a phenomenon out of its context seems to me a description of any bad study, case or otherwise.

Further, the boundaries between the phenomenon and the context are never "clearly evident." Their visibility is, one would think, a matter of authorial intentions or skills. Phenomena and contexts are constructions; if for some reason we want them sharply differentiated, we can always see to it. Take the Aston School's definitions of centralization, automation, and other "variables," which it clearly saw as quite distinct from one another and from the context. To me and other "fuzzies" (Rorty 1987), the boundaries between the phenomenon and the context are always blurred.

Finally, "multiple sources of evidence" (note the forensic language) are recommended in all research paradigms and, above all, by common sense.

Here, a case study is the study of development of a certain phenomenon. The process or focus is chosen by the researcher, and the time frame is beyond the decision of the researcher (a study can be terminated before the case is over; which does not terminate the case for other observers). The span of the development of the case is negotiated between the researcher and the organizational actors (alive or documented).

There is a possible variant to the approach, which may explain Yin's aversion to the term *historical* (provided that he understood it in a rather peculiar way). The development of a phenomenon can be studied *retrospectively* ("can you tell me what happened?") or *prospectively,* when the researcher tries to follow the chain of events, as well as following the chain of accounts, of course. Historical ethnographies—like those of Carlo Ginzburg (1966, 1976, 1995) or Marshall Sahlins (1985, 1995)—and contemporary ethnographies both address accounts that change with time, as new events demand new interpretations.

In a retrospective account, one story encompasses all the previous accounts; it is a history edited from the standpoint of today. This would be a problem if our purpose were to establish "what really happened," but if the correspondence theory is rejected, such a purpose is rejected with it. What differentiates the two approaches is that a prospective approach studies the process of social construction in its making; a retrospective approach is scrutinizing a construct that exists at the time of the study. In other words, in a retrospective approach, the time dimension is located in the accounts of actors; in a prospective one, it is located in the account of the researcher. Studies in the history and sociology of science and technology—the dynamic field that contains many exemplary organization case studies—use both approaches and do not differentiate between them (e.g., Knorr Cetina 1981; Collins 1985; Pinch 1986; Latour 1988a; Traveek 1992).

In what I shall call a *window study,* the balance is reversed. A researcher opens an arbitrary time window and describes all that can be seen through it. Here it is the processes that are negotiated with the actors: what is central, important, new, routine, and so on. A window study can turn into a case study (when the researcher decides to leave the window and follow the train of events), or into a series of mini-cases. As this description indicates, I am not proposing to establish a new methodology here, but suggesting a label (the demand for labels is insatiable, it seems) to cover what is actually the common but unnamed practice in organization research.

The degree of actual participation in organizational events may differ, regardless of the approach adopted. Participant observation is possible in case studies *and* window studies, although different events will be observed. The nonparticipant extreme is represented by document studies, while in between are interviews. What is reported here is a typical window study, an anthropologically inspired field study of several organizations related to one another in a pattern I have called a "constellation," to stress its difference from voluntary networks and from formal hierarchies. Let me reflect briefly on the kind of text that a "report from the field" can be said to represent.

## A Conversation between Texts
### Constructing the Field

At the outset of my study of public-sector organizations in Sweden, I realized that the conventional participant observation of all the units I wanted to include would have required ten years to perform. I needed another approach. I chose to repeatedly ask my interlocutors, who were located in various parts of the two focused constellations of organizations, to tell me what they had been doing at work over the past two to three weeks. This "observant participation" lasted about fourteen months. It involved ten to twenty visits to each one of the organizations concerned; it further included actual observation of selected events and extensive document analysis, resulting in a description of events structured along the lines of a dramatistic analysis (Czarniawska-Joerges 1992b). In the present text, the excerpts from that analysis enter upon a conversation with the selected texts from the field and from other conversations.

But how was the field delineated? I was making constructionist decisions all the time in the field, as well as afterward, while struggling to make sense of the material I had gathered. I found it misleading to speak of "organizations" as if they were clear-cut entities with obvious borders. I find it more profitable to study *action nets*, situated in *organization fields*, distinguishable from one another by the kind of meanings and products socially attributed to them ("banking," "city management," "health insurance"), where various types of unit are formed and dissolved, resulting in organizations rather than originating from them.

In practical action, actors or organizations may form action nets not

only with other organizations within the same field but also with many
other organizations that have nothing to do with "their" field but are necessary for a given activity to take place. Thus, a municipality will interact
with the government and with the Swedish Association of Local Authorities; but it will also, and perhaps above all, interact with the county council,
the local banks, the main local corporation, and so on. The traditional
picture of "the mayor, the priest, the doctor, and the police chief" may
lie at the root of the idea of the *action net* as I picture it. Contemporary
organizations, however, may be expected—thanks to communications
technology—to interact in just the same way with organizations that are
far away, and to be affected by organizations with which they may never
interact but that nonetheless constitute an important part of the same organization field. A municipality in the north of Sweden may decide to establish ties with a supplier of scanning software located in the south of
Sweden. A small Swedish town might decide to introduce the same governance structure as Bologna, which has been described in the local authorities' newsletter.

The reader may wonder what is the connection or the difference between the concept of the action net and that of the network. As I see it, the
concept of the network (Snehota 1990) is much closer to the rational actor
perspective than to the institutional one. In the network approach, actors
are the source of the network. They initiate the interactions, creating networks by repetition. A change in the actors or the loss of actors will deci-
sively alter the character of the network. Such an event, however important
to an action net, changes it only slightly. If one bank refuses to keep municipal accounts, the municipality does not stop having accounts; it turns to
another bank. Having a bank account is an appropriate thing to do in the
field of municipal finances. Actions are shaped by institutions that are more
durable than actors; indeed, they endow the actors with their identities
rather than the other way around. People are born to the existing organization fields, to the institutions that formed them, and although they may
spend their lives trying to change them and may even succeed by intention
or default, the relationship is reciprocal, but the balance of power is tipped
toward institutions. The focus here is on actions, as creating both actors
and the structures of the field. Thus, the construction of a new action net
may be indicative of a change in an existing institution or the emergence
of a new one.

The last concept that should be mentioned here is that of *institutional
thought structure* (Warren, Rose, and Bergunder 1974), an idea that is

akin to Douglas's "thought worlds" (Douglas 1987) but also to Mac-
Intyre's "canonical tradition" (1988). The concept was born, explain the
authors, at the interface between the sociology of knowledge and institutionalism. An institutionalized thought structure is a highly speculative
concept, an entity that cannot be proved to exist, cannot be described in
its totality, and cannot, of course, be measured. But it is important, not
least because the actors in the field frequently evoke it, directly or indirectly.
It is a set of basic assumptions or norms that are taken to be axiomatic;
that is, it is assumed that they exist, that they are shared by the majority in
the field, and their presence is evoked whenever an action is questioned
(literally as in a press interview, or metaphorically as when they are in-
fringed).

> What we are concerned with in the concept of institutionalized
> thought structure is the intricate interweaving or mutual re-
> inforcement of what is known as believed or conceptualized,
> on the one hand, about [certain kinds of problems], and the ac-
> tual configurations of specific organizations and procedures
> employed in addressing them (Warren, Rose, and Bergunder
> 1974, 20).

In literary terms we may be speaking of the repertoire of genres existing at
a certain time in a certain place, the perceived adequacy of certain genres
for certain situations, and the norms, rules, and most common textual
strategies defining a given genre. The concept of the institutionalized
thought structure is of central importance to this book because the organizational actors, and everybody else (that is, the media), all believed that
this structure typified Sweden at the time in the eyes of its inhabitants and
of the outside world; all believed that it was threatened from inside and
was shaking, possibly even changing.

All this shows that what is traditionally called "defining," or giving
meaning to concepts to be used in describing, analyzing, and interpreting
what was observed in the field, involves far more than engaging in a logical
exercise. It is actually a cosmological enterprise, a world-creation (Goodman 1978). In interpreting my material from the field, I shall be moving
within this cosmology of mine, created for the purposes of this book. It is
important to remember, however, that although the people in the field
share much of this cosmology, they do not always use the same terms as I
do; the analytical concepts may not carry the same meaning for them as

they do for me. But they are world makers just as much if not more than any researcher who attempts to write up "a study of the field."

## Back from the Field

When attempts to collect material from the field have been successful, the researcher is rewarded by a pile of texts. Some are written in numbers, some in words; in my own case, some were written by me (e.g., interview records and field notes) and some by other people (e.g., documents and press clippings). This does not matter all that much; the task is to interpret them and to come up with a new text that will bear this interpretation. What, then, are we to look for?

There are at least three versions of the answer to this question. According to the first, conventional one, texts are but a reflection of reality. We have to overcome the text, as it were, to get at what is behind it, at the true story of events. This is consistent with a theory of language as medium between objective reality (the world as it is) and our subjective cognition. When we write our own text, we communicate from our subjective understanding to the world via text.

In the second and more radical version, the text is all there is. The text is the world. Shocking as it may sound, this is not a new idea. There are well-known precedents—the Bible and the Koran, books containing the world as created by God. On a more mundane level, ethnomethodology claims that all the rules typical of a community can be found in any conversation between competent members of that community. From this it is possible to deduce that the only reading of a text is such as is permitted by the rules of reading that the text itself dictates.

The third version, the one I would like to opt for, is close to the previous one but expresses a different preference. Instead of looking at a text under a deconstructivist (or conversation-analytical) microscope, it proposes treating a text as belonging to other texts, as a material trace of a conversation that was or is taking place.

It is difficult to imagine a text analysis in the context of organization studies that makes a clear-cut choice among the three, however. Some kind of realism will always linger, either as a style in the texts we are analyzing or as a stylization of our own texts, undertaken for legitimating purposes. After all, every one of us sits in his or her appropriate iron cage, or rather in a whole collection of iron cages fitting into one another like Russian dolls. The very report on what one is presently thinking about ends up filled with reality claims, heavily decorated with all the institutional trimmings belonging to the genre. This difficulty plagued me throughout this book, and in the final chapter, I propose to tackle it by making a virtue of that vice.

As for the text-as-world approach, it need not be absolutist. As Latour points out, texts "build a world of their own that can be studied as such in *relative and provisional* isolation from other aspects" (1993a, 129). Any close or critical reading requires a momentary concentration on just this text alone. "Semiotics is the ethnomethodology of texts" (Latour 1993a, 131).

How, then, does one analyze conversations/texts, if not in the formalized approach of the conversation analysis? How does one read a text?

Eco (1990) speaks of two kinds of reader: the semantic (naive) reader and the semiotic (critical) one:

> The former [semantic reader] uses the work as semantic machinery and is the victim of the strategies of the author who will lead him little by little along the series of previsions and expectations. The latter [semiotic reader] evaluates the work as an aesthetic product and enjoys the strategies implemented in order to produce a Model Reader of the first level [that is, a semantic reader]. (Eco 1990, 92)

The organizational actors/authors write a variety of works and texts with a Model Reader[9] in mind—their collaborators and competitors, subordinates and superiors, clients and authorities, journalists and researchers. Their Model Reader is, of course, a naive reader. Like novelists, they write for their public, not for the critics. Unlike novelists, however, they do not receive enough systematic critique, which, although it is sometimes irritating, does provoke constant development and innovation in the long run. And here is where we come in—not to show our superiority or the sophistication of the semiotic reader, but to help to develop and change methods of writing. In doing so, nothing prevents us from enjoying and admiring the skillful organizational author. Ideal readers, adds Eco, are those who enjoy the first-level meaning of the text all the more because they know how it was done.[10]

## But Where Do Theories Come In?

Many analyses proceed by contrasting "a naked phenomenon" with possible theories and then choosing the one with "the highest explanatory power." Although I have made theoretical choices as well, I want to establish their credentials by a different route. The choice of a theoretical frame of reference is always situated in time and place and adapted to the purpose at hand. There is no one explanatory link between phenomena and theories that explains (interprets) them. To begin with, the description of a phenomenon is already made in terms that favor certain theories and disfavor others. If I perceive individual decision making as the central organizational process, it is very unlikely that a theory called new institutionalism will attract me by its "explanatory power." Obviously, it is the construction of the worldview that will influence both my descriptions of interesting phenomena and my choice of relevant theories. This is a limitation, however, not a determination. There are a great many phenomena and theories that can be counted as "matching" the interpretive approach, and it is only natural to expect that with time, and on encounters with new friends (those in real life and those in the pages of books and articles), both my interests and my perception of relevance will change, although fundamentals may remain the same.

What, then, is the role of theories in the interpretive approach? If science is a conversation, then theories can be seen as conversational devices, which facilitate conversation by imposing cohesion and stability on interpretations that are being negotiated.

This line of reasoning is related to the vision of the social world and social science as conversation. What we study is how people in other communities construct their world by conversing about it. (How did people in a municipality construct the idea of "company-ization"?) They construct cars and budgets; we construct facts and explanations, or maybe stories and interpretations. Once we get an idea about what their construction looks like, we are ready to contribute to a conversation. We do so first on paper; we converse with other studies, books, and authors. Once the research report is ready, we join a wider conversation; we receive comments, criticisms, and reactions of various kinds.

All this is related to the assumption that civilization, science, and education essentially constitute a conversation that goes on for something like five millennia:

> As civilized human beings, we are the inheritors neither of an inquiry about ourselves and the world, nor of an accumulating body of information, but of a conversation begun in the primeval forest and extended and made more articulate in the course of centuries. (Oakeshott 1959/1991, 490)

   This, then, is what I am trying to do here: to look at the narratives from the field, to compare them with one another and with the narratives of academia, in order to see what they say and what they do, what effect they make and how this effect is achieved. In doing this, I attempt to exemplify the possibility of alternating between semantic and semiotic readings. I owe the authors of the organizational texts the respect of taking them literally (Rorty 1992a, chapter 11). Equally, though, I owe them a reading that goes beyond the first level of meaning, and in this way delivers a "meaning added," a literary equivalent of a "value added."

# PART TWO

# Tales from a Public Sector

# FOUR

# Enacting Routines for Change

## The Swedish Public Sector as a Stage Set
### *The Demise of the Swedish Model*

The Swedish parliament, the Riksdag, makes decisions that are put into effect by the majority or coalition government, and then by central agencies. In other countries these are known as "governmental agencies," but in Sweden they are formally separate from the government. The National Insurance Board, one of the actors in the study presented here, is an example of such an agency.

The next administrative level is the county, with the county council, intermediate offices for some of the central agencies, and executive responsibility for medical services and social insurance among other things. The last level consists of the municipal councils and their administrative organizations.

At first glance, then, we have a perfect hierarchical system, a typical state bureaucracy in four tiers. But only at first glance. A unique history of alliance between king and peasantry (against the nobles) is also a history of considerable initiative and self-help at the local level.[1] Three major Swedish institutions[2] —local governments, social insurance offices, and saving banks—were born at the municipal level and functioned in many aspects as horizontal unions rather than hierarchical units. The historical sediment of this is visible in the remaining federal organs, but also in the fact that it is the municipalities that are the main tax collectors. A large part of the taxes collected by the state returns to the municipalities in the subsidies.

Nevertheless, the public image is that of an omnipotent state, eager to control its citizens and to waste their money, as opposed to anarchist, creative, and effective municipalities. Obviously, there are two-way connections between image and practice: the central government does like to control, and local authorities do usually have enough resources to be creative. Also, the point is not that the image is "incorrect," "distorted," or "exaggerated," but that the functionality of this particular and peculiar image has been declining in the period of a political crisis that Sweden is experiencing at present.

This crisis, and the measures that have been suggested for dealing with it, are not unique. The public sector in other countries, too, has had to put on the dunce's cap, particularly in the United States during the Reagan administration (Downs and Larkey 1986, 219). Yet there is also more to it, something specific to Sweden, which served for many years as a model for the successful welfare state. Thus, there is talk of crisis, or even of the "death" of the Swedish Model.

The Swedish public sector experienced a long period of economic expansion that came to a halt only in the late 1970s. Since then, a continuous campaign has been under way, aimed at making it more effective. Because of the failure of a program to control inflation, 1990 saw a first government crisis, something as alien to the Swedish political scene as it is normal to the Italian. Wildcat strikes and difficulty in renewing central labor agreements tended to be labeled a "legitimacy crisis."

The partners to the "historical compromise" (symbolized by the agreement signed in Saltsjöbaden in 1938 after a long and bitter fight between employers and labor) are changing positions. The Swedish Employers' Federation announced a retreat from the practice of collective bargaining. In connection with this, its chairman, Ulf Laurin, declared: "After a long illness, the 'Swedish Model' is dead" (*SAF-tidningen*, 16 February 1990).

The Study of Power and Democracy in Sweden, a five-year interdisciplinary research program, could be said to have carried out the peaceful burial of the Swedish Model. In the final report (*Democracy and Power in Sweden* 1990), the Swedish Model acquired a definite form as well as a farewell message. The argument was that a fifty-year-old package of solutions could not be expected to go on working unchanged; new solutions were in sight, as well as new problems.

One of the essential features of the Swedish Model was the open interaction between the parties on the labor market, free from state intervention. The fact that the state and the municipalities are among the biggest employers influenced the practice of industrial relations, which then found institutional expression (the pay freeze and a special mediation organ, both introduced in the spring of 1990). To counter yet another stereotype, it should be added that although the state and the municipalities are big employers, they are far from being big owners. Jointly, they own 5 percent of the stock market in Sweden (*Democracy and Power in Sweden* 1990).

This free play in the labor market arena was supported by specific institutions. The parties were represented centrally by a few homogeneous organizations. Nowadays, however, "organizations are neither few, centralized nor homogeneous" (*Democracy and Power in Sweden* 1990, 390). Local pay negotiations have become legitimate, even in the public-sector organizations.

These changes reflect the fading of the "historical compromise." The Swedish wage-earner funds, a system proposed by the Congress of the Trade Union Confederation in 1971 to increase employee participation in capital formation, proved to be an issue that powerfully polarized political opinion. According to the original proposal formulated by Rudolf Meidner, the large private companies were to transfer a certain percentage of their profits annually to "wage-earner investment funds" (Åsard 1980). A bitter ten-year-long fight between the two sides cast a shadow over the consensus culture, previously proudly claimed as typical of a "Swedish character." *Democracy and Power in Sweden* points out that although consensus remains a useful technique for handling difficult interactions in practice, its reputation as a normative value has changed. Public opinion today prefers more critical attitudes; consensus seeking is seen as "conflict avoidance," and the fight for equality has been redefined as "a pressure for uniformity." There seems to be an implication here that a fifty-year-old national image, no matter how positive, must inevitably reach a point at which it is no longer adequate, useful, or even flattering.

A new identity is needed and, according to the report, was being sought. The potential sources of the rebellion and of the new model(s) are the problems of women and immigrants in the labor market and growing inequality in economic standards, perceived influence, and access to knowledge. All in all, it may be a question not so much of a crisis as of a turning point. Besides, as it so often happens, actual practices still cultivate the old virtues, especially in the private sector, which is not under direct attack—or at least not yet; but by 1992, banking operations were an obvious candidate for the role of the next popular scapegoat.

## Selected Scenes

As Paul DiMaggio emphasized in his essay "State Expansion and Organizational Fields," "[a] field is always an analytical construct, and how one defines it depends on the phenomena in which one is interested" (1983, 249). It would therefore be both possible and justifiable to treat the public administration as an organization field, but any action net could then be of interest. I therefore defined two more specialized fields, municipal administration and social insurance, and tried to depict the existing and emerging action nets that originated around the field's recognizably central actors. In the case of local administration, this meant looking at the government (ministries), the Swedish Association of Local Authorities (SALA), and certain municipalities (local authorities) represented in this book by Big City, Northtown, and Little Village. In the case of social insurance, it meant the National Social Insurance Board (NSIB), the Association of Social Insurance Offices (ASIO), and social insurance offices, at present located at the county level—represented here by Big County, Northern County, and Middle County.

Social insurance in Sweden covers medical care, rehabilitation in case of accidents at work, and so on, for all citizens. Although the resources are administered centrally by NSIB, the activities are carried out by the County Social Insurance Offices (CSIO). The local origins of social insurance are still sedimented in its former federal organ, ASIO.[3]

I collected various narratives: the self-reports of my interlocutors, various documents, my own field notes, and the like. The initial classifying device with which I approached the collected material (my own and my interlocutors' narratives) was a categorization of these "tales of the field," as Van Maanen (1988) calls them, into stories, serials, and themes (Jean Matter Mandler, 1984).

A *story* consists of a plot comprising causally related episodes that culminate in a solution to a problem. Stories usually contain several stages that contribute to a final solution, albeit in a complex way; for example, via false solutions and the creation of new problems. They reveal a good deal about specific organizations, since it is precisely in the story context that actors improvise against the background of known rules. Stories have a clear chronological structure, with a beginning and an end (serials continue so long as they pass the test of popularity, while themes consist of minor scenes continually repeated). They combine traditional elements ("This is the way we do things in this organization") with spontaneous features ("But does it actually apply in this case?") and creative aspects ("Now we do it this way instead"). Stories are about critical, dramatic events in the life of the organizations.

A *theme* is linked to modern drama. There is no plot, only thematically related episodes ("scenes"), such as "personnel," "communication," and so on. The objective is to demonstrate "what people do and how they act in certain types of situations."[4] In organizational terms, scenes built around such themes show how relevant routines and rules are created, recreated, and changed in everyday life.

A *serial* does not have any plot, either. It consists of temporarily related episodes ("installments") that both vary and are repeated. A serial does not contain any solution: the point is that it can continue forever (or as long as anybody is interested in it). Organizational changes of various kinds may be regarded as serials of this type. Just as in stories and themes, the actors have to take into account "how people do things in this organization," but in this case it is a question of transforming a story (something that happened once and might never be repeated) into a theme (something that is incorporated into the relevant routines). Although there was originally a clear idea about what the serial was to be about ("decentralization," "company-ization," or "computerization") and how this was to be achieved, people were well aware that serials must be continually adapted to meet new conditions and requirements. Some actors depart, and new writers introduce new ideas. There are also a number of similar serials, with which the director and writers compete but which they also imitate. The serial proceeds slowly but surely; today's episode establishes the conditions for the next (the serial continues). Serials reflect the current fashion in the organization field within which the action takes place.

"Stories" are the most localized element; they come from specific organizations. "Serials" are recognizable in the whole of the organization field known as "the Swedish public sector," while the "themes" are sure to be found in large, complex organizations of many kinds. At the same time, all three are clearly linked, and all are in fact concerned with routines and change, construction and deconstruction, creativity and conformism.

I start with stories, as they can be seen as the basic unit of almost any narrative. In organizations the prescription for a good story is very simple indeed: mix well some random events, several attempts at control, and the corresponding amount of countercontrol, put in a warm place, and wait for results. Stories begin because somebody has had an idea and wants to realize it, or the other way around: because something has happened, and people in an organization feel they have to react to it. The stream of events begins to flow, and, as all streams do, it encounters various hurdles along the way. In traditional terms of organizational theory discourse, we (and practitioners) often talk about "friction." The encounters between "the old" and "the new" and the resulting "friction" are, in fact, a recurring topic in the stories that follow.

## Three Stories about Public Administration Management
### A New Budget and Accounting Routine in Big City

This story begins when the Municipal Court decided that Big City was overcharging its citizens for energy and water. The problem was not the level of the charges, however, but the obsolete accounting system that made a proper follow-up of incomes or expenditures impossible. As a result of this "legal friction," Big City's treasury director and his team decided to work out a "clean" accounting system which would show exactly where and when the existing money appeared.

In order to solve some technical problems connected with this, the authors of the new routine decided to introduce some unorthodox accounting techniques; these were commonsensical but at variance with the traditional principles of proper accounting. Tradition recommended the balancing principle, while the innovators wanted to introduce a cash principle. What matters, then, is how much money a given unit has, not whether the columns agree. The goal was to prevent the usual "end-of-the-year cheating," when all units overspend to achieve the required balance, and to encourage saving by guaranteeing that the sum saved can be used in the next budget year (and won't be appropriated by the central office). In short, the classical troubles (and solutions) of budget-financed activities.

As the proposal went against the lines recommended to the municipalities by the Association of Local Authorities, or rather by their group of auditors who opted for proper balancing, the innovators decided to introduce a double system, one traditional and one new, until the new routine could prove itself even to its opponents. Thus, an expected "professional friction" led to an increase in creativity and the careful planning of the introduction phase. The double work did not discourage the planners; to the contrary, they hoped that by presenting two sets of numbers side by side they could persuade even the hardest skeptics to see the superiority of the new system with their own eyes.

> You must understand that municipal accounting today is little
> else than a game with numbers. Our ambition was to change
> this state of affairs, to make an annual report actually say
> something. We wanted to relate it to actual operations and to
> tell the story of what we wanted to achieve, what has actually
> been done, and what the prospects are for the future.

Careful introduction was especially important since it was not only the external auditors but even more the municipal accountants who were not entirely happy with the proposal. It was partly a question of power, with one group of economists against all the others. But it was also a question of comfortable old routines, approved by the professional community.

> It is very difficult to abandon old habits—for all those people
> who deal daily with such questions in a practical context.

They may even agree with you in principle, but when it comes to practice, all they see are the problems. They refuse to see the opportunities for us in the change proposed. It's too threatening to their bookkeepers' souls. Some of them have built up all their professional lives around those bits and pieces that must eventually fit elegantly into their places in the final accounts. A proposal that aims at shaking the pieces out of place also means that they will have to lose some of their power and status.

This "hierarchical friction" led to the construction of an elaborate training program, in order to avoid complaints of technical difficulties. Special "service groups" were to explain the proposal to all affected units, while an "emergency group" was to take care of all the practical problems as they appeared. Much time and effort were put into the computer systems, because existing programs—created as they were to achieve a balance—could not cope with the cash principle.

The potentially most dangerous interface, however, was the one with the politicians. Although the aim of the change in routine was to provide simple and legible economic information, at the same time it would also create a transparency that precluded most well-known political techniques, such as painting a catastrophic picture of municipal finances. Furthermore, it reduced the distance between the political and administrative operations, giving the politicians both insight into and responsibility for previously mysterious financial developments. But the expected "political friction" did not occur; the majority agreed on the introduction of the new routine and the double system.

Work started. Service and emergency groups went around patiently explaining the ideas behind the new technique and relating it to the old system. They did this under the banner of the contact principle, whereby the new was to be inserted into the old, and both external and internal expectations were to be fulfilled. It meant in practice that the innovators' team reconstructed the computer system so that it encompassed both cash- and balance-oriented bookkeeping, registering the date of payment (new system) and the due date (old system), and meeting the requirements both from the Swedish Association of Local Authorities (SALA) and the stock market. Compared to many other descriptions of planned change, this is a very interesting feature insofar as the usual picture is one of innovation sliding toward old routines despite the innovatory zeal (Warren, Rose, and Bergunder 1974). Here, this element was carefully incorporated into the process from the very beginning.

The operational units appreciated the contact principle very much. Surprisingly, there were no problems in operating a double system; people claimed that it helped them to understand the point of the change. And when complaints did arise, they were of the usual kind, namely, that there is not enough money to do what is really needed.

Eight months later, when the project was acquiring full speed, the municipal councillor representing the opposition announced his intention of getting a majority in the Finance Council to vote for abolishing the change. Although he did not succeed, political discussion started up in earnest. The project proceeded more cautiously, and attempts were made to involve all interested parties in the discussion of the final version of the proposal. But this final version was put on ice by the opposition.

We leave Big City now, not knowing whether the proposal was finally accepted or rejected. I imagine it will have been be accepted, after negotiations have dealt with this last "political friction." In any case, there are at least two interesting aspects to this story.

One concerns the role of friction in planned change. Traditionally, it is interpreted negatively: it represents an obstacle to the realization of the innovators' idea, it threatens change, it reflects the conservative forces in an organization. In the present case, it would be hard to claim that all the types of friction encountered were pleasant, rewarding, or desired; nonetheless, friction did emerge as both necessary and energizing. An idea born in one head or in a few heads cannot "fit" all other perceptions. Friction reveals its faults, not as a "less than perfect" solution but as a pragmatic solution that is perfect only insofar as it works. A proposal can begin to function only when all the relevant sources of friction have been activated and the problems solved. This does not, however, exclude the possibility that too much friction can kill an innovation. Where does the threshold lie between "bad" and "good" friction?

A second observation concerns the remarkable way of combining the new and old ways of acting. Again, it is traditionally recommended that as soon as a new system, technique, or procedure is ready, it should completely replace the previous one, to avoid confusion. Failure to see to this, albeit very common, is always lamented. In this case we have two systems functioning in parallel in a way that is appreciated by all concerned. Is this the tale of an exception or a rule?

## Tax Reform

Whenever people tell stories about Sweden, there always has to be one about taxes. So here is mine.

An official investigation was under way concerning a possible reform of taxation in Sweden. The minister of finance had officially declared his intentions regarding local governments. The central government wanted to continue the "Robin Hood tax" (whereby "rich" municipalities are taxed more than "poor" ones), an issue that was especially sensitive for the Swedish Association of Local Authorities (SALA), which was supposed to represent all municipalities, rich and poor alike.

Two proposals, one from the government and one from SALA, were put forward for discussion. The content of neither of them was surprising to any of the parties concerned. "It is the negotiations before the discussion that really count," said one of my interlocutors. "That's when things get decided."

The government committee for indirect taxation proposed that more products and services should be subject to value-added (sales) tax. At the same time, however, the local governments were to be allowed to use this tax money in their own economies. This proposal met with some suspicion at the municipal level, where it was presumed that the government would reduce state subventions by the same amount.

Assuming, however, that the intentions of central government were honest, the sensible thing to do at the local level was to freeze all purchasing until the time of the reform (when the value-added tax could be appropriated) and replace by leasing. There was a little problem, though: leasing had previously been severely condemned in the public administration; the whole operation smacked of tax evasion, something that was possible in private companies but surely not in the public administration.

> It used to be thought immoral to do all this tax evading like certain companies on the private market . . .
> *What stops you from using the same argument today?*
> Well . . . that's exactly the crux of the matter . . . especially as it's quite obvious that it will hurt the taxpayers somewhere or other. Either the costs will be paid by the taxpayers in Big City or by the taxpayers in Sweden as a whole. On the other hand, if all municipalities do the same, there's no problem. After all, the state leases, too.

The reactions of the local governments varied. Little Village had already decided to transfer its housing operations to a sort of company, but in the present situation they changed their minds and did not want to sign the agreement before the end of the year (1990), so as to be able to appropriate the value-added tax (which a local government can keep for itself but a company has to pay to the state). SALA's auditors were consulted before this decision was made, and they wholeheartedly approved. The problem of the staff already employed by the company was solved by taking them "on loan" from the local administration, while all the managers were still employed by the municipal government.

> I think it's idiotic, but it's a legal loophole. Personally I am against such subterfuges, but all I can say is, this is how it is.
> *Are the tax authorities aware of this?*
> Sure they are. I talked to them; I talk to the value-added tax people. We're not the only ones doing this . . . but it's very opportunistic, I think.

This was not the only dilemma facing Little Village and the other municipalities as a result of the announced tax reform. At a conference organized by SALA, the association's own lawyers recommended that the municipal companies such as the water and energy services should pay their income in toto to the municipal treasury in advance, before the end of the year when the tax reform would come into force, thus avoiding the value-added tax.

> Some local governments refused to do this because they didn't think it was fair toward Feldt [then minister of finance], especially as he was furious about it. He threatened to stop state subventions to municipalities who did this. In our local government there was some discussion about it, but finally we accepted the advance payments.
> *Aren't you afraid that Feldt will punish you?*
> It would be very strange if he could.

My interlocutor was himself surprised by Little Village's lack of loyalty. But the argument for accepting the advance payments was that if SALA recommended it, it must mean that "the government hadn't really thought it through, this time around."

Eventually the government decided that it was illegal to accept the advance payments. The decision was not retroactive, but because most of them consisted of energy payments, which were to be collected three months later, the prohibition was effective.

There was a lot of gossip about which municipal authorities did accept the advance payments (among others, both Big City and Little Village did) and which refused to do so.

My hometown did not accept any money. If they got any payments, they sent them back.

*On moral grounds?*

On moral grounds, although it's very difficult to understand their kind of moral reasoning. One would expect it to have been the social-democratic municipalities which refused for moral reasons, but mostly it was the more right-wing municipalities which said no. They protest against other taxes, but when it came to tax evasion they suddenly became extremely moralistic. They said that as this is a Riksdag decision, we must obviously follow it loyally. But when it's a question of the Robin Hood tax, which is also a parliamentary decision, we must be solid in opposing it. I gave up any attempt to understand a long time ago.

At the same time, the government was discussing a ban on tax increases (obviously a very attractive idea in Sweden) but with the possibility of certain exceptions. This discussion did not get very far as the government fell soon afterward. The arrival of a new minister (from the same political party) gave rise to much speculation and to some extent disturbed the routine ways of preparing a reform. The working groups complained that they were informed too late of important developments. SALA and the Federation of County Councils did not agree with the government on ways of neutralizing the negative effects of the tax reform. All of a sudden, the newspaper headlines were shouting, "The Ministry of Finance got everything wrong!" The parliamentary committee called in all the parties. It resulted in an announcement that they differed in basic assumptions, not in detailed calculations. But this was not enough to pacify the offended officials at the ministry:

> When I saw SALA's material for the first time, I was furious! To think that we'd had so much time and so many opportunities to confront each other, to correct any errors and in general come to an agreement. . . . It is grossly unfair to come up with such accusations at the very last minute. They come out of the blue and criticize our calculations, as though they'd never seen them before! . . . I was a bit piqued at first, but then we called and talked to each other and explained why we were furious, and then we sent some papers around and everything is all right again, but . . .

SALA did not give up completely and demanded a meeting with the minister in order to express its disappointment and to demand drastic changes.
Much to the surprise of my interlocutor—a young official who expected
to see dead bodies being carried out of the meeting—the two sides ended
up issuing a common statement informing the mass media of their agreement that the reform must not hurt any municipality in the country and
announcing that they would be working together to achieve this desired
state of affairs. Clearly, they were doing what is called "touching base"—
in this case, the base being the institutionalized thought structure which,
as the antagonists had to be reminded, can be challenged, but only up to
a point.

We can leave the reform here. Tension was high, the action dramatic,
and the actors colorful. And yet we find the same elements as in the previous story, although not less well balanced. There is again a mixture of old
and new, but sometimes there is too much of the new and at other times
too much of the old, and the whole process becomes unbalanced. There
are obviously routines for introducing change, and one must not deviate
from them. Also, there are clearly routines for handling frictions—direct
and calm negotiations—and one must not deviate from them by attracting
the attention of the media. But what is to be done if the aim is to introduce
new routines, so new that nobody knows them?

Let us summarize the plot in a simple way. The government's main
intention was to replace administrative control instruments by economic
ones. Thus, a set of financial regulations was introduced, and, after some
hesitation, the actors began to act in what they perceived as an economi-
cally minded way. Soon, however, this turned out to be wrong; they were
expected to show solidarity and to act out of loyalty to the government.
Some actors did in fact act in this way, but not those who might have been
expected to do so (after all, actors' identities depend on a certain way of
acting in certain situations). An interesting question now arises: by acting
as they did, were the right-wing councils loyal to the state or disloyal to
the ("economic") spirit of the reform? Similarly, was the social-democratic
government acting against its own ideological base, or was it changing its
base by the way it was acting? There is much discussion about "political
talk," allegedly not followed by action; less attention is paid to action without ideological justification. This omission is not surprising, as the critics
of "lack of action" are usually journalists or researchers—great talkers
themselves.

It was interesting to watch the actions of SALA. Their role is to represent every municipality's individual interests, and to encourage solidarity—a paradoxical role, but one that until now had been "resolved" by SALA acting in cooperation with the state. But now we could observe a dramatic (or was it simply dramatistic?) break, performed in front of the media so it could be clearly seen from every direction. SALA represents its own opinion which in turn is built of its own perception of the collective and individual interests of the municipalities.

The local actors were perfectly willing to take part in this centrally arranged spectacle, but its openness was somewhat disconcerting. It is all very well to be enthusiastic about experimental theater, but it is also very difficult for an experienced conventional actor to act in it. What exactly were they playing? If we switch the metaphor from a play to a game, close enough but more comfortably rationalist, we could say that some of the local actors assumed the government was willing to play a calculating, zero-sum market game. When the government began to lose, however, it also got angry. Rather childish and immature, thought some. And what sense does the game make, anyway?

> *If every step one takes meets with a predictable reaction on*
> *both central and local sides, wouldn't it be better to stop the*
> *game?*
> Well, at the local level, people don't believe that everything can
> be centrally controlled, and this opens up the possibility of
> extra wins for the municipalities. . . . But this is not certain,
> either, the investigation about the reform isn't complete,
> and until it is, we're all taking tentative steps on unfamiliar
> ground. . . . Maybe we'll all be proven wrong, but at least we
> can say that we tried.

And so the rules are constructed during the game, or the script is created during the play. One does not know what one wants (or, rather, does not want) until one sees it (Weick 1979). In this case, uncertainty grew as time passed. More and more actions turned out to be forbidden, up to the point where the whole idea of reform seemed to peter out. This was probably affected by the general sense of prolonged political crisis. The tax reform was intended to prevent the crisis; when it did not work, nobody seemed to know what to do next. Paradoxes were resolved—in such a way that it was difficult to know how to proceed. This kind of story is very difficult to interpret in terms of institutional theory. In the next story, things go more as they should.

## The Rehabilitation Program

Another obligatory story in the Swedish repertoire naturally concerns the
social insurance system.

The story of the rehabilitation program starts, in fact, from quite a
different story. A new political climate in the country allowed for a proposal whereby the obligation to pay for the first two weeks of sick leave was
transferred from the social insurance office to the employer. The proposal,
dubbed the "employer's takeover," sent the social insurance offices into a
panic; after all, dealing with short-time sick leave has been their main occupation since the advent of the social insurance system in Sweden. According
to rough calculations, the change would reduce insurance office operations
by 25 to 30 percent, or thirty-five hundred to four thousand employees in
a year, to use the common measure. What would all these people do?

The panic receded when a government committee on rehabilitation
presented its final report, in which it stated that the number of long-term
sick, and the length of such sickness, had both increased, and in order to
reduce the consequent cost to society, an extensive rehabilitation program
must be activated. The social insurance system, various labor market
actors, institutions responsible for industrial welfare, and the medical services were all regarded as being crucial to this process and were expected
to collaborate in the program. More specifically, the social insurance offices
were given the responsibility of initiating the cooperative effort and coordinating the necessary resources at the county level.

The relief in the insurance offices was palpable. Nevertheless, new
tasks meant new worries. The participants mentioned above were known
for conflicts rather than cooperation. Besides, it is easy to coordinate resources, but what resources?

> You cannot achieve a major transformation of the rehabilita-
> tion system without spending a little bit of money on it. If you
> don't pay, it will be no more than an empty gesture. Take our
> county, for example [Northern County]: we have a shortage of
> physicians here, whereas in Stockholm they could make an
> army of them. Mind you, I am not saying they make an army
> of them—they'd do better to send some here.

Despite his facetious tone, my interlocutor from Northern County took his
task very seriously. The county office applied to the National Social Insurance Board for funds for a project on methods of cooperation between
authorities—and received them. The reference group that was to design

and supervise the project gathered for its first meeting. Everybody liked the idea very much, but sectorial thinking was stronger than the cooperative intentions. The physicians, for instance, got the idea that they could sell hospital beds for a good price to the rehabilitators. Other actors were indignant at the thought of such base commercialism. Before a full-fledged conflict could develop, an external consultant reminded the gathering that she was being paid by the hour and persuaded the antagonists to draw up and accept a plan of action for the immediate future. The first step was to consist of a series of interviews conducted by the same consultant with all the potentially interested actors, to discuss existing and potential methods of cooperation and existing and desired resources.

In the meantime, NSIB came up with its own interpretation of the rehabilitation program, announcing that this must be accomplished within the limits of present resources.

> This, naturally, led to protests. The social insurance offices complained: "What do you mean, you said yourselves that two thousand people would be needed to realize the rehabilitation program properly." To which we answered, "Yes, but we never said that these people were to come from outside. The two thousand people have to be mobilized from within current operations."

Both sides were partly right, in the sense that not just anybody could join the ranks of the two thousand. As one official document put it: "Rehabilitation is a very special job. It needs great commitment, patience and perseverance on the part of those who want to help people who have ended up in trouble."

A dry document cannot properly express what everybody in social insurance knows very well. In some ways rehabilitation can be compared to helping the handicapped: it deals with accidents, misery, suffering, and unequal life chances. People who do such work meet daily a side of life that others try to avoid and forget. There is a certain touch of heroism in working with the handicapped, however, and the gratitude of those who are helped can give a worker an incomparable feeling of usefulness and meaning in life.

Rehabilitation work is less heroic. There is nothing romantic about people with lumbago, work-induced neuroses, or disfigurements. Such people are often very bitter, disappointed with themselves and their lives, looking for scapegoats as often as for help. Moreover, people working in rehabilitation always have an unpleasant feeling that any day they themselves may be on the receiving end. In short, rehabilitation needs very special skills, both professional and personal. Awareness of this fact led to the creation of a special working group at NSIB to describe the competence required for this special job.

In the meantime, the reference group in Northern County met again. The atmosphere was one of exhilaration. Representatives of the medical services, the county government, the county hospital administration, the municipal administration, the white-collar union, and Samhall, a state-owned company that employed people with limited employability, were all there, and all agreed that the task facing them was enormously important. Another reason for the festive mood was that the government had decided to allocate special resources for experimental operations to be conducted by two selected insurance offices, with a view to designing the future role of the insurance offices in the rehabilitation program. Northern County was very interested:

> This is an incredible lot of money, SKr 18.5 million ($3.1 million) a year, and the talk is of two years. But the darned thing is there's a rumor that the two offices are already decided, and of course it's not us. But the government document says clearly and explicitly that it is the NSIB and the ASIO together that are to appoint the two experimental offices. So I called ASIO today and warned them—don't let the NSIB act behind your back again! I talked to our board of directors and realized that they were with me on this, so I made them promise to declare our interest in other quarters as well. And you know what the NSIB said? They said all interested offices are required to put in a "tender." What tender, I ask you! What are we playing at now—a "head office and subsidiaries"? A market? This is silly! They behave as if we've all suddenly become private companies.

But all in all things were not too bad. The budget bill contained a substantial sum assigned to the rehabilitation program which was received very positively by NSIB:

> This bill means an incredible lift for our board. It proves that the government has confidence in us, that they believe in our ability to undertake active rehabilitation operations. It gives us a nice start, and it gives us the opportunity to buy services on the open market.

Several members of the reference group in Northern County were absent from the third meeting without giving any explanations, but the next meeting, the one after the budget bill, was fully attended. It had become known that the social insurance office would be able to pay SKr 500 million ($83 million) for the rehabilitation services in the next budget year. All of a sudden the office had found its new role: as a purchaser of services on the open market.

> Well, we didn't know quite what to do. We first had to build out our own organization so that it properly covered all the needs, so we really didn't know what we could promise. . . . We were trying to estimate what would be, let us say, a sensible level of purchase . . . perhaps using the Labor Market Offices for testing and other services—how should I know, maybe fifty to sixty employees over the next year? What would it cost, a million perhaps? How should we know? We'd never thought in these terms before.

The other actors seemed to know a bit more and had had more experience. Samhall initiated a series of meetings to discover what real chances there were that the social insurance people would be buying workplaces for their clients in Samhall.

> They claim that they have unique competence in just this field, i.e., on-the-job training and so on. But I have my doubts because they also showed us their throughput figures, and, to tell you the truth, there were not many people who returned from Samhall to workplaces in the labor market. It shows that many fail, they get to a kind of a dead-end station, where people remain until they retire, which is not a definition of successful rehabilitation. I have a feeling that all they want is to attract some money their way.

My interlocutor was very dubious about the "commercialization" of the public sector. Would it not lead to forgetting the public sector's true mission? Besides, how is it possible to develop a "competitive mentality" when all these organizations are operating under what are practically monopoly conditions?

At a "semi-informal" meeting in Stockholm, the undersecretary of state declared: "It should be profitable to rehabilitate. One must first invest and then collect the gains. It is important to understand that it is impossible to achieve very much by cuts alone."

We leave this story now. It seems to lack a clear ending, so it is not impossible that it will develop into a serial. Other than that, it seems to contain all the well-known elements. It spins around a paradoxical task: those who are deprived of an important mission (possibly because they failed in it) are supposed to develop another important mission; the old organizations are to bring about renewal; the reform must follow the routines for reforming; and units that are typically public-sector bodies are expected to play a market game.

The collective reaction was a mixture of excitement, curiosity, fear, and suspicion. Of course, it is very pleasant to spend money, but how is it all going to end? Are we really allowed to play the market? If so, how do we do it? Shall we play the "head office/subsidiary" or the "buyer/supplier" version of it? Old habits drag down the new ambitions, but perhaps it is all to the good not to let the kite fly too high? And, of course, the unavoidable or maybe necessary frictions are there: between hierarchical levels and within the newly created "market-cum-organization-field" of rehabilitation.

This was an example of an attempt at constructing a new action net. Such attempts can end in the establishing of a new formal organization ("Local Rehabilitation Committee" or something like that), but it can also lead to an institutional transformation. (What is the main activity within social insurance? What are the permitted practices? Who are the appropriate partners?) Thus, the construction of a new action net entails changes of routines, like any organizational change, but it might go much farther—creating new organizations and dissolving the existing ones, or even establishing new patterns of action and justifying them as new institutions.

## What Is the Point of the Stories?

These are just three of many stories. Each one is a unique combination of random events, interests, intentions and counterintentions, and existing routines. One can see these stories as a meeting in time in which routines (institutions) represent the past, chance (the unpredictable events) represents the present, and intentions stand for the future or for time that does not exist yet. This encounter leads to a construction of meaning; actors interpret what is happening for themselves and for their audience. In other words, narratives are created and negotiated.

What happens when all possible stories have been told? We might almost feel that once, when there was only one story to tell, such as biblical or Homeric epic, time must have stood still. But this is very unlikely in public organizations. Life itself produces new topics for stories every day. But even so, we might expect that age and experience, at least in the case of those who remain a long time in the same organization, would lead to a classification and a sort of standard elaboration of events into a limited repertoire of stories: "the needs of strangers," "the bureaucratic organization," and so on.

But there are other forces underlying the ever-evolving organizational dynamic and the corresponding storytelling. And the chief of these is the paradoxical and therefore unsolvable nature of the basic problems that constitute the mission of the public sector (Brunsson 1986). Were the problems solvable, the public sector might well have ceased to exist.

## Paradoxes as Tension-Producing Devices in the Organizational Drama

A study is supposed to reach some "conclusions," and if it fails to do this, it must at least contain a "summary" of "what has been learned in the field." So prompted, I came up with the following list, modeled upon a rather famous text.

### Ten Paradoxical Commandments for the Public Sector

1. Follow routines in order to change.
2. Invest in order to save.
3. Differentiate in order to achieve equality.
4. Complicate in order to simplify.
5. Decentralize in order to control.
6. Give up power in order to influence.
7. Do nothing in order to be able to act.
8. Concentrate on the future in order to control the present.
9. Keep forgetting in order to learn.
10. Pursue change in order to maintain the status quo.

In this picture, the Swedish public administration is seen as revolving around and thriving on paradoxes. As the Servant of the Public, it has to reflect, accept, and attempt to realize all the opposing values that govern society: equality and individual rights (paradox 3), constant renewal and tradition (paradoxes 1 and 9), democracy and efficiency (paradoxes 5 and 6), order and freedom (paradox 7). As a result, the people employed and acting in public organizations acquire superior (although enforced) understanding of the economic (paradox 2) and control aspects (paradoxes 4, 5, 8, and 10) of organizational processes.

These organizational paradoxes can be subsumed under what Göran Ahrne has called "the bureaucratic paradox" (1989). It can be formulated as follows: bureaucracy as a means contradicts its own goal, in the sense that the less humane it becomes, the better (that is, the more smoothly) it functions in the service of humanity.

All these aspects can in fact be found in the public administrations of other Western democracies. Warren, Rose, and Bergunder certainly acknowledged their existence in a study of "model cities." It is the "paradox of change" that seems to be the most acute. The socialization process instills in the citizens of democracies a belief that their society is basically sound, and that all it needs is incremental improvement, "muddling through," not replacement. Further, the norm-prescribing interaction implies that such improvements must be carried through by collaboration, not confrontation. As a result, the organ created to bring about change "rather accurately reflected the same structure of power that it was ostensibly meant to challenge and change" (127).

This does not mean that private organizations are free of paradoxes. It might be claimed, however, that the paradoxes in private-sector organizations are less acute. The stakes in the public sector are so serious: life, death, illness, misery, not just profits and losses. But this can be disputed; after all, profits and losses only thinly disguise misery and happiness, harm or justice. The more important difference is that profit organizations live and work in a shorter time frame. Theirs is not a world prepared to wait for slow and long developments: paradoxes are often coped with by decoupling over situations and issues (March 1988) and are not immediately visible.

On a more general level, the above observation is hardly surprising at all. "Social systems as seen by an observer are paradoxical systems," points out Luhmann (1986a, 179), arguing that this is a necessary trait of self-referential operations, needed for a system's self-reproduction and resulting from a system's self-observation. This insight is not, however, often used in understanding organizations and organizing, commonly interpreted with another set of metaphors.

## "Good" and "Bad" Friction and Other Consequences of Physical Metaphors

Organizational power, influence, and change are generally described by physical metaphors. The spreading of innovation, for instance, is traditionally discussed in terms of "diffusion." This is a good example of how meta-phors of the field (Manning 1979), when employed unexamined for analyt-ical purposes, can become misleading. Admittedly, people speak of ideas as though they were things, objects moving in time and space by virtue of some inherent properties. As in the use of the other field metaphors, this also has an economic value, rendering the less well known in terms of the more familiar, the immaterial in terms of the material. But adopting the metaphor for analytical purposes takes us into a blind alley. Let us follow Latour (1986) in his analysis of the metaphor.

The model presents diffusion as a movement started by some "initial energy" (initiative, order, command, instruction); the initial energy is usu-ally connected with leadership and is seen as coming from an individual source. According to the law of inertia, the objects will move uninhibitedly unless they meet with "resistance." This resistance takes the form of "resis-tance to change," "political resistance," and so on. Resistance produces "friction," which diminishes the initial energy. Friction, in the social as well as in the technical world, is a negative phenomenon when movement is desired. That is, so long as the model of diffusion is accepted.

> [The] model of diffusion may be contrasted with another, that of the model of translation. According to the latter, the spread in time and space of anything—claims, orders, artefacts, goods—is in the hands of people; each of these people may act in many different ways, letting the token drop, or modifying it, or deflecting it, or betraying it, or adding to it, or appropriating it. (Latour 1986, 267)

Ideas do not diffuse; it is people who pass them on to each other, each one translating them according to their own frames of reference. Such encoun-ters between *traveling ideas* and frames of reference, that is, *ideas in resi-dence,* can be called "friction," but now the term has a positive ring to it. There is no initial energy; all ideas exist all the time, as Merton shows convincingly in *On the Shoulders of Giants* (1965). It is precisely from friction, that is, the meetings between ideas, between ideas and their trans-lators, and so on, that energy arises. Insofar as one can speak of inertia of social life—habits, routines, and institutional behavior—it is this that checks the movement of ideas. Without friction, there is no translation; at best it is a case of "received ideas," Flaubert's definition of stupidity (Kund-era 1988). Friction can thus be seen as the energizing clash between ideas in residence and traveling ideas, leading to the transformation of both. Translating friction into terms that are concerned not with the movements of physical objects but with human discourse, we arrive once more at *inter-ruption*.

Translation can be seen as a general phenomenon one of whose facets is the interpretation of texts. As presented in Latour's model, friction between traveling ideas and ideas in residence leads to the changing and enriching of both: *translation as transformation*. However, constant reproaches from the authors translated (Kundera 1988) suggest that the literary translation avoids friction by giving priority to the translator's version of reality (translation as co-optation).

Silverman and Torode (1980) see this situation as typical of the conventional approach to text interpretation, which looks at a text or a conversation through the filter of its own version of reality. In this sense, interpretation is reductionist, in that it seeks to reduce the workings of one language by the domination of another. Interpretation, in their opinion, aims at the smooth diffusion of ideas, to be accomplished by denying and removing resistance.

I propose to regard interpretation as translation: expressing the utterance of the Other in one's own language. Such translation always involves domination, or displacement (my version wins so long as I am speaking), but it can be done with a greater or lesser degree of respect for the text translated (on polyphonic texts, see Tyler 1986 and chapter 12 below). But even the most apologetic translations co-opt the text by reading it anew, and even the most liberating interruptions also impose their own language upon the text in question, thereby transforming it. An interruption can be seen as a device for making friction a visible and welcome element of translation, a reflective transformation.

In other words, if we treat "appearance," "reality," and "difference" as frequent topics of organizational speech acts, interruption (interrogation of the text) is something that organizational actors constantly do to one another, and what the researchers do to them. Interruption happens when innovators are interrogated about their "true" intentions ("What are you *really* trying to protect by these new accounting procedures?") and, when they fight back, interrogating the resistant actors ("What are you *really* trying to protect by opposing our innovation?"). What was previously called friction because it disturbed the smooth flow of ideas is now seen as interruption, which still emphasizes a disruptive character but also indicates the positive effects of questioning received ideas—whether these come from leaders or consultants, from inside or outside.

## The Dramatic Value of Paradoxes and Interruptions

What happens when the system observes itself and sees paradoxes, when an actor reflects upon what has been done and finds it paradoxical? Should it not lead to a shock, a feeling of impotence and frustration? So long as there is a next opportunity for action, for communication, the process of reproducing the system "does not stop in face of logical contradictions: it jumps" (Luhmann 1986a, 180). One is tempted to speak of creative leaps; after all, as Burke has put it, "it is in the areas of ambiguity that transformations take place; in fact, without such areas, transformation would be impossible" (Burke 1945/1969, xix). Paradoxes, until recently the villains of organizational drama, constitute its dynamics and, even more important, account for its transformations. Without paradoxes, change would not be possible. An institutionalized thought structure reconstructs itself, which means that organizations can almost be described as *autopoietic systems* (or, more exactly, configurations of autopoietic systems), systems that carry within themselves the instructions for their reproduction (Diener, Nonini, and Robkin 1980). Paradoxes and interruptions threaten the present state of organizational reality but might be the only hope for its future.

Here, however, it is time to make an ethical caveat: does the acceptance of paradoxes and the celebration of friction mean that everything that happens in the public administration is good, positive, valuable?

First, there is an unavoidable touch of tragedy in the paradoxical. Here again the public sector reflects and imitates life—*la condition humaine*. The motto of profit-oriented companies is optimism; they thrive on action, energy, and growth. The public sector is by definition pessimistic (Brunsson 1986). Second, not everybody copes with paradoxicality equally well. It requires a certain ironic disassociation which is much easier to achieve at executive levels than in the lower reaches of the hierarchy, where it is hard to see the whole and easy to see the threat to one's own part of it. What seems paradoxical higher up appears confusing or absurd lower down. Third, an amusing paradox is always a close neighbor of bitter absurdity, and it can reproduce itself in a spiral that moves on or gets stuck in a vicious circle. There is nothing inherently "good" about paradoxes.

Similarly, frictions or interruptions, aesthetically unpleasant as they may be, are seen here as "strategic spots at which ambiguities necessarily arise" (Burke 1945/1969, xxi) and where a plot can take a turn. Again, friction can lead to frustration, but the smooth flow of events is nothing more than repetition; drama arises from interruptions, and paradoxes are its fuel. An interruption stops the flow of routinized action, of received ideas; it leads to ambiguity, which calls for reflection, and reveals paradoxes, which, in an organizational context, call for "deparadoxification" (Luhmann 1991).

This does not mean that I am calling for espousing an enthusiastic attitude toward friction instead of the previous, negative one. Reflective paradoxicality must also be maintained at the level of analysis. Friction or interruptions have the function of blunting innovations by translating them into versions closer to (or less threatening to) the institutionalized thought structure (Warren, Rose, and Bergunder 1974). From this point of view, the first story is a classical one: an innovation is blunted, and maybe even finally repelled, by various representatives of the institutionalized thought structure. The accountants know how the accounting should be done; SALA knows how the relationship between itself and its members should work; and the politicians know what an annual report addressed to them should look like. What they are trying to do can be seen as co-optation of ideas: in this way, they can eventually impose their own rationale, or rather the rationale of the organization they represent, on the innovators.

The two other cases are unusual in this respect. Here we have attempts at change that clearly target the existing institutionalized thought structure. While such attacks usually come from outside or from the margins, in these two cases they originate from organizations of the highest status in the field itself. The result is that other organizations react, predictably, by trying to blunt or repel the innovation. At the same time, however, promises are made that the changes in the institutionalized thought structure will not directly threaten the legitimacy of other organizations in the field. Once the field has been reorganized, runs the message from the top, there will be a (new) place for (almost) everybody. Thus, we are dealing with a primary contest here, what Warren, Rose, and Bergunder call a serious threat to an institutionalized thought structure, which calls for the cooperation of the organizations it threatens.

Most studies of organization fields focus on innovations initiated by particular organizations that might threaten the prevailing thought structure in the field, or emerging thought structures in fields under construction. A self-changing institutionalized thought structure, like a picture of somebody lifting himself up by his bootstraps, belongs to the domain of literature and art. Dino Buzzati, Jorge Luis Borges, Julio Cortázar in literature, like M. C. Escher in art, have accustomed us to the sort of disquieting insights that subvert the world as we know it. Such insights help us to understand how changes in institutionalized thought structures can occur at all. The paradoxes, when revealed, paralyze routinized action, thus opening the field to ambiguity and reflection, and enabling random and intentional actions that subvert existing institutions. In the first story, where the paradox was neatly incorporated into the design, the most likely outcome was a change that would improve the status quo. The third story showed how a drastic change proposal can be blunted and co-opted into the existing order. But the second story could easily be reckoned among the "impossible figures," like those drawn by Escher or the Swede Oskar Reutersvärd, in which those who constitute a certain order are the ones who try to change it. Sweden is known for having accomplished this impossible task at least once in its history. Will it be able to do it again?

# FIVE

# Serials: Innovation and Repetition

People usually think of television when they hear mention of "serials" today. But the origins of serials are much older than the beginning of television. Movie serials go back to the days of silent films, when people used to go to the cinema every week. Psychology was not particularly important in such serials compared with ordinary films. Heroes and heroines were familiar, and the audience anticipated developments in the action rather than any evolution in the personalities of the characters.

Even farther back, before moving pictures, there were oral accounts of a similar kind. Serials can be traced back in time to sagas, of which the best known are those of Old Norse origin. Unlike stories, sagas never finish. The main heroes and heroines are practically immortal, and new things can always happen so long as someone is prepared to go on with the story and anybody is interested in listening.

Analogously, there are unsolvable problems in the public sector, which continually provide material for fresh episodes. Hence the idea of portraying developments as a kind of serial. By relating these serials to a specific cultural choice mechanism, namely, fashion, and analyzing them in terms deriving from literary theory and culture studies, I hope to gain a better understanding of their somewhat puzzling evolution.

## Company-ization

Company-ization is the Swedish answer to the British challenge: resolving public sector's problem with privatization. The latter is in turn often perceived in the United Kingdom as something that came, like soap operas, from the country where all organizational fashions seem to start, namely, the United States. Company-ization is a serial being played out in many municipalities, and some are already showing later episodes than others. In Little Village, however, the serial had barely begun when I arrived.

### Episode 1, in which We Get to Know Something about the Intentions of the Main Actors

It has been decided in Little Village to transform the Public Housing Board, the Industrial Board, and the Property Administration Office into limited companies. Here are the beginnings as presented in a conversation with two municipal officials, who were my main interlocutors during the whole process. One of them remained in municipal administration, the other joined the new company.

> The background is the general change in the public sector, where company-ization has become extremely popular. More-over, the two boards didn't have any employees of their own; they bought services from the municipality, which resulted in a sort of corner-store trading situation, in which it was ex-tremely difficult to arrive at a clear picture of results. But then people also believe that the change is going to produce greater efficiency. I don't really understand that . . . but I wish them luck. At any rate, I think that the employees need a carrot, if they are to become aware of costs and things like that.

All possible motives are presented in this utterance: the municipality fol-lows the fashion, politicians hope for greater efficiency (something that can be presented to the public), employees perhaps acquire a carrot, and municipal managers get something interesting to work on.

A management group was formed, and tasks were assigned for a planned investigation to precede the actual change. The group was led by the managing director, who can also be regarded as the main personage behind the creation of the company. In the past he had been head of the Property Office, a function in which he had learned a lot about property maintenance and how difficult it was to take the requisite measures. As a rule, these last depended not on needs but on the means that the municipal-ity decided to allocate. Façades could fall down and pipes leak, but budget decisions took no heed of such things. The head of the office had been one of the main authors of the idea that a company should be formed to look after municipal real estate.

Perhaps it is hardly necessary to add that the administrative units with clear costs and revenues were those that were given a corporate form in the first instance. There are also certain types of operations that seem to be better suited than others to such a form: operations that appear to have a practical nature and most closely resemble the management of a private household; that is, they are characterized by commonsense rules and vis-ible effects.

Preparations began to get seriously under way. In line with the original proposal, the two boards were to be dissolved, and assets and liabilities were to be transferred to the municipality, together with their capital. At a later stage, the municipality was to inject these into the company, reinforced by the amount of equity capital the municipality wished to invest in the company. In addition, the municipality was to determine the amount of compensation for plant, inventories, and other items that were to be transferred to the company. My interlocutor was delighted at how smoothly it went:

> It's extremely easy to form a company. You can go out and
> buy a standard document containing all the articles of incorpo-
> ration, and in fact this is what people do. But now the Swed-
> ish Association of Local Authorities has drawn out even more
> detailed articles which apply specifically to property offices.

Soon everything was ready: a proposal for the articles of the company, a proposal for a service contract with the municipality, an outline of the basic financial requirements, and an employment plan. The Municipal Council had a look at all this and expressed its approval.

### Episode 2, in which We Learn That the Route to the Promised Land Passes through the Sea of Legalities

When some representatives of Little Village visited SALA in Stockholm, they learned that the planned tax reform would affect the municipality negatively if they formed the company too early. Municipalities were to be able to deduct from their taxable income the value-added tax (VAT) they paid on their purchases, but companies would not—not even those owned by the municipality.

> And then we got a whole lot of advice about how we should
> arrange things, how we could get around these regulations so
> as to avoid paying VAT. It's all a question of legal dodging. If,
> for example, a foreman in a work group was to be employed
> not by the company but by the municipality, the company
> could buy his services; then no VAT has to be paid for his
> work. So it is a question of waiting for the final formation of
> the company until 1991, in order to keep the costs down, in
> other words, in plain language, to cheat the government in a
> legal way.

The person who told the story repeatedly expressed his astonishment. This could have been caused by the fact that he was not sure of my reaction (would I see such duplicity as an outrage or as the symptom of sound eco-

nomic thinking?). I do not think he was sure himself. If the state comes up
with certain regulations, this must mean it wishes to achieve a certain effect. Maybe what it wanted to achieve was just this sound economic thinking? If this was not the government's intention, however, maybe one is still
correct in opposing the central government when it acts against municipal
interests? In other words, should the central government be seen as a higher
level in one's own organization, or as an opponent in a game?

Five months later, the Municipal Council decided to inject the necessary equity capital. Three days after that, a constitutive meeting was con-
vened to appoint the board members and auditors. On the same day,
the board held its first meeting and appointed an authorized signatory and
a managing director. One month later, the company was in existence—
almost. The application sent to the Patent and Registration Office was answered by a piece of prior-to-decision information, namely, that the clause
giving the Little Village municipality the sole right to acquire shares in the
company did not comply with the Companies' Act, which states that every
physical Swedish person has the right to acquire shares.

> Part of the problem was that our articles followed a standard
> pattern which we had received. I contacted the lawyers at the
> Swedish Association of Local Authorities and SABO,[1] and
> they said that many articles which were accepted contained
> this same clause and that nobody bothered to object, but actu-
> ally it is right [that is, what we are doing is wrong].

This assumption on the part of SALA, that the public good must be defined
by practice and not stipulated in articles, was something that both my interlocutor and I regarded with considerable interest:

> The funny part was that both SALA and SABO now have to
> change their recommendations. I asked how it could happen
> that such an error could be found in so many articles of incor-
> poration. They implied that a particularly zealous official had
> been dealing with our application, and that he had noticed
> this particular clause and started to look at it more closely. If
> it had been another official . . .

They then had to remove the offending paragraph, after which it was just
a matter of finding a name that was not already being used, and the legal
aspects would be completed.[2]

*Episode 3, in which We Can See How Difficult It Is*
*to Bid Farewell to Old Friends*

While the company was unsure of its own official existence, its budget was being prepared in the normal manner. And, as usual, the Property Management Office had to decrease its demands, and, as usual, the maintenance accounts suffered. It was only to be expected that the ensuing negotiations with the municipality would not proceed as smoothly. A series of complex and slightly strange bargains were struck. Finally, the company purchased equipment from the municipality for "clean, fresh money."

> But that was the idea—that everyone should try and think more in financial terms—raking in the cash for their operations and not giving anything away. We haven't really made a great bargain, but on the other hand, when we get paid by the municipality, we will add the capital costs to our invoices. So we will get the money back that way. Since we have had to pay a lot for our plant, we add a supplement for every assignment we carry out. But in total, I think it will be cheaper, and I also believe we will have a more efficient organization in the end.

This episode may give food for reflection to those who believe that market transactions are always simple, while transactions within the public-sector administration are always complicated. In fact, the use of internal prices is a well-known method for establishing financial discipline, but it meets with similar problems in business corporations. It is also normal that mistakes have to be made before people learn how to operate in a new role. All in all, optimism predominated:

> It used to be a bit difficult to distinguish between the municipality and the Housing Board, and so on. But now you can see the difference. There is a clear distinction now. Here is the company, there is the municipal administration, and we are quite separate. We can already see a new way of thinking.

Not everybody was equally pleased about this "divorce." Most of the new employees were members of the Municipal Workers' Union, and it was therefore decided that the company should join the corresponding employers' association (Municipal Enterprise Cooperation Organization). This meant that the rest of the employees, who belonged to another union, were to switch to the new union. They had no objection to this, since the agreement proposed was more favorable to the workers. But the other union was not prepared to give up without a struggle; one could see it as a question of survival, since so many municipalities were setting up companies, and the employees were changing their union membership. The battling union found a surprising ally in the corresponding employers' organization, which tried to stop the company when it wanted to cancel its membership. The situation was truly a paradoxical one. First, the employer forced its employees to accept better conditions, while the union tried to prevent it. Next, the union was helped by "its" employer organization; together they opposed another pair composed of a union and an employer association. The corporate state has its own complexities . . .

### Episode 4, in which We See That It Is Not So Easy to Dangle Carrots If You Have to Keep Your Head Down

> The question now is to make the employees really positive. This means there has to be some form of reward system—a carrot, in other words. . . . At the moment, you can hear the apartment janitors saying, "I'm not going to do that, that's not my business, I don't get paid anything extra for that." The problem is, how can you create a different spirit?

While people were thinking about the color of the new overalls and other ways of creating a "corporate identity," the dream about the flight from bureaucracy was unpleasantly interrupted. Reality was more tied to the past that anyone wanted to admit.

> All our employees come from the municipality, where they were all registered with the municipality's pension fund. The personnel office is now sending in reports notifying them of the termination of their employment, while the new employer—that's us—has to register everything all over again. This means that they have to fill in forms describing all the jobs they've had in the whole of their lives. In my view, in the age of computers, it would be extremely simple to transfer this information from the municipality to the company, but no, definitely not, that doesn't work! Our people are going crazy.

In this situation, it was not really helpful when it was announced that, in order to avoid paying VAT, all supervisors had to remain in municipal employment, whereas the rest of the staff was "on lease" from the municipality. In motivational terms, the losses were very evident:

When it became clear, a few days before New Year, that we
still had to operate as a municipal public service unit, you
could see that the fighting spirit went out of most of the
people here. Some said, "What are we doing here?" Things
were not what we'd planned. It was as if the whole balloon
had been punctured.

Everybody was invited to attend a Christmas lunch, which improved the
atmosphere (in the municipal administration, this was not a custom). But
this was an exceptional measure in an acute situation. The company did
not dare "to stick its head up," as my interlocutor put it, and to accept
favorable orders from actors outside the municipal sphere; they continued
"to keep their heads down" and to hide their new identity. As a result,
people's spirits kept rising and falling, until they crash-landed when it came
to pay negotiations:

Everybody who works here has had to write job descriptions
for the tasks they now perform in the company. And the Municipal Staff Employee Union had made pay demands. They
had asked for dramatic pay increases, and it was not possible
just to say "Yes!" Then the representatives of the Municipal
Enterprise Cooperation pointed out that our 1989 earnings—
in other words, what applied before we were transformed into
a company—had not been negotiated. The final outcome was
that the negotiations were broken off . . . and that created a
very uncomfortable situation.

The situation was uncomfortable because there was no money to pay for
such substantial increases, and also because negotiations that are broken
off are always a problem. And matters were to get even worse.

The next day, the atmosphere here was something which I
hope I never experience again. The girls had heard that nobody thought they were worth anything, and they were very
upset. I sat all day talking with them. The managing director
was away that day. He had gone up into the mountains.[3] It
was an awful day, oh my, oh my. . . . We talked and talked so
that the girls would understand that it was not just malice on
the part of the company, but that the pay demands were rather
too high. They had misunderstood lots of things as well—for
example, they thought they had been refused any increase at
all. But we are not a production company—our only revenue
is from property rents. I hope this hasn't ruined the positive

spirit which was created when the managing director initially talked to everyone, and emphasized that they all had a valuable contribution to make. But I don't know anymore what they were up to. . . . It turned out that our representative had repeated things to them which were never said during the negotiations.

*But why were the girls affected in particular?*

It's more difficult to deal with girls, because they get so downhearted that they start crying. That's one of the worst things, in my opinion. The guys, the technicians that is, are not so sensitive. They were extremely angry, in fact, and that made it much easier to talk to them.

This is like a scene from a saga of the early capitalist era: the family idyll disrupted by brutal reality. It could be said that this is all part of the formation of a company: again, everyone needs to learn how to react in a new situation, and vague ideas about "how to do things in the business world" do not get one very far.

Perhaps at this point the reader may be wondering whether the serial as I describe it is not so very different from a story, since it also develops over time. And to start with, this is true. When David Lynch made the first three episodes of television's "Twin Peaks," he never thought it would run to twenty-two installments. A serial starts as a story, but it does not reach a conclusion; it is a chain of interconnected stories. Each episode is a skillful mix of problems that are solved and problems that arise. And even if the actors continually push the message that things will get better, the spectator discovers that there is a certain balance between what gets better and what gets worse: the serial has matured.

In Little Village, more details that had to be dealt with were continually being discovered. The atmosphere got better, and it got worse again. The central authorities came on the scene, offering assistance and making demands. The municipality supported and then obstructed the company's development. Customers and suppliers cooperated and then turned against the company. And, for the most part, everything cost more than anybody had imagined.

### Review

Obviously, there are many episodes still left in this serial. Even now, however, it is possible to see the problems that typically recur.

First, people are beginning to realize that they must try to learn not from the business world but instead from the process in which they are themselves involved, to translate rather than to transfer. The companies that are formed are not ordinary companies but "companies which are totally in the service of society and operating on society's conditions," as one of my interlocutors put it. This means that all the "magic" solutions and systems have to be evaluated in practice, on the basis of how well they work in this particular context.

Second, it appears that the central problem is one of confused identity. When the process started, municipal administration was to lift its bureaucratic hand from the operations. The staff was promised "a completely different atmosphere." Subsequently, however, everything proved to be much the same as usual, and the few things that were different were regarded as negative, such as new pay negotiations. The search for a new identity can be analyzed as an attempt to change the Swedish public organization field. The interesting point about this attempt to change the existing field is that the actors are uncertain of their identities, and the structures are not given. Identities and structures arise from interactions, actual conversations. The actor identities can be created with the help of models, but their relevance is confirmed or rejected in concrete interactions, that is to say, in practice. It is not enough to select an attractive model and copy it. The new identity has to be accepted by the main actors involved, as it entails a positioning vis-à-vis these Others. "Company-ization in Little Village" shows how the actors oscillate between old and new identities, surprising both themselves and others.

This also applies to structures, or the rules of action and narration. The government's action (or, rather, inaction) has created new space, a certain freedom, a vacuum, but not new rules. New rules of this kind must be created through action. You know only what is right or wrong when you (or somebody else) have already acted. "Company-ization in Little Village" is a clear example of this. It differs from the trial-and-error method, in that there are no "discoverable" rules; there are no "umpires" who know better, even if it is evident that the municipalities, for example, would be happy to see the government in a role of this kind, and that the Association of Local Authorities is aspiring to such a role. This is an excellent example of the uncertainty that is built into the process.

Third, despite all the problems, most people consider that "company-ization is a good thing." If we ignore the ambiguous question of efficiency, two advantages are emphasized. One is that "company-ization appreciably reduces the tax base for municipal operations"; in other words, it earns its keep, and this is in line with widespread demands. The other advantage is that "creating new organizations is always agreeable, because it inspires people with new courage"; in other words, it has positive effects at the internal level, but it does not appear to make things simpler for the public administration. Company-ization creates new paradoxes which the public sector must learn to live with in the future.

This was another example of constructing a new action net, although less radically innovative than in the social insurance story in chapter 4. Nonetheless, new kinds of action were tried out, and new kinds of collaborators invited themselves in. The main result was what I called at the outset a hybridization. Brunsson (1994) assures us that the public sector is not alone in this: while public agencies company-ize, private companies politicize. As Latour (1993b) pointed out, old dualisms cannot be stretched enough to give names to new, hybrid forms, and no amount of modernist purism will force practices into their traditional compartments. New names, perhaps whole new vocabularies, are needed. This is also the way institutions are changed.

## Computerization

*Is it time to start thinking about a new system?*

It is always time to start thinking about a new system. Technology always moves quickly, but it is moving even more quickly today.

The computerization serial is been played out primarily in the Swedish social insurance offices. Some of the events taking place in the municipalities resemble what is happening in the insurance offices (the technology usually breaks down, for example), but it is not possible to speak of a fully equivalent serial in the municipalities. This is because computer equipment, computer know-how, and computer utilization are all at a much less advanced stage in the insurance offices. My interlocutors explained it as follows:

> Social insurance offices became famous for their extensive computer support at an early stage. But from 1977 onward, nothing happened. We are no longer in the forefront, but perhaps in the rear.

An official investigation concluded that an enormous serial (known to insiders as "Phase 90") was to be financed, and a professional "director" (project manager) was called in from the world of business. Important input providing the basis for insurance decisions was to be stored locally; the central database was to be decentralized, and local networks were to be extended.

### Episode 1, in which We Learn Something about What It Is Like in the Local Offices

From a computing point of view, the local offices differ considerably from one another. Some know very little about computing, while others are computer freaks. In Northtown, neither resources nor know-how was available.

> We had a meeting to discuss how the knowledge which the experimental offices possess should be disseminated to the other offices, so that the usual thing would not happen, i.e., that a year and a half later we'd be told which way to do things. Furthermore, the offices designated as "experimental" are the same ones which have had similar projects before. This increases the gap between the computer-mature offices and those that don't know a darned thing.

There were other insurance offices that tried to get computerized on their own, such as the Centraltown office.

> Computerization is on the way, at the same time that the offices are acquiring computer technology for their own administrative operations. We have two computer systems, one which is for the current production of insurance, owned by the Agency for Administrative Development and by the NSIB. But we can also purchase our own computers, PCs and similar small computers and our own equipment for managing our administrative work. At least until six months ago, our manager believed that developing our technology and technical support was the route to take. And some of the guys think that technology is swell.[4] We have pumped thousands and thousands of kronor into EDP development, the acquisition of technology, EDP courses, and the like, but it has all simply gone up in smoke, because we are behind the times with our personnel costs. The insurance offices still take the line that they are primarily interested in retaining personnel and paying salaries, and that the acquisition of computers takes second place.

At some intermediate position between high ambitions and an awareness of inadequate knowledge, there were insurance offices that calmly recognized that change was unavoidable but that there was still a long way to go. At the central level, the first stage was an investigation, followed by the creation of a project management group (involving a power struggle between ASIO, the Association of Social Insurance Offices, and the National Social Insurance Board over who had the main responsibility for the project). But then things moved very rapidly.

### Episode 2, in which We Meet the Project and Its Leader

On 30 June 1991, every local office in every county in Sweden was supposed to be equipped with a new health insurance register. These registers were to consist of an electronic health card, a database containing all the relevant information about the people insured.[5]

> By the fiscal year 1991–92, all the local offices are to be re-equipped and to be managing themselves. However, many are not well prepared—our office here for instance—and that means we need time to talk about what it means for us. The staff have to be prepared for a tough job and a lot of effort, which at the same time is also exciting and interesting.

But who could convince the wary, overworked staff that the new change was to be exciting and not merely oppressive?

> He comes from Gothenburg and has many years of experience in the private sector of EDP operations, EDP companies, and in recent years he has been working as a consultant, and has also had assignments in the public sector. The whole thing is really exciting. He is moving now at a hell of a pace, gathering the various loose ends together, fixing things, and in September he is going to present a proper implementation plan. (ASIO)
> He's been working with this for five weeks, and he really knows nothing about social insurance, but nonetheless he's found where the problems lie, I think. He's examined the current situation, the project organization, and the timetable. I must say he's impressed me. He seems to be a decent fellow, and it's going to be interesting to see what happens. (Northern County)
> For the first time, it felt as though the things would really become clear. Everything had been very vague, unfocused, hard to understand. And the result was that nothing was happening. People are afraid of technology; they hear these

strange words which don't explain very much, and where anyway the idea of what is to be achieved is pretty abstract and
foggy. But this guy is admirably simple and clear. He is excep-
tionally good at explaining things, and in addition everybody
seems to accept him, including people from the local offices.
(NSIB)

These comments tell us a lot about the new leader; on the other hand, they
also tell us that the initial computerization serial in the 1970s failed to
make computers popular in the local offices. A predilection for formal language and the power privileges granted by restricted access to knowledge
meant that computers were accepted by a certain elite category but were
regarded as evil spirits by most other people ("ignorance creates uncertainty, and then it is easy to demonize technology"). But now the talk was
of "cultural change," and the main question was whether the changes were
going too slowly or too quickly.

The "too slowly" group seemed to be winning this battle, and so pilot
offices were selected, and the experiment began.

### Episode 3, in which We Are Allowed to Watch the Experiment

The project consisted of two parts: the creation of a central administrative
organization, and local development projects.

There is a proposal for an administrative organization which
involves budgetary control and a common fund which is allo-
cated to this organization. If the people involved, who come
from NSIB and the local offices, cannot reach a common decision, the board will make it, as before. So the challenge lies in
being able to choose common priorities within the budgetary
frame. This is going to be very exciting because it appears to
involve the whole organization in a totally new manner which
I honestly feel should be extremely satisfying even for the local
offices, which have frequently demanded a decisive influence
over the EDP operations . . . so I think that a crucial problem
has been solved here. (NSIB)

The idea of budget process as communication, and budget as dialogue,
was regarded as something new, since, unlike the municipalities (Brunsson
1989), the local offices had a fixation on the past.

The other aspect is that the experimental project conducted in
Scania in southern Sweden, which is the real test of whether

we can handle such a sophisticated system, means delegating responsibilities to local offices and developing a major component of the future local system. This then has to be approved centrally by the board, but the real responsibility is at the local level. (NSIB)

This is a problem that also appeared in some of the decentralization serials: the "central unit" has its doubts about the competence of the "local units."

When I listen to what is being said here at the board, I hear mostly skeptical voices, and what they are really saying is, "We're not going to manage this," and it's largely a question of inadequate competence and skills at the local offices. (NSIB)

Note the "we" form when what was meant was "they." This works both ways: the central unit does not believe in the competence of the local units, while the local units assume that the people at the central unit simply cost a lot of money without doing anything sensible or useful.

Perhaps this is precisely where a cultural shift is needed. This is what one of my interlocutors believed.

It would be a victory for the organization if it could be proved that it was possible to develop a computer system for local offices, which could then be used all over the country. There are many people who don't believe this at the moment, many people are waiting for it to fail and to take it on themselves, to take care of things later after it's all gone to pot. It's something of a tradition to think this way in an old centralized organization like this. "Let them play with this for a bit, then we can fix it later." Part of our development work is aimed at getting beyond that kind of mentality, to make ourselves extrovert and consultative, to learn to help each other instead of just starting new investigations. (NSIB)

An interlocutor from ASIO doubted this very much:

We have a well-established central authority culture here. I don't think it's anything special to just the National Social Insurance Board. Appointing an investigation committee is a method employed by central government and Parliament to get out of difficult situations. In the private business culture you have to take decisions very quickly in order to get ahead. (ASIO)

Both interlocutors were alluding to "investigations" in four subprojects that had been launched prior to the appointment of the project leader. After his arrival, Phase 90 was linked directly to line operations, and eight (of twenty-six) insurance office managers joined the leadership group. This group first discussed two important questions: the choice of operating system and issues of information and training. Two further items concerned the contents of the health insurance register (software required) and the allocation of responsibilities between the central and local levels. This last question was handled in a completely new manner:

> It was a somewhat disorganized meeting, and that meant that
> it was a good one. A whole lot of questions came up which
> were not actually on the agenda, and meetings of this kind
> usually turn out to be the best. Things were a bit more sponta-
> neous, and it gives more scope if you're allowed to say what
> you think. (NSIB)

It was hoped that it would be possible to locate most of the responsibility at the local level (even if some people hoped this would prove to be a disaster). The office selected was to determine the content of the register, to develop the technical aids, to handle the database, and so on. This was all I was told, since things were at such an early stage that it was impossible to say anything more concrete.

## Review

There is something very peculiar in this serial, which I would like to emphasize. It is hard to imagine anyone in private business saying (in public), "We're not going to manage this." If anything, the problem in business is that people go on believing they will manage, long after the company has gone bankrupt. But in the public sector, the opposite applies.

Pessimism is a trademark of public-sector organizations, according to Brunsson (1989), because people are forced to be realistic. While municipalities at least have their future-oriented politicians, who are eternal optimists, the local offices are dominated by public officials who are oriented toward the past and who are pessimists. This pessimism, realistic as it is, can actually have a negative effect on the future.

The idea that "people are afraid of technology" can operate as a dangerous self-fulfilling prophecy, just like "people are opposed to change." Everything depends on how the initial contact turns out. True, it is almost inevitable that during introductory meetings people are on their guard against the new technology and anxious about change. But it is hardly "people's" fault. One point often neglected is that changes of this type threaten those whose power is based on existing circumstances. The "fear of machines" is to some extent the result of a clumsy introduction to technology, but it is also the result of more or less deliberate attempts at "demonization" by people whose power is threatened.

There are two well-known demonization narratives in contexts of this kind. The best known can be called the *deus ex machina,* whereby a new technology is introduced not as a political decision (which it always is, of course) but as being determined by technological development as such. To counteract such fatalistic feelings, the leader of Phase 90 found it necessary to declare, "Phase 90 systems are not expert systems. They are really rather simple register maintenance systems" (internal teaching material).

The second narrative is more sophisticated and is often told even by people who want to counteract demonization. It can be called *periodization.* In the teaching material quoted above, references—sometimes critical—are made to "the transition to an information society." It is assumed here that there are three periods, dominated by "the traditional mentality" (which is then not discussed anymore but is always present in the background), "the information society" (which is the period when "occupational skills of the future" will be needed), and "the transition period." Two interpretations are implied. According to one version, the problem is said to be that "certain people with a traditional mentality" (you? me? her?) "will not manage the transition." In the other version, there is fear that crucial positive aspects of the "traditional mentality" will be "lost" during the transition period.

The symptoms are reversed in the two versions, but the process is depicted in the same way. Something clear and definite has existed in the past, designated as "the traditional mentality," "culture," and so on. Something else is equally clearly determined, namely, "the future." Between the two is the present, the transitional period, of unclear and shady status. The present is seen as the most problematical: it is now that we can choose between the fear of "not managing the transition" and of "impoverishing an occupation."

Both fears can be dispersed by a little reflection on the ephemeral and arbitrary nature of such divisions. The future is something that we do not know much about. Giving it a name ("the information society") is an interesting rhetorical technique that at best (or worst) can operate as a self-fulfilling prophecy. Whether the society of the future becomes an information society will be revealed only when we emerge into the next period, into the postinformation (or post-something) society.

Interestingly enough, the "traditional mentality" is equally vague. When an attempt is made to anchor the label in time, it turns out that every period has its own traditional mentality and that people always believe they are living in a "transitional period." On the other hand, extremely few people maintain that they themselves have a traditional mentality of which they are proud. Most of us want to manage the transitional period and would like to arrive instantly on "the other side." In other words, the three terms mean nothing more than "then, now, and later," and the borders between them are completely flexible.

Niklas Luhmann (1986b) points out that periodization is a well-known technique for creating meaning. This is achieved more successfully in time past than in the future. The most difficult, of course, is the present since it is always in motion. Thus, people speak of "transition," that is, a period without a name. Like all human inventions, periodization is meant to be useful to humankind. But sometimes it escapes our control and begins to haunt us.

## The Material: Why This? Why Now?

Sometime ago, current TV serials were being discussed in a radio program. One Swedish expert concluded that the public was tired of unrealistic sagas such as "Dallas" and was longing for realistic serials that describe life as it really is.[6] This critic was right on the first point but wrong on the second; the Swedish public chose a hyperrealistic serial called "Twin Peaks." An observer may then ask, why this particular serial? And why just then, at that particular moment?

There is an answer that applies to both TV serials and public-sector serials: *fashion* (Czarniawska and Joerges 1995). Fashion can be conceived as a societal competition mechanism that influences the market by distorting both demand and supply (Blumer 1973). Its essence is a collective selection of lifestyles, things and ideas; it focuses on finding and at the same time creating features that are typical of an epoch (Simmel 1904). In terms we have used before, it gives us words for describing a period once we have delimited it.

Managers often regard it as their duty to follow the latest fashion. Fashion expresses what is modern, and in our society what is modern means what is valuable. This argument applies, above all, to top managers and organizational leaders who see it as their duty to renew and develop their organizations. Company-ization and computerization are "in"; this is what is being done in the public administration at present, and not only in Sweden.

To perform this duty, however, is only one part of the leader's role, which also involves the opposite: defending the organization from the latest fads and other frivolities. Organizations are supposed to be serious. But how can one tell what is frivolous and what is not? When the first attempts were made to introduce submunicipal councils (Czarniawska-Joerges 1988), everybody laughed at the ideas behind the reform; it was "empty talk." But now the system has become a holy cow; people laugh at company-ization instead.

The difficult thing about understanding the fashion mechanism is that it is only possible to know if something is fashionable ex post. The initiators risk making fools of themselves, while those who jump on the bandwagon later feel twice as safe. Fashion, as a collective choice, releases the individual from the responsibility implied by individual choice. Fashion represents both conformism and creativity, tradition and change (Blumer 1973). It is a paradoxical phenomenon that fits well into the paradoxical reality of the public-sector organizations.[7]

In the world of fashion, there are always "fashion leaders" (Sellerberg 1987) and public opinion leaders, just as there are movie directors who are "in" at the moment. These people also have their counterparts in the organizational world. Hinnings and Greenwood (1988) discovered in a study of the British public sector that the same organizations always started any new developments. Such new developments then became known via the Association of Local Authorities, various professional associations, and the transfer of personnel. We have the same phenomenon in Sweden, where the municipality of Örebro acts the part of "model municipality."

The local TV station chooses a repertoire that is fashionable. Serials—the core element in the postmodern theater of television—are particularly sensitive to shifts in fashion. Organizations can stage their own stories, and no one knows much about how local custom deals with the various themes. But serials are different. Viewers, in this case citizens whose direct experience is mediated by the professional rendition and interpretation of events, have to keep up with the Zeitgeist in order to participate in the mainstream of events. In addition, the characters in serials are extremely appropriate for reflecting public-sector operations. Unlike other forms, where there is a clear intrigue that has to be solved in the limited time and space available within the framework of the drama, serials are characterized by the fact that there are "no resolutions, constant repetition and interruptions" (Alexander 1991, 111).

## The Device: Low Culture, Feminine?
### *Serials and the Mass Production of Art*

It should be obvious by now that it is the specificity of serials as an experience-material organizing device that made me choose them as an analogy for, or, better still, as a device for organizing, this part of my own research material. It should be equally obvious that it is a sensitive choice. Clearly, the kinds of serials I have in mind are those that are best known under the derisive name of "soap operas," a name derived from the fact that Procter & Gamble, the soap producers, sponsored the first serials, and which in time came to denote "low-culture" products. Does this mean, then, that public-sector operations can be compared to low-culture production?

Let us say first that they can certainly be compared with mass-culture production. The relationship is in fact a synecdoche, whereby the part symbolizes the whole in the sense that the public sector is a mass producer of welfare, of which culture is but a part. So what has to be analyzed and, if necessary, defended is the "low-culture" attribute attached to their operations.

Umberto Eco points out that it is only modernist aesthetics that have equated the artistic value with novelty, and have set a low value on the pleasure derived from repetition—a domain of crafts and industry as opposed to Art. The earlier classical theory of art lacked this differentiation. "The same term (*techne, ars*) was used to designate both the performance of a barber, or shipbuilder, and the work of a painter or poet" (Eco 1990, 83–84). The modernists, however, decided to distinguish the two in the face of unprecedented technological development, which permitted mass replicability. Consequently,

> A popular song, a TV commercial, a comic strip, a detective novel, a western movie were seen as more or less successful tokens of a given model or type. As such, they were judged as pleasurable but nonartistic. Furthermore, this excess of pleasurability and repetition, and this lack of innovation, were felt to be a commercial trick (the product had to meet the expectations of its audience), not the provocative proposal of a new (and difficult to accept) world vision. The products of mass media were equated with the products of industry, insofar as they were

produced in series, and the "serial" production was considered
alien to artistic invention. (Eco 1990, 84)

This artistic puritanism, says Eco, is very difficult to maintain in an era
when iteration, repetition, and mass production permeate the whole world
of artistic creativity. People speak of a "new aesthetic of seriality."[8] In the
universe of the mass media, things are offered as original and different
even though the audience realizes that they are repeating something already
known. Despite this, or maybe because of it, the offering is liked, accepted,
and sought after.

There are many examples of this, ranging from repeats of the same
movies (where *Casablanca* probably beats all records), through remakes
(*Superman*), and on to sophisticated quotations (*Dead Men Don't Wear
Plaid*). But it is serials that are of interest here, both the series type in which
every story is separate (in this respect, all three serials quoted here are
installments of an eternal serial called "Reforming the Public Sector") and
family sagas. "The saga is a series in disguise. It differs from the series in
that the characters change (they change also because the actors age); but
in reality the saga repeats, despite its historicized form, celebrating in appearance the passage of time, the same story" (Eco 1990, 87).

What is it that the audience likes about serials? They reward the viewers by confirming their talent to predict; developments proceed as expected
after various deviations and peregrinations that are enough to stir up a
pleasant feeling of suspense but are resolved just as we thought they
would be.

It is beginning to sound as though the serials were meant for an un-
demanding consumer (we will be returning to this problem); indeed, this is
a frequent criticism of the public-sector services as well. In fact, says Eco,
the serials are meant to satisfy both a naive and a smart consumer, what
he calls a naive and a critical reader. The first just enjoys the developments
in the series without much questioning. The second enjoys the seriality of
the serials, "not so much for the return of the same thing (which the naive
reader believed was different) but for the strategy of the variations" (Eco
1990, 92). And this is an argument heard quite often from public-sector
veterans, who know that given the goals of the public sector, repetitions
are necessary, and who consequently appreciate the way the variations are
effected. This is why it is possible to reconcile repetition with innovation.
Eco makes a provocative comparison between Balzac's *Human Comedy*
and the TV serial "Dallas," and comes to the conclusion that each of the

Balzac novels told us something new about French society whereas each installment of "Dallas" tells us the same thing about U.S. society, but "both use the same narrative scheme" (Eco 1990, 93).

In other words, a successful serial achieves a balance between *order* and *novelty,* between *scheme* and *innovation.* It can do this in a way that is visible to a sophisticated audience, which only contributes to its success. Serials do not hide their devices; they celebrate them.

### Feminine Narrative

Belonging to a "low culture" is only one of the dubious attributes of serials. It has also been claimed that serials present a "feminine narrative form" in contrast with the masculine tradition, which emphasizes goal orientation, preestablished conflict, and a climactic resolution (Alexander 1991 summarizes the argument, but see also Fiske 1987). If we compare this with what Merelman (1969) claims to be the main drama techniques used in politics, we can produce a comparative list such as the one appearing below.

| Conventional Drama Techniques | Variation of the Technique in Serials |
|---|---|
| Personification | Confused |
| Identification | Many possible (static, fragmentary personalities) |
| Suspense | Open structure of events |
| Unmasking | Repetitions |
| Climax | No resolutions |
| Catharsis | Interruptions |

There is no need to attach final labels to those two dramatic modes, but it is evident that the techniques in the left column are typical of "action serials," for example, which, as Fiske (1987) has pointed out, attempt to recreate masculinity by breaking the form characteristic of "soap operas"—as presented in the right-hand column. Soap operas in their turn broke the form typical for the classical drama (the left column again) by assuming a rhythm typical of everyday life, replacing dramatic resolutions by a variety of small problems that arise while others are being solved, by introducing several possible identifications and open-structured events, and by blurring the genre.

If we continue to dwell on the analogy between the public-sector organizations and TV serials, we will see that the left column represents a mode of action that can be described as "problem solving," whereas the right column describes what was so aptly called "muddling through." Further, I would not hesitate to call the public administration more "feminine" than private business for two reasons, one symbolic and one literal: the public sector deals with matters of life and death (rather than profit and loss), a domain attributed in Western ideology to females; and the public sector mostly employs women. Insofar as serials characterize the public sector (and I claim that they do), it is a characteristic appropriate to the assumed "femininity" of the context.

I would like to draw the reader's attention to yet another analogy. The public sector's serials, as described above, cleverly imitate reality by portraying women as the unintended victims of a course of events. It is the "girls" (*tjejer*)[9] who cry in "Company-ization" and the less qualified women who "will not make it" and "are afraid of technology" in "Computerization." The present anti-public-sector campaign in Sweden can be seen as the "masculinization" of organizations, with the emphasis on "competition," "autonomy," "free choice," and other elements from masculine drama. The serials and the public sector truly belong to those "places and situations where literary tradition and real life notably transect," and which reveal this "simultaneous and reciprocal process by which life feeds materials to literature while literature returns the favor by conferring forms upon life" (Fussell 1975, preface). If we replace "literature" with "art," the picture will be complete.

# SIX

# Talking Numbers: Preferences and Traditions

In my search for metaphors, I turn this time to a special category of texts: those that help to enact a narrative, such as stage directions and screenplays. If such metaphors seem far-fetched in the context of budgetary processes, I would like to point out that at least in connection with the public administration, the idea is not new: the symbolist analysis of organizational action first focused on budgets a long time ago. Murray Edelman's *The Symbolic Uses of Politics* (1964) led Thomas Anton to claim that the budget is a symbol of responsibility, and budgeting a game of status maintenance, in which one side is for growth and the other for cuts (1967). On the basis of his studies in Norwegian municipalities, Johan P. Olsen called for a new perspective on budget behavior and proposed "ritual" as an appropriate metaphor (1970). Geert Hofstede, reinterpreting his own doctoral dissertation (*The Game of Budget Control*, 1967), came to the same conclusion (Hofstede 1987).

Olsen's work inspired the Scandinavian researchers in particular, and they have followed up on his ideas, speaking of budgets as rituals of reason, a language of consensus (Czarniawska-Joerges and Jacobsson 1989), automatons, combats, and dances (Jacobsson 1990), and, in true Scandinavian fashion, budgeting as beer drinking (Rombach 1990). The plethora of budget metaphors filled the academic discourse especially since an increasing number of researchers agreed with McCloskey (1986) that metaphors and stories are the basic stuff of economics. Morgan (1986) discussed the use of metaphors in organizational theory; Boland (1989) continued the argument in an accounting perspective. It is this tradition I wish to continue in the following four cases.

## The Budget Bill as a Screenplay

One possible image of the budget bill represents it as a document reflecting the economic decisions of the politicians in the government that are to set the frameworks for public-sector activities over the coming year. This set of decisions is then submitted to the scrutiny of Parliament, and, following its approval (usually contingent upon certain changes), it assumes a controlling function over all the public-sector organizations.[1]

The way the budget bill functions could thus be compared to a screenplay. The author, like the scriptwriter, prepares the text, which reflects his
or her creativity. The use of a team of scriptwriters is not unknown, just as
it is not unknown—I was told—for a strong minister of finance to dictate
practically every item of importance in a bill. Once the screenplay has been
accepted for production, it starts to control the actions of the director, the
actors, and the rest of the people involved in the production.

The analogy seems very fitting. The problem is that the conventional
picture of both screenplay and budget bill writing is inaccurate. In contemporary movie production, with its roots in the 1930s, the traditional role
of the playwright has been completely changed. An instructive picture of
this process is to be found in F. Scott Fitzgerald's novel *The Last Tycoon;*
here the protagonist, the movie producer Stahr, is alleged to have been the
inventor of the new method.

In this version, the screenplay is written by a team of writers, none of
whom can claim authorship. In fact, authorship can be attributed to the
producer or sometimes the producer and the director; the very people who
never write anything. The task of the writers is to guess at the ideas and
feelings of the leading characters and put these down on paper. Their contribution is a knowledge of technicalities: language, the art of writing dialogue. Creativity is not forbidden, but it does not play a crucial role in the
formation of the screenplay. In fact, all their attempts must be approved by
the producer, the director, or both, and are very often altered.[2] What is
more, the idea of a screenplay that is ready before the shooting starts is
completely false: in fact, the screenplay is ready when the movie is. The
writing takes place parallel with the acting; new ideas and scenes are tried
out or changed as a result of factors such as a star's dislike for a given
scene, or a cold caught by an actor playing one of the main characters.
If there was an original story behind the film, its author might discover,
for example, that the sad ending has been changed to a happy one, or even
that the message is almost the opposite of what he or she had intended.
The author's frustration is similar to that of many experts who submit proposals as a basis for a political decision.

The task of writing the budget bill certainly seems very similar to that
of producing a screenplay. Here it is described by my interlocutor, a young
official at the Ministry of Finance, who was preparing her first budget bill:

> In practice, every official with budget responsibility writes his
> or her bit. Then you give your diskette to an assistant in the

Administrative Section who has a coordinating function for
the whole thing. She gets the diskettes from the all people in
our ministry and puts them together. It is nothing but a collection of texts. This is then sent, according to a special address
list, to the representatives of the various ministries, as the
whole thing must have support of the whole government.
They all have a chance to come up with comments. For example, I got my pages back—they tore them out of the whole
text and made comments in the margin. Next, I corrected my
bit and sent it to the assistant again. She sent it out for comments once again, and then it went to the printer, and as it
was already on a diskette, there was no need to check every
letter, because if it was correct as written, it would be correct
as printed.

*Does this mean the minister of finance doesn't read it at all?*

No, he doesn't. We deal with it at the administrative level. If
there are any issues which aren't clear, or if the officials in a
given ministry think something we said doesn't correspond to
the agreement reached by the ministers, then we go and ask a
vice minister. It only goes to the minister if the vice minister is
not sure himself, but this is very unusual.

On the one hand, the process is much more democratic than in Hollywood,
in the sense that there are a great many people who read the script. On
the other, the process is also more hierarchical, in the sense that once the
intentions have been made clear, the actors involved do not bother to check
the writers' product. But, I asked, how do the officials know what to write?

We take the basic material, we look at it, we check what different actors said about it, what was said in earlier investigations, in old budget bills, and what we believe the minister
wants, judging from his recent statements. What helps a lot is
the fact that I am present when various talks are taking place,
so that afterwards I can try to interpret the minister's opinion
and then write what I believe the leadership wants on this
question.

The budget bill is the final result of a whole year of such interpretations,
during which the politicians seem to learn their own preferences at the
same pace as the officials do, in the process of ex post facto sense making
so aptly described by Weick (1979). Although the process appears to be

mutual, the official version assumes the traditional one-way communication scheme, whereby politicians "explain" and officials "express." If the results are unsatisfactory, the writers take the blame: they "misread" the politicians' intentions. Here, again, the power allocation is very similar to the movie business.

But it is not usually the first version of the budget bill that leads to conflicts. The budget bill is actually composed of three texts: the proposal, the counterproposals, and the supplement to the bill, which includes and responds to various criticisms.

The counterproposals come from the opposition parties, but are dealt with by the same officials.

> One part of our task is to see what different parties have said about various issues, whether there is a risk of the government's proposal being rejected. The other part is to check the quality of the counterproposals. They are not all written at the same level: some parties calculate the economic consequences of their proposals, and some write flamboyant tales, without bothering about the consequences. The various ministries go through counterproposals that relate to their own activities and try to calculate the costs. They leave it to us [the Ministry of Finance] to check whether the proposal needs to be complemented and to present them all in a uniform way. We present the results so that the officials in various ministries can explain to their ministers what is the position of other political parties. Budget debates or general political debates are prepared on this basis.
>
> *But isn't it a waste of time, making so much effort to calculate the costs of something that has an opinion-forming role only?*
>
> Why do we do it . . . well, one party can claim, for instance, that their proposal leads to significant economies, and if we calculate it properly, it proves to be just the reverse. But we have to do it. Otherwise, people might think it was enough to say, "Our proposal is much better!" Somebody must check out this kind of statement. But people who've done it before me also say that it's donkey-work.

Here again, one is reminded of that part of the scriptwriter's job that consists of writing dialogues in an infinite number of versions, which are discarded one after the other.

But perhaps the most important aspect is the supplement to the bill, which is written after all the important groups have expressed their opinions. Movie production then enters the final stage, when the only thing that counts is what will remain in the script. At this point, it is important that the contents of the supplement do not leak to the press too early. Or, to be more exact, that what leaks does not make it sound as though the supplement ignores the views of any specific interest group. Because, just as in movie production, leaks are quite common, as my interlocutor learned in her first attempt at producing a budget bill:

> A newspaper reported that the government reached an
> agreement with [the Liberal Party] on a two-year freeze in
> municipal taxes, although this was not yet official. But it had
> leaked out somehow, created turbulence, and, in a sense,
> changed the basic assumptions . . . just before the talks were
> to begin with the politicians from the Swedish Association of
> Local Authorities. These talks are at the political level, but
> most of the preparation is done by the officials, so it is very
> important that as little as possible leaks out during the talks.

This time, the turbulence surrounding all parts of the bill was unusually great—a situation that creates an excellent opportunity for us to grasp the workings of the process: it is through the unusual that we understand how "the usual" proceeds. First it was SALA who refused to accept the original proposal, telling the press that "the ministry has made an error in its calculations." This was not *comme il faut*. But, as we know from the story in chapter 4, the misunderstanding ended peacefully in a common press statement; this evoked the institutionalized thought structure common to the adversaries, thus astonishing the young official. She did not like the reaction of the opposition parties, either:

> We did what we usually do, that is, we collected all the coun-
> terproposals and calculated the costs, if the people concerned
> didn't do it themselves. . . . The counterproposal is getting a
> lot of space in the press these days, so the minister of finance
> had to mention it in his speech to Parliament. The opposition
> parties became very upset. For instance, we pointed out that
> the Conservative Party came up with a balance which was 50
> million kronor below that of the government. They stood up
> several times, shouting, "That's a lie, it's a lie, it's a lie!" And
> so it started—the political mud-throwing, using our figures as
> the basis. None of us thought it was very pleasant.

Unlike the movie scriptwriter, the writers at the Ministry of Finance try to achieve as little dramatic effect as possible. To no avail: the basic dramatics of the situation win.[3] One can well imagine, however, that film scriptwriters are not very happy, either, when their work is used for publicity purposes by the leading actors, producers, and directors.

Like all metaphors, the screenplay metaphor has its correct and incorrect aspects. The usefulness of metaphors, however, lies not in proving their identity with the phenomena in question but in creating an alternative image of what is taken for granted. With this in mind, I would like to apply Barthes's (1979) distinction between "author" and "writer," and consequently between "work" and "text," to the situation I have been describing here. Faithful to individualist interpretations, the conventional viewpoint insists on seeing not only literature but politics and the economy as being populated by "authors," powerful creators of their own (and other people's) fates who call whole new worlds into being in their "works." This romanticization of social reality blinds us to the fact that the world is full of "writers," who in writing their "texts" reproduce social reality rather than creating it. The institutional thought structure can be seen as a gigantic matrix containing the blueprints of texts for all occasions.

The writing of the budget bill reveals some further aspects that could be relevant to other texts as well. For instance, it is a case of collective writing, in the literal sense of the term. In the very concept of the "writer" the image lurks of an individual who gathers in signals from the collective consciousness. In reality, more and more texts—budgets, laws, screenplays—are being written by teams, by groups of people united in an organized effort (see also the concept of a collectively imagined Leviathan, as presented by Callon and Latour 1981).

Finally, there is the matter of control. Much has been said about the inability of budgets to function as control instruments. This interpretation could be revised together with the conventional concept of control. A mechanical concept of control could be replaced by a social one, and the time frame reversed. The budget bill, in my opinion, fulfills an important controlling function, not after it has been but *while it is being* written and accepted. It is during the negotiations leading to the production of the text that resources are divided, policies fixed, and decisions made. Completed budgets are like books on the shelf: they do not exert a direct influence anymore. They do so only when they are taken off the shelf and read again. And when does that happen? Obviously, during the next budget process. Budgets influence budgets, not "reality out there."

## Stage-Setting in Municipalities

The ritual character of budgeting processes in municipalities has been emphasized by many researchers. While it is usually the process that has been conceived as ritualistic (Olsen 1970; Hofstede 1987), I have observed that the contents, too, are ritualized. The text, written by the collective writer, has essentially one main topic: how can we economize?

The municipal finances in Northtown had been unexpectedly good over the few last years. It had become clear that a new text would have to be written on this topic: how can we spend the money sensibly? A task of this kind produced a general feeling of uncertainty, especially as the central government decided to postpone the section of the budget bill concerning the municipalities and include it in the supplement to the bill which comes much later.[4] There was nowhere to turn for advice or instructions. In what follows, the head of the Finance Office describes the process.

> We had a very unusual and somewhat problematic situation
> with the budget directives for the coming year. We hadn't
> needed them much over the past few years, as we could use
> the existing long-term plan and budget directives, and our
> task as officials was simply to translate this into money terms.
> But now we had something like 10 million to 15 million kro-
> nor extra, and it was the politicians' job to decide what to do
> with it. We came up with a proposal, but it turned out to have
> very poor support, even within the government party. So there
> were problems.

As my interlocutor saw it, there were two problems: the governing party had difficulty in achieving internal consensus, and the politicians were generally unused to deciding priorities between potential operations, that is, operations that did not yet exist. As a result, the mayor hastily accepted the officials' proposal just as it was, without any political consultation. As the proposal was based on previous political decisions, it was "coherent but not current," and this provoked opposition when the proposal was presented in a political setting.

> *But isn't it better if the officials decide how things should be*
> *done? After all, you have the knowledge, the expertise, and*
> *the experience?*
>
> No, it's not our business to decide what to invest in. That's
> clearly a political issue. We are not even supposed to have
> opinions about that. We're supposed to know how much

things cost, what effects to expect from various alternatives,
that's our expertise, but not about whether more money
should be spent on this or that.

My interlocutor refused to rise to the provocation in my question, which
in turn was inspired by research showing that officials run the show, telling
politicians what to do (see, e.g., Brunsson and Jönsson 1979). One interpretation might be that he was insisting on the "ought to" picture of reality.
But an alternative interpretation could be that the picture commonly
painted by studies like the one mentioned above—that of officials controlling politicians—is an illusion arising in routine situations when nobody
actually controls anybody, but everyone is controlled by a routinized procedure. Actions and interactions are institutionalized, and there is no need to
produce a new script for each performance. In a routine situation, the officials appear active simply because they are doing something, that is, preparing the document. This is hardly an act of control, however. A "same
procedure as last year" procedure does not demand the writing of a new
text; it is enough to brush up on the old one. Yet when it came to writing a completely new text, it turned out that everybody had forgotten how
to do it.

The meeting of Northtown City Council took several hours to discuss
the problem.

> There was a discussion about principles first, on how specific
> the budget directives must be. Some people claimed that the
> only way to do things is to collect the proposals from line com-
> mittees [that is, those that supervise actual operations, unlike
> the staff committees] and then sew them together. This was, in
> fact, how we used to do things before—no framework, no
> budget directives. The big parties usually prefer this method,
> whereas the small parties demand that the budget directives
> must be discussed in the council meetings. It is their only op-
> portunity to exert some influence, after all. Ultimately it is a
> matter of democracy.
>
> *And what was the conclusion?*
>
> There wasn't one. After that, we discussed the content, and
> there was a long debate for three or four hours. It was very
> similar to a debate in Parliament, where the government says
> that the situation is fine and the opposition tries to show that
> it is very bad indeed. But this time, everybody agreed that
> things were in fact very good, so the issue was how good they

really were and whether you have to economize even when
times are good. It was the Conservative Party that demanded
that, in spite of healthy finances, the committees must be required to economize. According to Conservative opinion, economizing is the only way to increase efficiency. Besides, good
finances today do not mean good finances tomorrow. What
everybody seems to be afraid of is that positive directives will
lead to budget demands that will greatly exceed all the limits.
A positive presentation of the finances has the psychological
effect of increasing the level of aspiration. In my experience,
one has to create a crisis situation to be able to induce thinking about economies.

The uneasiness was therefore caused not only by the fact that the ritual
had to be suspended, but also by the fact that it ran counter to a certain
control philosophy that was popular in the public sector.

If you want to introduce changes, you must begin by building
up a sense of crisis. This is the basis of all changes, at any rate
changes that are to lead to economies. What makes it difficult
is the fact that it isn't enough to lie and say that there is a crisis. It has to be a credible crisis.

This control philosophy requires a slight change in metaphor: in order
to understand better the character of typical budget directives written in
accordance with this philosophy, one should think of it as a specific part
of a screenplay: stage directions.

We will leave Northtown here, to discuss more general matters. But
first the reader might be interested to know that the good finances turned
out to be illusory, and soon—much to everybody's relief—they could go
back to the "same procedure as last year." It is important to note that although the accepted truth is still that the Swedish municipalities have an
"expansive" mentality, at least twenty years have passed since "expansion"
was replaced by "stagnation." The fact that budget requests are always
higher than previous requests does not necessarily reflect a financial situation; it has more to do with the role of the administrator (Anton 1967).

Once more, the concept of the scene-act ratio introduced in chapter 2
proves useful in understanding what is happening. Once the curtain goes
up, the public gets a pretty good idea of the kind of play it is going to see.
This is because one of the most crucial dramatistic principles is that the

characters of the actors and their actions must match stage scenery. Achieving a correct scene-act ratio can thus be seen as the main task of the stage directions: the scene directions must be coherent with acting instructions.

A screenplay includes both stage directions and acting instructions; a theater script contains the stage but not the acting instructions. In this case, stage directions have many interesting functions. While the actors' lines, in order to become a play, must simply be said (written word becomes spoken word), the stage directions are words that have to become actions and things. This miraculous transformation must take place in such a way that another miracle becomes possible: the fit between what is said and what is done. There must be a table if the actor is to bang on it, an action that requires an angry line, not a smiling one. All this is possible because the stage directions, this seemingly uninspiring text, take care of the fit between the "scene" and the "act," between the set and the action, saying how it is to be achieved.

Which comes first? Most actors in the public sector believe that the set determines the action (although in the theater and in constructivist perspective, it is the action that creates the scene), and therefore the "crisis effect" is used industriously (see also Edelman 1977). A situation like that in Northtown, where the set seemed to be painted gold, produces uneasiness not only because it supposedly provokes careless spending but also because it questions the need for control.

Brunsson (1989) points out that it is also a more general question of legitimacy within a given field. A good financial situation in a private organization means work has been well done, while the same thing in a public organization can be interpreted as meaning that taxes have been too high. Indeed, many of the public sector's efforts to imitate business companies (under the pressure of public opinion) lead to paradoxical effects, so that the action not only does not fit the scene but even appears to contradict it. A management course in the Bahamas is clear proof of success in a business company; in the public sector, it would be an obvious sign of scandalous waste. The public repertoire has to be limited, even though the limitations meet the harshest criticism. A proper budget is a set of stage directions written on one theme: "How great are the economizing requirements?" as my interlocutor put it. And he went on: "Usually, it is a discussion about 'shall we take away 1 or 2 percent from this committee?' In a more grandiose variant, the demand is for a reappraisal of all the activities. Then we know what we are doing."

## Open, Closed, or Empty Text? Three-year
## Budgeting in Social Insurance

Three-year budgeting is one of those new-old reforms that are character-istic of the public sector in Sweden (Czarniawska-Joerges and Jacobsson 1989). Launched as a brand-new instrument that would promote eco-nomic thinking and financial control in the public sector, it reminds the skeptics and the veterans of the "program budgeting" of the 1960s and the so-called State Economic-Administrative System (SEA) of the 1970s. At any rate, the social insurance system was one of the areas in the public services that was to be initially subjected to three-year budgeting. The re-actions were mixed:

> It reminds me a great deal of program budgeting in the 1970s, a reform that failed. Unfortunately, the reactions are also simi-lar. Many people are just sitting back waiting for instructions what to do. My response is that there will be no instructions, as there's no one who knows better what to do than we do ourselves. We are best at evaluating our own performance. If we get supplementary directives, that's OK, but it does not free us of our duty to develop our operations. We must get away from all this theorizing and focus on practice, if we don't want to end up with just a lot of fine phrases again. I person-ally dislike the term *three-year budgeting,* as it immediately focuses attention on money matters. This is not what's most important. The crucial issue is long-term thinking about our performance. (NSIB)

The government issued a set of very general directives on three-year bud-geting that were to be successively specified in a dialogue between minis-tries and the state agencies. The dialogue went quite smoothly, apart from a few irritations:

> The National Audit Bureau and Government Administration Office are not exactly familiar with how the particular agen-cies really function, so that everything becomes very general and somewhat abstract. . . . All too often their only knowl-edge is general to the point of superficiality. They probably don't have time or the ability to understand how we really work.[5] The problem is that different agencies are perceived as similar, whereas in reality we deal with very different problem areas and are at different points in the development process. (NSIB)

All in all, the officials at the board perceived the governmental directives as open to interpretations and saw them as something positive, a sign of government's confidence in the board's ability to work things out for themselves under the new—loose—framework. ASIO, however, reacted[6] somewhat differently:

> The directives began with a very general statement to the effect that we should have active control through results and a corresponding result analysis. We felt this could have been better explained; it was simply stated in one sentence. At any rate, we felt the social insurance offices should be given a chance to prepare a realistic description of their activities, to sketch a realistic basis for the start of the reform. . . .
>
> Next we spent some time discussing the two proposed alternatives for the basis of the budget process: unchanged level of resources, or the present level minus 5 percent on the administrative side. Here, the unions protested that it would be a very passive reaction just to accept such instructions and say nothing. We might agree with that to a certain extent, but we also believe that one has to be loyal to the government. The idea is not to yell for more resources for our sector, but to learn to like the situation as it is. However, we felt that more scope could be opened up for creative input from the offices themselves, so we were back to the issue of results. (ASIO)

The social insurance offices had little doubt about how to interpret the directives. They had no illusions about "a text open to creative interpretations."

> From now on, the allocation proposal [a kind of "budget bill" for insurance] will come as a central directive, straight from the state authorities. This strengthens the role of the national board, as it is they who cooperate closely with the Ministry of Social Welfare. (CSIO)

Or, in an even sharper tone:

> Commencing in 1991, we will get these three-year budget perspectives, and then we won't be able to make any serious plans, as Parliament will be able to change everything and negate them all. (CSIO)

Were the instructions too general or too specific? They seem to have contained a collection of slogans plus one concrete stage directive ("present state minus 5 percent on administration"). This explains the cautious comments. Apart from this last directive, the text could be regarded as open to interpretation. The question of intentions arose: was the major part of the text left open in this way by intention (and the specific directive was a slip), was it open because the authors did not know what to say, or was it open because there was nothing to say since all decisions would be made from above?

This problem has its counterpart in a more general discussion on open and closed texts (Eco 1979), which in turn is related to the discussion of the difference between *meaning* and *information* (Eco 1989). Taking his inspiration from statistical and mathematical information theory, Eco reinterprets them both into a theory of communication that can then be applied to poetics (that is, innovative texts). Eco's argument can be summarized as follows.

According to information theory, the information carried by a message is the negative of entropy and is equivalent to meaning. Indeed, language is an order (a code) imposed on the disorder of noise. Consequently, reiteration (redundancy) increases the possibility of the message being received and understood. "[T]he very order which allows a message to be understood is also what makes it absolutely predictable—that is, extremely banal. The more ordered and comprehensible a message, the more predictable it is" (1989, 52). In a real interaction situation (as opposed to a machine simulation), information is *additive:* its value depends on its novelty for those who receive it. This is why poetic discourse introduces disorder by challenging the order established by the accepted code. The new text cannot be interpreted according to previously accepted rules: it is *open* to new interpretations. In time, some of these interpretations may win over others and acquire legitimacy; a new order is established and a new rhetorical convention created, while the text becomes "closed." Temporarily, however, meaning and information are opposed to each other. This process can be schematically illustrated, as shown below.

| Convention | ContraVention | New Convention |
|---|---|---|
| redundancy | ambiguity | ambiguity removed |
| meaning | information | meaning |
| (closed text) | (open text) | (interpreted text) |

With its consensus-seeking orientation, the Swedish public sector, or perhaps the whole political scene in Sweden, is an acclaimed master of the left

column. At conferences, congresses, and meetings, as one of my interlocutors put it, all the participants say "what everybody knows and expects to
hear." Having participated in two such conferences myself, I was surprised
to see how little he had exaggerated. Nevertheless, the wider cultural transformations—the postmodern winds, as it were—find their reflection, albeit
indirectly, in the practices of the organizations I was studying. There was
consequently an awareness of the need for greater openness, for leaving
room for interpretations and thus for creativity, a recognition of the inade-
quacy of traditional control methods.[7] What Eco says about art can as well
be said about organizational genres:

> In its advocacy of artistic structures that demand a particular
> involvement on the part of the audience, contemporary poetics
> merely reflects our culture's attraction for the "indeterminate,"
> for all those processes which, instead of relying on a univocal,
> necessary sequence of events, prefer to disclose a field of pos-
> sibilities, to create "ambiguous" situations open to all sorts of
> operative choices and interpretations. (Eco 1989, 44)

One can suspect that the directives were meant to be open (the stage was
to be set in a cooperative effort), but the old habits prompted the authors
to include a bit of concrete instruction, thus arousing the suspicions of
the readers. But no text *is:* texts *become*—in practical uses, in concrete
interpretations. Everybody could yet be proven right. If things go well,
the openness may persist, creating a plethora of innovative interpretations,
some of which will eventually become institutionalized. It is possible, however, that the power game will interfere and somebody will see fit to "close"
the text on its way down the ladder, just as the local offices gloomily predicted.

## A Rhetorical Battle: The Budget in Local Insurance Offices

In contrast to municipal councilors and administrators, people in the social
insurance offices tend to see budget processes as time-consuming, relatively
meaningless, and frustrating.

> We first had a preparatory meeting, and then we had a proper
> meeting, and at both we talked about the money we need and
> why we needed money and the fact that we needed more
> money than other people, and so on and so forth. It doesn't
> lead anywhere. Naturally, it is very difficult to allocate money,

and it is very difficult to budget in the public sector in general,
so all this is very tricky. (CSIO)

As everywhere else, it is a ritual, but a sad ritual without much suspense.
There are attempts to change it, to enrich it, but they also fall flat. One
idea was to come up with operative plans, real texts rather than just dry
numbers.

> We make operational plans because we are required to, but no-
> body really thinks about what to use them for.
> *Aren't they related to the budget?*
> You know how it is with such . . . plans. Of course, they should
> be related to the budget, but we do the budget first and we
> write the plan afterwards. It is feasible, but somewhat peculiar
> nevertheless. (CSIO)

The difficulty in relating numbers to plans, some of my interlocutors
claimed, lay in the fact that social insurance offices are not used to thinking
in economic and financial terms.

> Economics is not just some figures heaped together. Econom-
> ics often means choice. This is a discussion we are trying to ini-
> tiate—to get people to think in economic terms. Sometimes
> we get very good discussions, good presentations, sometimes
> very bad discussions or none at all.
> *What does it depend on?*
> It depends on many things. Partly on the documents we get
> [from the board]. They are difficult to understand, and they
> are so specific that most of the people in the office decide they
> haven't time to immerse themselves in such details. (CSIO)

The difficulty experienced by people who did not have special economics
qualifications for understanding the financial information was pointed out
at many levels. "It takes a scientist to be able to compare one year to another in financial terms, as prices change several times within a budget year.
The labor agreements became so complex" (CSIO).

All this could have been said by the municipal employees, too. But in
my opinion, one crucial difference was that budget processes did not have
a dialogue character in the social insurance offices. It could be said that in
the municipalities, people use budget processes as a pretext to talk to each
other (Czarniawska-Joerges and Jacobsson 1989). In insurance offices,
budget-related texts *replace* conversation. Although I admired the idea of

"shadow budgets" (budgets written with no consideration for constraints, just stating wishes and needs), I learned that such budgets are written on a paper that is then handed to the boss; nobody ever mentions it again. If anything, said my interlocutor, frustration simply grows when one sits alone musing over the differences between what one wants and what one has. What is more, the budget process is structured in a punitive way:

> You feel as though you're at school—first we gather together
> in a small group and march upstairs, where the director sits
> with all those budget people. . . . All in all, our director is a
> very nice person, pleasant to be with, smiling and sociable.
> Nevertheless, the atmosphere is unmistakable: "Now, Mary,
> it's your turn to show me your homework." (CSIO)

If this sounds like a personal reaction, I might add that the board established teams (later known as "death squads") that were sent out to any offices that found it difficult to keep within their budget frames.

This unusual attitude toward budgets can be better understood if we look at it in a wider context. The favorite texts in social insurance offices are performance measures. These measures are traditionally the basis for resource allocation, not budgets (budgets are plans, wishes). The lip service paid to "economic thinking" requires that the ritual of budgeting must be retained. But there is no joy in it. Why this preference for one type of numbers and distaste for the other?

Romain Laufer and Catherine Paradeise (1990) describe the historical battle between the two types of numbers, as represented by statistics (the legitimate numbers of the state) and economics (the legitimate numbers of the free market model). Economics, with its model of the human being as *Homo oeconomicus*, assumes that exchange is the natural pattern of human interaction and prices are therefore the universal language of humanity. The economic models are based on mathematics and are meant to be symbolical (that is, to stand for terms of exchange). Statistics were invented by humans and use arithmetic to count categories—receptacles for things and people, not relationships.[8] The two can be contrasted as below.

| Statistics | Economics |
| --- | --- |
| culture | nature |
| categories | prices |
| arithmetic | mathematics |
| pragmatic counting | symbolic counting |

A ritual battle between the two continues on the ideological front, with alternating winners, while in practice the duality collapsed a long time ago. During the period of expansion in the public sector in Sweden in the 1960s and early 1970s, when the public sector dictated the norms, the introduction of prices into public-sector activities would have been read as a betrayal of its humanistic ideals. The insurance world, traditional as it is, still holds to these old ideals.

In the meantime, the private sector incorporated statistics and cultural categories into its system without advertising the fact too much (see Laufer and Paradeise's interesting interpretation of management by objectives in this spirit). This was recognized all along in certain circles, as can be illustrated by a quotation from Péteri's history of economic research in Communist Hungary. He cites the party daily newspaper as saying in 1949: "Statistics, as all the other sciences, used to be a class-science in the service of capitalists and that is why it should remain to be in the interests of socialism as well" (Péteri 1993, 149).

The fall of the Berlin Wall and its consequences brought back the ideal of the free market and of prices as a universal language, an ideology that is more easily accepted in municipalities than in social insurance offices.

> In all of this, the figure has lost its symbolic value. From a natural regulator, it has become a cultural indicator of the self-image that the firm projects, for its own use and for the use of others; from the expression of a natural relationship, it has become a pure simulacrum of the objectivity of nature, providing a presentation of the order of the world from the standpoint of organizational categories (Laufer and Paradeise 1990, 60).

In Laufer and Paradeise's tone there seems to be a trace of nostalgia for the age of the truly free market, when a benevolent anarchy ruled the behavior of economic agents. Were there ever such times? Rather than taking sides in this obsolete battle, it seems more worthwhile to study the phenomenon itself, with its institutional setting and consequences. An interesting example of such an attempt appears in a recent article analyzing the role of Luca Pacioli in the emergence of modern accounting (Thompson 1991). The article in itself is an interesting example of the institutionalization of a metaphor, insofar as it "critically assesses" the uses of rhetorical analyses, presupposing their established character. Let us follow Thompson's example and try to assess the advantages and disadvantages of text-related metaphors for numbers.

## The Uses and Consequences of the
## Text-for-Numbers Metaphor

The purpose of the above discussion was to enrich existing knowledge of the organizational phenomenon known as "budgeting" by employing the simile of collective writing. The texts thus produced acquire various functions through pragmatic interpretations arising from specific contexts. In this light, my interpretations can be given analogous status: they derive from the context of the research, informed by a need to problematize and demystify. They are neither superior nor inferior to the interpretations of organizational actors, irrespective of whether they coincide with these or oppose them.

However, this glib relativistic conclusion may not satisfy the realists, who have a legitimate right to know whether there is any reality behind the text. Collectively written or not, budgets are supposed to *represent* or, better still, *correspond to* (someone's) reality. And even if their reality status is weakened by the fact that they always concern the future—that is, a potential reality—the question of correspondence (concealing the greater question of control) must be tackled.

I think that even the most obstinate realists would agree that the budget *is* a text, and a collectively written text at that. The point of dissension concerns the use to which such a text is put in organizations. The traditional image would have it that the budget commences its controlling function once it is written. It sets constraints, at least mental constraints, on the actions undertaken during the budget period. An alternative image would have it that the budget exerts its greatest influence while it is being written, that it is an inscription of a reality rather than a causative force.

What about budget directives, then? In both the cases under discussion—budget directives in Northtown and directives for three-year budgeting—it was a matter of setting the scene, establishing the framework for budgets to come. In both cases, the actors were forced to recognize, uneasily, that a set of instructions concerning the future (and which therefore cannot be safely based on last year's budget) must be an open text, open to many interpretations that might lead practically anywhere. Budgets inform reality construction, like all other texts.

The final case, concerning budgets in social insurance offices, addresses yet another issue: the legitimate rhetoric in which organizational texts are supposed to be written, with periods of change revealing the ideological clash between two traditions.

All in all, the text metaphor shows its usefulness, paradoxically enough, by stressing not the symbolic function of budgets (in the sense of *standing for* reality) but their political and practical function (as *part of* a specific reality). Budgets-as-texts reproduce a certain political order, complete with its unavoidable drama, while organizing (controlling and coordinating) the actions of a large cast of actors. In this sense, what the texts say is less interesting than what they do—to return to the distinction made by Silverman and Torode (1980). The reality in question is the reality of text itself.

But how relevant is the metaphor? Stories compete with metaphors in economics, says McCloskey: "Stories criticize metaphors and metaphors criticize stories" (1990, 96). The partial character of every metaphor distorts the story; the literalness of narration kills the metaphor and thus the interest. But:

> [w]hatever difficulties a story faces in the light of the model, or a model in the light of a story, economists use both. Like other human beings, they use the phrases "just like this" and "once upon a time" routinely for their work. Economists are concerned both to explain and to understand. (86)

Economists are thus both poets and novelists, in practice as well as in research. A budget is a narrative (situated in the future), but it is written with the help of basic economic metaphors. This is why the text metaphor is so apt—because it is a kind of a meta-metaphor, able to include both activities practiced by economists.

But this poetic argument does not suffice. It is hard not to agree with Solow when he points out that many analyses made with the help of metaphors "stop at the 'look, Ma, a metaphor' stage" (1988, 34). The text metaphor seems to be promising because it is borrowed from a discipline that just now is in the forefront among social sciences.

Economics, for centuries under the individualist spell, still has a very feeble grasp on the social and consequently on the organizational. Serious steps are being taken in this direction. On the one hand, there is institutional theory to take care of macro-view; on the other, there are ethnomethodological and phenomenological approaches to document social processes from micro-perspective (e.g., Silverman and Jones 1976; Boland and Day 1989; Boden 1994). The exponents of both perspectives claim that each one is sufficient. To me, there is still a need for a theory that allows for a smooth passage between the two, which combines them rather than assuming their separate existence. And it is here that the theory of text seems to be most promising.

To support this view I would like to recall Ricoeur's suggestion that in the same way that "understanding" can be reconciled with "explanation" in text (by combining semiotics and hermeneutics), so the "motives" can be reconciled with "causes" in interpreting human action (Ricoeur 1981). An interesting example of such an attempt is provided by a study of investment calculations (Jansson 1989, 1992). Jansson shows how, in organizational practice, the rationalist rhetoric of investment calculus is strategically used in political negotiations; how organizational actors strategically use their knowledge of what is taken for granted in a given context. Instead of setting up a contest between the subjectivist rhetoric of motives and the objectivist rhetoric of causes, he shows how the rhetoric of causes is put into the service of the subjective motives. More studies of this kind are needed to explore the patchwork of romanticist and modernist rhetoric (Gergen 1991) that is so typical of contemporary life in large organizations.

# SEVEN

# A Quest for Identity

The Swedish public sector is on trial. In the political arena, there is talk of a crisis of legitimacy. At the administrative level, it would be more appropriate to speak of an identity crisis. Thus, what is currently required is the creation of new identities that clearly demonstrate the break with the past (that is, the tradition of powerful public authorities with a supervisory function) but nonetheless avoid the mechanical imitation of models in the private sector. In order to interpret this process, I will be employing the concept of organizational identity introduced in chapter 2, which is based on four elements:

- A definition of individual identity as a *modern institution* (i.e., temporal and local).
- An (institutionalized) metaphor of *organization as person.*
- A description of an individual identity as *emerging from interactions* between actors rather than existing in the form of an essence that is consistently exhibited.
- An analogy between organizational narratives and autobiographies as *narratives constituting identity* ("autobiographical acts").

## Six Characters in Search of a Role

The organizations under study, whose identities may be until further notice conventionally termed "municipal authorities," "the Swedish Association of Local Authorities," "the government," "social insurance offices," "the Association of Social Insurance Offices," and "a state agency," were involved in the search for a new identity—all of them from different starting points and with varying results. The old stage setting, the Swedish Model, has been dismantled, and it is hard to say what the new one will be.

The "government's" ideological identity was under threat at the time of the study, and it still is. The same might be said of the other five "characters in search of a role." The "municipal authority" was doing rather well, at least in its external manifestations. Parts of the municipal administration have been turned into limited companies. They speculate on the financial markets, they speak the same language as the local population (or at least try to), they use visual presentations in attempts at marketing themselves, and they try to depict themselves as "suppliers in the service sector." New action nets have given rise to new identities. But things have not been working so smoothly at the internal level—the municipal administration's traditional identity as a miserly employer that expects sacrifices on the part of its staff continues to be a burdensome image. The "Swedish Association of Local Authorities," on the other hand, is having considerable success, at both the internal and external levels. SALA's internal identity was fairly easy to establish since it is a highly professional organization. In the outside world, gales are blowing, from the government directions and from the large municipalities, but SALA is nonetheless fighting for a new role as a "molder of public opinion" (an example of which we have seen in the tax reform story) and a "guide." This also applies to the "Association of Social Insurance Offices," but in this case it is more a question of tornadoes blowing from all possible directions. ASIO itself is more political than professional, and this is a disadvantage when building up a consistent organizational identity.

The "social insurance offices" were facing considerable problems in their search for an identity since there are many external mandatory restrictions and very little autonomy. The "parent body," that is to say the National Social Insurance Board, had even more serious problems of identity since it is perhaps the state agency that has been the most bitterly attacked and most heavily criticized.

Chapter 2 contained a description of the material of modern identity as given by Meyer (1986): self-respect, efficiency, autonomy, and flexibility. It is precisely this modern identity that organizations in the public sector were once again trying to find after the identity they acquired with the emergence of the welfare state lost its legitimacy. Self-respect was redefined by the public as self-righteousness, efficiency was regarded as nonexistent, autonomy was seen as a lack of contact with the outside world, and flexibility was political opportunism.

The problem was exacerbated by the fact that it is not just individual identities that are disintegrating but also other institutions. In the case of individuals, building up an identity is described as an interaction between an individual (who is developing) and relatively stable institutions. But in this case, we have the reverse situation—there are "individuals" who used to have strong identities, and there is an organizational environment of institutions that are in a state of radical change. We will be analyzing the institutional aspects of this process later. Our immediate focus is on attempts to find a narration expressing a new identity through changes in legitimate rhetoric (McCloskey 1986).

Public-sector employees were well aware that their rhetoric must change—particularly when they presented themselves to the outside world. But the traditional rhetoric still existed, holding back every attempt to achieve change. Perhaps it would be appropriate to speak of several kinds of traditional rhetoric that used to be accepted as legitimate in discussion within and about the public sector.

## Traditional Rhetoric

We can start with three conventional kinds of rhetoric: political rhetoric, officialese, and the language of experts.

*Political* statements are usually poor in *logos,* the logical argument, but this is counterbalanced by rich *pathos,* appealing to the audience's emotions. Hyperbole is favored: threats are described as black and sinister, while promising developments are depicted in all the colors of the rainbow. This rhetoric is also often employed by the Swedish media (journalists report what politicians say, and politicians learn to formulate their ideas in media terms).

*Officialese*—the language of bureaucracy—has three main characteristics. It is full of *congeries* (the obvious is reiterated), and its *logos* is unnecessarily complicated (it can take time and require some expenditure of energy to perceive the repetition). The third characteristic is the low *aesthetic* level, which is partly the result of the first two characteristics but is also the product of conscious[1] or unconsciously bad (clumsy) rhetoric. Figures of speech such as metaphors and irony are avoided in favor of empty parallelism, phrases that are identically built, therefore achieving the effect of monotony. In terms of narrative strategies, suspense is avoided, and the *ethos* and *pathos* kind of appeals—references to the authority of the speaker or to the character of the listener—are both sacrificed to *logos,* the force of an impersonal argument.

It is true that officials who can write well have existed throughout the ages, but it is also true that officialese has always been under constant fire. Of course, "writing well" means different things in different eras. In the 1960s and 1970s, the language of experts became the ideal. *Expert* rhetoric is based on the "objective truth," in contrast to subjective (moral) truth (not lying) or cognitive truth (believing something to be true). Expert rhetoric is designed to give the impression that the expert in question has direct contact with reality, while the readers suffer from distortions resulting from their subjectivity. *Ethos* is therefore the basis of the argument. There is an imitation of science—the argumentation consists of "proof," and "confirmation" is achieved by employing statistics—and a great many metaphors are employed (derived from the world of science and describing objects and their characteristics), resulting literally in an impression of "objectivity," that is to say that the argumentation involves material objects, not symbols or ideas. In addition, the expert would hotly deny that any rhetoric was being employed. This amounts to the denial of *ethos,* a claim to credibility based on the authority of the speaker, replaced by an institutionalized claim that it is *logos* only, that is, the force of argument as such, that persuades.

## Trying to Change

I chose for scrutiny two articles in *Dagens Nyheter* (the leading Swedish daily) that were widely discussed by my interlocutors and that in my view represent attempts to change the traditional rhetoric—with mixed success.

An article by the head of the Municipal Finance Department of the Association of Local Authorities appeared in *Dagens Nyheter* on 25 January 1990 under the headline "Put a Price on Services":

> The final goal has been scored in the municipal pay championship. The cost is about 12 billion kronor, or a further 6 percent in local taxes—a figure that corresponds to municipal expenditure for cultural and leisure activities.
>
> How are local authorities going to manage this? They have budgeted for a pay increase of only 7 percent, but the current award amounts to 13 percent.

The writer first sets the scene by trying to gain the reader's sympathy and interest by employing a sports metaphor.[2] A dramatic atmosphere is created by the mention of a terrifying figure: 12 billion. Some tension is built up by employing a mysterious analogy: is the "pay championship" linked in some way to culture and recreational activities? Finally, the writer promises an answer to a vital question, and here it comes.

> Municipalities must find a connection between pay, achievement, and the public's willingness to pay for services. I believe that it is essential . . . to let "consumers" decide the value of these services to a greater extent by establishing prices in the form of fees. This will provide both employees and politicians with a litmus test for what people are prepared to pay. At the

> same time, employees will be able to see clearly that excessive
> pay increases affect people's propensity to demand local author-
> ity services. This will establish a correlation between cost and
> job security.

By employing the pronoun "I," the author demonstrates that the proposal
has been formulated by an individual, not by an organization, thus reduc-
ing the negative "official public relations" implications of the article. The
use of quotation marks around the term "consumers" makes us aware that
the "market orientation" has been borrowed from another context, while
linking into this orientation. The market myth permeates the entire article,
rather than coming directly upon the reader as a boring lecture on a familiar subject. The positive effects of the market are subtly hinted at: politicians and officials will receive congruent financial information (and not, as
is customary, information that merely leads to conflict). Finally, employees
(the union) will also receive a salutary lesson in the workings of economic
mechanisms.

> How does this fit in with fair allocation policies for services for
> the care of children and old people, on whom increased charges
> would have the greatest impact?
>     Local authority activities will continue to be centered on
> education and care for the young and the elderly. Education will
> probably continue to be free, and welfare services will also be
> largely financed through taxation.

The reader who was afraid that marketization would apply to all aspects
of the public sector has been reassured, since what are currently felt to
be central aspects of public services are excluded from the proposals. But
subsequently matters become more specific:

> Local authorities will be unable to continue to provide all types
> of services free, for example in the cultural and recreational
> sectors.

By employing the phrase "for example," the writer demonstrates that his
proposal is at a preliminary stage and that other types of services (unspeci-
fied) may be included subsequently. There also appears to be some justification for selecting the examples mentioned:

> Why should local authorities continue to subsidize forms of
> consumption that are largely utilized by well-paid and well-

educated citizens? By all means subsidize activities for children
and young people, but let adults pay the going rate.

The use of contrasts is a well-known rhetorical technique. We are faced
with a choice between sympathizing with the "well-paid and well-
educated" or with "children and young people." The remainder (pension-
ers, the underpaid and the poorly educated) belong to "a relatively small
group which will then be under pressure" and which is to receive support,
"but not within the framework of the current financial system. It is not
possible to subsidize 98 percent of the population in order to reach the
final 2 percent." And now we come to the punchline:

> Put a price on culture and leisure services, and let the individu-
> als themselves decide whether these are attractive enough to
> merit consumption.

In a deconstructivist spirit, one can contrast this statement with how it
would have sounded in the 1960s. Most likely, it would run along the following lines: "Culture and leisure activities must be freely accessible to all,
not only to the privileged few. Yet it would be naive to believe that it is
enough just to say this. We have to launch an active program popularizing
cultural activities and meaningful ways of spending leisure time." Different
times, different rhetoric.

The language of the marketplace dominates the article. "Putting a
price on" something, "letting the individuals decide," and the "consumption" of services are all central features of the market myth. The article
continues by outlining the consequences of implementing the proposal and
of the alternative (maintaining the status quo):

> Today, most nonmandatory municipal services tend to be sub-
> ject to a gradual deterioration in quality and attractiveness as a
> result of extensive savings. Ultimately they become so poor that
> people find better alternatives outside the local authority struc-
> ture. Privatization will have been achieved without any political
> decision being made.
>
> This is definitely not a perspective that can attract people
> to seek employment in the local authority sector. Who would
> want to work in an organization of this nature?

This is the dark side of the picture. There are three nightmare visions: poor
quality, privatization, and negative recruitment. But now comes the good
news:

The best way of experiencing challenge is to work with activities that are in demand. Instead of having to deal with continual requirements for cutbacks that affect services negatively, local authorities must dare to invest in services that people demand and are willing to pay for—getting us to give priority to a high-quality cultural program, rather than some gadget bought in a chain store or a second-rate video. That makes it fun to go to work again!

It should be noted that although certain clichés are employed ("experiencing challenge," "dare to invest"), the language is hardly bureaucratic. Everyday expressions ("chain-store gadget," "fun to go to work") are employed to increase the impression of immediacy. The contents of the article indicate clearly that it is written from an official perspective. The positive vision offers improved finances and a better work situation for employees.

I would like to suggest that this article is a model attempt to change communications at the "official level." I will clarify this by comparing (in a speculative manner) the rhetoric employed with the three conventional rhetorics mentioned above.

Compared with political rhetoric, the article has a well-balanced structure, logical argumentation,[3] and skillful but calm use of figures of speech. The fact that it is addressed to "well-paid and well-educated citizens" (whose interests are attacked in the article) is an unconventional and daring attempt to persuade a group that is likely to suffer from the author's proposals.

The article also contrasts sharply with conventional officialese. It is very well constructed, with skillful use of metaphors and appropriate high-flown phrases to calm the reader down before delivering the next knockout blow. It employs *enthymeme*, assuming and demanding that the reader supply missing (and shared) premises, and it avoids repetitions (congeries).

Nor does the article comply with the expert tradition. The figures are clearly estimates ("about 12 billion kronor") and they are used as part of the argument, not to prove that a particular point is correct. Expert rhetoric normally avoids the use of "I," and also subjective touches such as "I believe." The expert prefers "It is essential" rather than "I think it is essential." The know-all tone that characterizes expert rhetoric is no longer in fashion in public-sector communication in Sweden. *Ethos*, that is to say the credibility of the speaker, is built up by the sincerity of the opinions, and not by an appeal to some hidden authority.

In another article published in *Dagens Nyheter*, headed "Scrap the National Insurance Board" (13 April 1989), a principal administrative officer in the board's employ wrote:

> Several articles that have appeared in these pages have dealt with activities in the public sector. Among other things, views have been presented regarding methods for restricting the development of costs, thus benefiting the taxpayer.

Thus, the article establishes its legitimacy by linking into an ongoing discussion. It is claimed, however, that something is missing in this public debate:

> Evaluation of the Insurance Board's operations is not undertaken in a manner that gives the state information as to whether the resources invested in the board have provided the yield that was intended. What specific services does the board produce? Who demands these services? Are they necessary, and, if so, do they give value for money?

The first sentence quoted above implies that the government receives "information as to whether the resources invested have provided the yield that was intended" from all other government bodies, with the exception of the National Insurance Board. The reader is confronted with a conspiratorial hypothesis, and this impression is reinforced by the rhetorical technique characteristically employed in this context: *interrogatio*. Rhetorical questions, of course, mean asking questions that have an apparently given answer. In the above case, the answers will be a triple no. This total negation means that argumentation has to start from the beginning again:

> There are twenty-six insurance offices in Sweden and each office is a separate legal entity managed by a board. . . . As a result of the broad representation on these boards and committees, the general public has good insight into the operations of the insurance offices. In addition, the offices have jointly formed an organization to promote their interests—the Federation of Social Insurance Offices—which provides the local offices with administrative services. . . . There is an established contact network with the general public, providers of social care, employers, other organizations, etc.

These are just a few sentences extracted from a full column of description of the status of the local insurance offices. Unfortunately, the effect created by the technique of the rhetorical question is swamped by the volume of information provided. The conspiratorial introduction is allowed to fade away, and when the author returns to his original point ("This is the perspective in which the need for the board's supervisory function should be discussed"), the reader has forgotten the introduction, and the original drama has dissipated.

Now, however, comes the dark side of the picture:

> The central control of data-processing operations and the day-to-day workload of the local offices mean that the offices rely on up-to-date instructions from the board on services required with regard to the general public. If there are delays in making payments due to the malfunctioning of the computer system or because personnel are waiting for new instructions before they can explain the position to the public, local office staff have to deal with the complaints.

The description is unclear, and this effect is reinforced by the complex language employed ("services required with regard to"). The reader is distracted by several hidden implications. Why doesn't the computer system work? Do the local offices always have to wait for the board's instructions? What is the connection between the two? In addition, the argumentation is weakened by the conditional use of "if," which implies that the problems described have not (yet) happened.

> Central control by the board also inhibits the creativity of the local offices, hindering initiatives to achieve more effective routines and improved service to the general public.

This arouses the reader's suspicions, since "creativity"—something that is desirable per se—is not exactly what is expected of a local insurance office. However, the reader is pacified by mention of "improved service," which is a familiar albeit empty concept.

The article examines the various departments at the National Social Insurance Board and finally presents a proposal:

> There are major opportunities for achieving more efficient administration in the social insurance sphere, thus significantly reducing costs. It is no longer justified to continue the board's supervisory activities. Local offices should be entrusted with the task of administering social insurance and the benefits system on their own responsibility. . . . This would provide greater scope for creative initiatives to reduce the risks of injuries, im-

prove the health environment, and undertake rehabilitation measures, in conjunction with employers, worker protection organizations, employment offices, and local care services. . . . A review of the board's role in the social insurance field is therefore required from an economic point of view. It is important that this review adopt an unbiased approach and have access to a broad range of expert resources, including people with experience of structural change and business know-how.

Here we have a mixture of political and bureaucratic rhetoric. On the one hand, a solution of several societal problems is promised, while on the other, the article employs all the expressions commonly found in bureaucratic documents that are devoid of content. On the one hand, a proposal is presented that is totally at variance with conventional practice (when have there ever been "unbiased" official reports?), while on the other hand, a coupling is made with trendy ideas (expert resources from the business world) that the general reader may find unpalatable.

I use the phrase "general reader" deliberately since I regard this newspaper article as directed at insiders rather than the general reader. This is a narrowly targeted communication attempt. Even in my own case, as someone relatively familiar with the problems involved, the provocation achieved was extremely weak. The inconsistent *logos,* in combination with the officialese language, diluted the message to such an extent that I wonder if other readers could understand how revolutionary the ideas expressed actually were. What appeared to be an attempt to talk to strangers proved to be primarily addressed to the writer's own circle. The board ignored the rhetoric but focused on the message, as the following quotation from an interview with a top official shows:

> It is extremely sad and unfortunate to find that someone employed by the board advertises his views in the press in this manner. The person in question has suffered from the reorganization that has taken place at the National Social Insurance Board. Naturally, he is bitter and thinks he has been unfairly treated.

But this does not mean that his ideas are idiosyncratic, the official continued:

> He expresses opinions that are held, by and large, in many quarters and that are represented in some local insurance offices. . . . It is felt that central control is too extensive. The de-

> gree of control required is an ideological question. We assume
> that an insurance system should be applied on the same basis
> all over the country and that a centralized body is required to
> ensure that this happens. . . . But is it really correct?

This is an important discussion that I do not intend to get involved in. The
point I am trying to make is that Insurance Board staff are used to reading
between the lines. What was clear to them appeared to me as confused
rhetoric and an unclear message (as it also did to younger members of staff
and new employees, as the interviews showed). Of course, it is difficult to
change the predominant rhetoric when "insiders" actually understand
what is being said very well. This may explain why officialese is still alive
and kicking, despite so many attempts to kill it.

## Long Live Officialese

Everyone in the organizations I have studied agreed that traditional communication modes fail to meet contemporary requirements. But at the
same time, both the diagnosis and the cure seemed to be trapped in the
same frame of thought that had originally caused the disease. It should not
be forgotten that any attempts to improve the particular officialese stem
from the same institutional thought structure that originated it. Hence another paradox known as self-censorship: heavy editing of the authorial
voice is instilled internally; the rhetoric of control needs to be controlled at
the outset (Hatch 1993).

  While individuals may not be aware of all this,they are aware that there
is a language problem. Yet they continue to believe that "simple" and "correct" language is enough to solve the problem. In other words, there is
continued faith in the modernist, naive-realistic view that words refer directly to phenomena in the real world. There is a firm belief that if you find
the "right" word, everyone will understand. This is reinforced by a fear of
rhetoric as such. It is condemned in advance as "empty" or as being merely
a matter of "verbal initiatives."

  This, claims Fisher, is where the practical use of the narrative paradigm
is at its highest:

> The narrative paradigm challenges the notions that human
> communication . . . must be argumentative in form, that reason
> is to be attributed only to discourse marked by clearly identifi-
> able modes of inference and implication, and that the norms for
> evaluation of rhetorical communication must be rational stan-

dards taken exclusively from informal or formal logic. (Fisher 1987, 58)

The narrative paradigm, says Fisher, attempts to reconcile two conflicting trends in the history of rhetoric: rhetoric seen as pure argumentation (persuasion) or as pure ornamentation (aesthetically pleasing).

But how are we to evaluate whether a given rhetoric is persuasive or aesthetically pleasing? Within the constructionist perspective, the dialogue and its conditions, including the participants and their identity, are created and re-created in the interaction itself. This is why a rhetoric is never "right" or "wrong" in itself. Rhetoric and identities must be tried out and accepted in action nets within the relevant organizational field.

## Autobiographical Acts in Social Insurance

We have already noted that one of the most threatened identities was that of the Association of Social Insurance Offices (ASIO), and this was where visible attempts at regaining identity by authoring and negotiating autobiographies could be observed.

### Textual Strategies: The Stock of Actors

As the heading to this section implies, there was no single autobiography: there were many attempts, formal and informal, which fought with one another, tried to dominate or subvert the others, and so on. Accordingly, different textual strategies were used in different biographies. The biography that ASIO is authorized to write is the biography of social insurance in Sweden; therefore, its main elements must at least be recognizable to all the actors. There is thus a common stock of actors; it is the roles into which they are to be cast that differ in the competing versions.

In what follows, three categories of Narrators will be mentioned: the first consists of my interlocutors, presenting their versions in conversations with me, supporting one or another version of the common autobiography. Sometimes they strengthen their argument by quoting one of the other categories: writers within the social insurance system who have written PR brochures or official histories (the official task of the ASIO), or researchers who asked or were invited to study the history of social insurance.

There are basically three main collective Characters: the National Social Insurance Board (NSIB), the Association of Social Insurance Offices (ASIO), and County Social Insurance Offices (CSIO). Naturally, there are many other characters in this organization field, such as the representatives of the employees, the Ministry of Social Affairs, and so on, but they could be described as the audience (readership) and judges of the autobiographical acts.

The role of the Author is the most controversial. Historically —and on this fact there is complete agreement—this role was occupied by a popular movement (*folkrörelse*). The disagreement concerns the present, as usual. Some claim that the state has taken over the authorial role, and that all other versions are just a question of sentimentality and nostalgia; others say that, yes, the state has such an ambition which is abominable and must be ended, and others again claim that the original Author is still at work.

## The ASIO Story

ASIO has a virtual monopoly on autobiographies of Swedish social insurance, since its task is to produce most of the PR brochures. So here is a concise history of Swedish social insurance as presented in a glossy brochure entitled "Association of Social Insurance Offices: A Presentation." I translate it in extenso so that I can then concentrate on comments and interpretations and avoid repeating historical data.

> The association was created in August 1907. At the dawn of the twentieth century sickness benefit clubs constituted the biggest popular movement in Sweden. The creation of a countrywide organization was considered important, not only to meet the need for a uniform and effective system, but also to attract public attention to the idea of universal obligatory insurance against ill health.
>
> Originally there were around one thousand small voluntary sickness benefit clubs which dealt with cases of illness, infirmity, and funerals. Half of them had fewer than one hundred members, and their finances were very modest. When the association came into being it began the laborious job of organizing and changing structures so that the effective insurance offices of today could materialize.
>
> In 1931, a decree recognized the sickness benefit clubs, which made it possible to rationalize their work and to improve the allowances.
>
> In 1955, obligatory social insurance was introduced. The whole country was insured, and benefits were much improved. The authorized clubs were transformed into public sickness benefit offices.

From 1962, they were known as insurance offices. The name "sickness benefit office" vanished because the offices now took care of many other matters, such as the national old-age pension and the national supplementary pension scheme.[4]

Since then, the offices have acquired many other tasks. During the 1970s, these included, for example, payment of advance allowances, dental insurance, work-related disability insurance, and parental insurance. This last has been successively extended.

The historical presentation begins with the date when the association was created, but there is no mention whatsoever of even the existence of NSIB, or its historical predecessor, the National Insurance Institution, founded in 1902 to take care of work-related accidents. Obviously, the Author here is the popular will, and the two main Characters are the local offices and their association. The date when the sickness benefit offices and the insurance institution became one, 1962, is given as the time when the name was changed and new tasks were taken on. There is no mention of the present crisis, although elsewhere (the brochure has eight pages) there is a list of wishes for the future that includes rehabilitation activities. It takes quite a lot of detective work to discover what the text does not say.

Personal accounts reflect much more tension and uncertainty, but the general lines are the same. Here is the story as rendered by an executive of the association:

The system of general insurance was born of the need for support primarily in cases of sickness and infirmity. It originated in the guilds, whose members joined together to supply such support rather than leaving themselves in the hands of fate. The movement spread all over the country, and there was always this tendency to cooperate, first at the local level and then at the county level, so that the advantages of such a cooperation became increasingly evident. Hence the creation of the association. After this, we witnessed the development of the social security system, and our association acquired a role quite different from, let us say, that of the SALA or the Association of County Authorities. Today we have a social insurance system, and the NSIB has an important role there, even a leading role within the social insurance system, if you will—as the government's supervisory authority, but the association consists of the social insurance offices themselves.

The key to understanding the present situation, in the executive's opinion, lies in a proper understanding of the past:

> The offices are autonomous legal persons; they have both local political boards and local social insurance boards which make difficult decisions, very much in accordance with the social insurance tradition as a popular movement. This is also why we feel that we have an advantageous start in this decentralization process which is expected of us now; a decentralistic attitude has permeated our activities from the beginning, this has always been our way. . . . And the tension that accompanies it, the tradition of the popular movement versus the tradition of central authorities, this is also something very characteristic.

It is indeed, and not only in the case of social insurance. This paradox of a very strong tradition of local autonomy and central control permeates everything in the Swedish public administration. Some actors, like the municipalities, gain from it, claiming that their decentralized character has been "forever"; some, like the state actors, suffer most; and the whole issue is debated and twisted and turned again on the spit of public attention as rotated by the media.

But declarations alone are not enough; an external ally was found in the person of a historian who studied social insurance in Sweden and identified three phases: the "solidarity culture" (from the turn of the century to the beginning of prosperity in the 1960s), the "regulation culture" (up to the present), and the "service culture" (for the future). This was the kind of biography that fit in well with the association's image, not only because it offered an attractive vision of the future expressed in fashionable "cultural" terms, but also because it made a link between the original culture and the culture of the future. According to this view, the service culture is "a kind of need-controlled culture, in which citizens themselves decide what they really need."

Naturally, this was not the only version of the history and future of social insurance in Sweden.

## Voices from the Field

Many people in the social insurance offices supported the most important points in the association's version. Here is one voice that emphasizes the role of the social movement and its links with the workers' movement and opposition to centralized authority:

> Social insurance offices, which today are legal persons, ori-
> ginated in the authorized sickness benefit clubs which were
> closely linked to the workplace; every guild had its club whose
> task was to save its members' skins, starting in the nineteenth
> century. It wasn't until the late 1950s that they were combined
> with the state offices taking care of pensions. So, you see, a so-
> cial movement was suddenly merged with an administrative
> tradition, and this battle of values is still going on. We still feel
> strong links with the workers' movement and want to be faith-
> ful to the idea . . . of serving the common people. This is why
> we oppose losing our legal sovereignty and becoming a part of
> the state. (Centraltown)

Another voice tells a history of battles in which the metaphors of identity emerge clearly from a pun (in Swedish): the same phrase can mean both "we became an authority" and "we were declared responsible adults." There is a bitterness in this woman's story, in which the supervisory organ is presented as having deprived the insurance offices of their autonomy, their right to be a "person."

> Don't forget that social insurance offices are not part of the
> state administration; they are legally autonomous persons. The
> fact is, though, that the state budget finances the administra-
> tion of insurance, although the insurance money comes from
> the employers. But there is a state supervisory organ which
> has the right to prescribe the terms of our operations. The end
> of the 1970s was characterized by powerful centralization,
> and it was then that NSIB became our supervisor and started
> telling us in detail what we were to do in the local offices.
> They prescribed every step in our operations. But the last few
> years have seen a kind of a revolution; there is talk of decen-
> tralization and deregulation, and consequently we are now
> recognized again as being quite sane and responsible. (Cen-
> traltown, another interlocutor)

Observe the shift in Characters. The Author is the same, the social movement; and the offices are still onstage. The association has faded away; now
a slightly vague enemy—the central authority—appears in the stories.

It seems that the association did not limit itself to writing about its
history. Sometime before I started my study, the association had publicly
questioned NSIB's right to control insurance operations. The main claim
was that the supervisory role concerned the administration of insurance

funds, but not the management of the insurance offices. The board appealed to the government:

> [The association's] perception did not tally with ours. In our
> view it is quite clear both in the law and in the budget bills
> that NSIB is a management and supervisory body for the in-
> surance system and its administration. . . . We have now re-
> ceived a very clear answer in the present budget bill, which
> states that NSIB manages social insurance operations, but it is
> also pointed out that we must take the views of the offices
> into account and must cooperate with them.

Regarding the clarity of the various statements, opinions were divided. My interlocutor in Northern County felt that the ambiguity was the same as before, and it was simply that "the association is now singing small, and doesn't dare take up the battle again." He was not very optimistic about future developments, either:

> The association is trying now to change its role and to lobby
> the government and Parliament. They want to represent those
> interests of the offices that are not reflected by the NSIB. Per-
> sonally, I find it all very frustrating because for us it simply
> means lots of double signals. It would be unjust to blame it
> on the association; this is how the whole system is organized.
> To tell you the truth, we belong to the state. The autonomous
> standing of the offices is a chimera because they are totally
> financed by the state.

The last word has not been spoken yet, but it is perhaps interesting that the NSIB was very dissatisfied with its lack of printing capacity (all PR production is located with the association). NSIB officials have pointed out many times that the quality of their documents (of which there are thousands of pages—all sent to the offices) is unsatisfactory. In their computerization programs, particular attention was paid to the layout software.

NSIB took over the responsibility for training and development that formerly resided with the association. If it succeeds in becoming the official Narrator, there will no longer be a multiplicity of autobiographies.

## Tentative Identities in Fuzzy Organizational Fields
### Authors and Critics

This search for a new identity can be interpreted as an attempt to change the whole organizational field of public administration, and not only the subfields under study. Actors are attempting to adopt new identities at a stage when a change in structures has been announced but not specified. Accordingly, not even NSIB is certain of an identity in the situation when short-term sickness benefit is to be paid by the employers. Models and histories proliferate, but in practice their relevance in relation to new identities is confirmed or rejected in conversations. It is not enough to select an attractive identity and then to present it with the help of an appropriate rhetoric. The new (or the old-new) identity must be accepted by the other actors involved, by those who are operating on an established stage with a clear identity (e.g., the private sector), and by other people who find themselves in a similar situation.

When the field has been restructured and the new stage institutionalized, it is highly probable that someone will acquire a new identity as "umpire." In the case of company-ization, the Association of Local Authorities had a good chance of becoming umpire. ASIO has similar ambitions but on shakier grounds. But the last word has not been said yet; it will depend, as usual, on random factors and on the association's identity-creation skills.

It could perhaps help us to understand the process better if we compare it with some other similar studies of organization fields. Most studies of this kind are concerned with one of two typical cases: new actors who are trying to enter an existing field or new actors who are trying to construct a new field (DiMaggio 1983; DiMaggio and Powell 1983; March and Olsen 1989; Meyer, Boli, and Thomas 1987; Olsen, Roness, and Soetren 1989; Sahlin-Andersson 1989). Here, however, we have a case of established actors trying to construct a new stage, to restructure the old field, according to the prevalent control philosophy whereby the stage determines the actions and the actors. The old identities of these actors, their habitual ways of acting, shackle them and restrict their freedom and creativity. This is most clearly evident in the insurance offices, whose established identity was both clear and precisely specified. So long as their action nets remain the same, it is difficult to enact a new identity. This is why the formation of new action nets, as described in chapters 4 and 5, raises high hopes of creating new identities.

Processes of this kind obviously involve big risks. There are concrete risks, such as the municipal currency speculation scandals, and there is also a considerable risk of public ridicule. The transformation is taking place onstage. The citizens, who want good entertainment without paying too much, are sitting expectantly in the audience, along with competitors who would like to see a real fiasco and critics from the media who will be writing their reports on what "actually" happens.

Can the narrative approach offer any help? Probably, on at least two counts. Public administration organizations, like everybody else, are only partly the authors of their auto-narrative. Acknowledgment of this fact can extend their understanding of the situation, without pushing them toward fatalism. Further, conscious attempts can be made to limit the role of other authors and to increase their own.

This last opens the way to a further important insight connected with the difference between "search" and "quest." Up to now, "search" has been a legitimate term in organization theory, and this may be part of a problem rather than a solution. The idea of the "quest" in medieval ballads, for example, did not refer to a search for something already adequately defined such as oil or gold; the quest was a search that created its own object.

> It is in the course of the quest and only through encountering
> and coping with the various particular harms, dangers, tempta-
> tions and distractions which provide any quest with its episodes
> and incidents that the goal of the quest is finally to be under-
> stood. A quest is always an education both as to the character of
> that which is thought and in self-knowledge (MacIntyre 1981/
> 1990, 219).

A search for excellence, or for a new identity, assumes that such an identity already exists and is waiting to be discovered. This may be correct only if the new identity is to be "written" by somebody else, for example, the private sector. If the public administration wants to remain its own author, then it must embark on a quest during which a new identity will be formed as an autobiography, but one that accords with what are "legitimate" autobiographies today. This, however, must be discovered in the process of formulation itself. A quest, unlike a search, never ends; it alternates between striving for resolution and immediate relaunching, between the certainty required for action and the demolition of certainty that results from reflection, between the very human dreams of sitting still and moving forward fast.

## Local Knowledge

It is not only the place of the narrative in theory that is presently being discussed, questioned, and reestablished. The construction of local knowledge may be changing in analogous ways, both as a part and as a result of the quest for identity. Some people worry that the quest is going too fast and losing important values on its way, others that it is not going fast enough. It depends, of course, on who is watching whom.

> To those who are observing political trends in this Northern Kingdom it may look as if the Swedish model is now changing, that the era of modernity and the rule of Social Democracy welfare state is terminated. "Being modern" is, however, not only a simple attitude that may change with the new fads and fashions. It is a matter of existence beyond political trends, especially if it has been a form of life for generations. It then turns into a condition deeply rooted in human mentality. In the Swedish case, modernism is closely linked to a special kind of mentality we may call "managerialism." (Guillet de Monthoux 1991, 27)

Guillet de Monthoux continues his argument by claiming that the traditional pictures of "peaceful interorganizational cooperation" on the one hand and the dramatic contrast between the public administration and private enterprise on the other are not really relevant. What is most important to an understanding of contemporary Sweden is the managerial mentality permeating all Swedish organizations (which in turn permeate the whole of Swedish society). Sweden is one big firm. Everything can be managed, when left in the hands of corporate managers. This tradition is so strong that no "legitimation crises" are going to affect it—"Sweden . . . will probably become a cute little island of modernity in the European post-modern ocean" (40).

There may be a good deal of truth in this, especially as the Swedish type of modernism has proved to be extremely successful, in spite of all pessimistic prophecies. "How Bright Are the Northern Lights?" asked Mancur Olson, and answered comfortingly that "a society can, if its policies and institutions are intelligent, prevent destitution and even make fairly generous provision for its least fortunate citizens, yet still remain a prosperous and dynamic society" (1990, 91).

Both Olson and Guillet de Monthoux see Sweden as a modern project through and through—the difference is whether they see it as a reason for optimism or pessimism. Another possibility is to look for reasons for the survival and success of the modern project in its postmodern practices.

The postmodern condition as described by Lyotard (1979) is characterized not by disappointment with the modern project (in fact, it can be seen as an inseparable part of it) but by skepticism regarding modernism's legitimating metanarratives: that of *functional system,* as designed by experts, and that of *emancipating freedom,* as created by a political consensus. People who populate organizations are well aware that experts represent only one voice in a polyphony, not to say cacophony, of voices, and that a final consensus can never be reached. What is more, there is no greater danger to the system than its efficiency (Antonio 1979; Lyotard 1979), whereas consensus can be seen as the condition for a dialogue rather than its purpose. Much is said about the collective policies of Swedish trade unions; less attention is devoted to the unique capacity for collective action revealed by Swedish business (Pestoff 1991).

As for the public administration, its organizations are cheerfully bad-mouthed but little known, in Sweden or anywhere else. Mary Douglas has written a very interesting article entitled "The Social Preconditions of Radical Scepticism" (1986). In it she scolds the contemporary intelligentsia for erasing the borders between appearances and reality, which she sees partly as an expression of powerlessness, partly as a defensive search for sophistication. In ironical mode, she turns on Western intellectuals, telling them: "Choose the more sophisticated path if you will. As you do so, . . . you will separate yourselves from dirty politics, and look down on those *crude officers of public administration,* whose minds such complicated doubts would never cross" (Douglas 1986b, 83, emphasis added).

With all respect to Douglas, she knows little about the minds of Sweden's public officers, who hosted every possible doubt—and survived. They are the true masters of radical skepticism, which does not prevent them from forming and maintaining a commitment to reality—against all the odds, it might seem. Indeed, they are more like the intellectuals than any other group I studied. They live wedged between appearance and reality, that is, between politics and administration, and they spend a good deal of thought on it. Like intellectuals, they try to influence politics by argument, and, unlike intellectuals, they have access to reality via the organizational hierarchy. Maybe this gives them more power, in the common sense of the word; but it also gives them the power to live with paradoxes without frenetic attempts to resolve them.

Berg claims that the key to an understanding of contemporary developments in the Swedish organizational context lies in certain typically postmodern traits: "the deconstruction of organization structures, the rejection of grand strategies, the emphasis on expressivism, and the importance

of coding" (1989, 213). While in the field, I witnessed a growing awareness of the fact that every organization hosts a multitude of small narratives, multiple interpretations, plural realities. These stem from ideological
differences, professional variations, or generation and gender differences.
Actors are forced to choose one version of the world to act upon, but this
does not make any particular version permanent or valid for the future.
Reality is constantly being renegotiated, thus giving new meaning to the
concept of a "negotiated economy" (Hernes 1978). Of course, this meaning is spurious, and in times of crisis and desperate action a single totalizing
narrative might have a better chance than in times of relative prosperity
and quiet reflection. But as things are now, not only is the number of voices
not diminishing; it seems to increase daily (for example, Sweden moved
rapidly from having two television channels to about ten for an average
household, and a total of 129 theoretically available)—as everywhere else,
a veritable Babel of voices.

Does the narrative approach combined with institutionalism help to
understand these multivoiced developments in Sweden? No simple summary could replace the variegated interpretations I have been trying to review in this book. As for a general overview, however, this can be outlined
roughly as follows: what happened in Sweden, starting in the late 1970s
and culminating first now, was that the institutional thought structure that
can be said to have prevailed for the last fifty years or so began to be called
into question. This may or may not be announcing a period of radical
change. What one can clearly see is the mobilization of the adherents of
that thought structure, with the help of many devices: not only reformulations and a search for new narratives, but also the blunting and dilut-
ing of the changes that go against the core of the structure. Nevertheless,
the sharpened dialogic relationship, to borrow Bakhtin's phrase again—
the visible confrontation between those who defend the institutionalized
thought structure and those who attack it—increases the likelihood of an
unintended innovation, which may yet produce a new identity, unplanned
and unexpected by any of the parties involved. The difference between a
"search" and a "quest" for a new identity is not only a semantic difference;
it is also a political one. If the present explorations can be limited to a
search, there is a comforting certainty that nothing really new—that is,
nothing we cannot foresee on the basis of our present knowledge—will
happen. As for what the possible novelty might look like, by definition
nobody can know it, or thus establish in advance whether to rejoice or to
fight against it.

Thurman Arnold, writing *Symbols of the Government* at the time of the Great Depression, ended his book thus:

> The writer does not pretend that he or anyone else can invent a formula to remove us from this sea of doubt. Such formulas are not constructed by individuals. They come from a place from which language and poetry come; they grow up with the institutions which they support. However, if they are to be successful, this much is required of them: they must permit practical institutions to function with security, and provide them with freedom to experiment; they must be supports and defenses; they cannot be guides. (Arnold 1935, 232)

Replace "he" with "she," and this ending will do for my own tale from the field as well. What Arnold is saying is that there is always a need for normative narratives, and that they fulfill their function properly if they are loosely coupled to practice; if they emerge from a public debate and are not dictated from above; if they legitimate (provide the legitimate rules of accounting for practice) rather than trying to influence practice. The crisis in the practical institutions we are undoubtedly observing in Sweden today calls for a new set of such narratives.

# PART THREE

# Interpretive Turbulence in Organization Fields

# EIGHT

# Paradoxical Material

Why have I, as an author, chosen to repeat these stories, to report these serials, and to describe these themes from the Swedish public sector? First of all, I wanted to show that narrative knowledge constitutes the core of organizational knowledge, that it is an important way of making sense of what is going on in the everyday life of organizations, and I felt I could do this in and through narratives told by the actors to me, to themselves, to other actors, and to observers. The material was the everyday organizational life; the devices, that is, the ways of structuring it, varied according to the local fashion and, no doubt, the intended audience. But the choice of devices is in itself part of organizational life.

Now I would like to claim the right to comment on the stories in a way that is closer to the paradigmatic knowledge, although of such a kind as tolerates the existence of paradoxes in the field and in the text.

## Paralogy as a Source of Innovation
### On Unity and Rupture

One of the themes that run through the whole material reported here is the presence of paradoxes in organizational life as reported by practitioners and theorists, by actors and observers. According to Burke's dramatistic method, people assume a dialectical stance in face of paradoxes, in order to achieve the dissolution of the paradox-induced drama: "Encountering some division, we retreat to a level of terms that allow for some kind of merger . . . ; then we 'return' to the division, now seeing it as pervaded by the spirit of 'One' we had found in our retreat" (Burke 1945/1969, 440).

Burke quotes examples of how this works in practice:[1] a dramatic act turns into a lyrical state (after reaching agreement, the opponents raise their glasses and toast each other with shining eyes and smiles); action is reduced to movement ("Now Mary will go and type what we decided"); reflection upon the drama replaces the drama itself ("John is here to provide us with reflection on our way of functioning as a group; it's your turn, John"); or an impersonal agent resolves the drama—in the theater God, in organizations the state or the market).

Such "resolutions" are, of course, well known in organizational life (especially in "stories" that most closely follow the classical drama mode) and are accompanied by a sense of the accomplishment of a dialectical transformation. But, as serials so convincingly show, this is an illusion. In the theater, a solution is necessary because the audience must go home. In the organizational theater, the same audience returns day after day and must pick up the thread again. At the end of every installment of the "Company-ization" series, the actors believe the company has become a fact; at the beginning of the next, they learn that it has not. Although much energy is put into solving paradoxes, they always reemerge.

This observation will hardly seem surprising to a dramatist. As Overington points out, Burke's understanding of "dialectic" is a very special one and consciously distant from that of Hegel: it is "the concept of contradiction and the ironic presupposition that one approaches a fuller, more true explanation for social action by taking opposing perspectives on that action" (Overington 1977a, 135). Discussing the "paradox of substance," Burke said that the dialectic substance "derives its character from the systematic contemplation of the antinomies attendant upon the fact that we necessarily define a thing in terms of something else" (1945/1969, 33), a statement that may be seen as an allusion to the diacritics of Saussure.

Merleau-Ponty, commenting on Saussure, explains how language creates its own paradoxes, which, rather than debilitating its power, in fact enhances it:

> [W]hat we have learned from Saussure is that, taken singly, signs do not signify anything, and that each one of them does not so much express a meaning as mark a divergence of meaning between itself and other signs. . . . This is a difficult idea, because common sense tells us that if term A and term B do not have any meaning at all, it is hard to see how there could be a difference of meaning between them. . . . But the objection is of the same kind as Zeno's paradoxes; and as they are overcome by the act of movement, it is overcome by the use of speech. And this sort of circle, according to which language, in the presence of those who are learning it, precedes itself, teaches itself, and suggests its own deciphering, is perhaps the marvel which defines language. (Merleau-Ponty 1964, 39)

In the above examples, action resolves paradoxes, whereas reflection[2] reinstates them. Another way of putting it would be to say, following Luhmann

(1991), that reflection produces paradoxes whereas action requires that they be removed. This very insight, in a more or less conscious form, was always at the core of organizational wisdom: this is what Brunsson (1985) means when he says that decision making, understood as the consideration of alternatives, inhibits action. What is needed, then, in accordance with the Burkean logic of inquiry, is contemplation of the opposite possibility: that paradoxes not only paralyze action but also enable it.

## Protecting Paradoxes

The usual criticism of paradoxes and the urge to "solve them" is connected with the fact that they violate logic. This is correct: two opposing statements within the same sentence are not logical, they are *paralogical*. But what is logic if it is not a linear, one-dimensional set of rules that came into being through the praxis of the Indo-European languages? The fact that we adhere to and roughly agree upon such a set of rules makes it easier for us to communicate with one another. Logic is a conventional way of describing one's image of the world which can then be discussed and negotiated with other people. Logic is a device. Consequently, as Luhmann (1986a) points out, paradoxes are not attributes of social systems but the result of using the logical analysis as an observation tool.

A static two-dimensional picture such as a map or a photo has serious defects compared with the dynamic three-dimensional reality it purports to represent. Yet we accept it without protest (its stands to reason that we did not spend our three-week holiday sitting and smiling in front of a hotel), because we realize the conventional character of such "representation." We start to rebel only when some smart constructivist tells us that it is not a representation but is itself a part of reality. Exposure to linguistic paradoxes rouses a protest much more quickly. Words are, after all, devices with which we shape our reality.[3] In everyday life, we take it for granted that language reflects reality, or at least that it represents reality as it is.

A pragmatic reflection shows that there are no grounds for assuming any correspondence between language and reality, be it iconic, symbolic, or other: "*no* linguistic items represent *any* nonlinguistic items" (Rorty 1991, 2). Paradoxes are irritating not because they go against the "essence of things" but because they ruin the conventional order of the surface that is our life.

Essentialists of various denominations are against paradoxes because reality ("as such"—a favorite essentialist expression) cannot possibly be paradoxical. However, there are—and always have been—approaches that insist that a paradoxical image of reality is "truer" or simply more practical. The paradox of the existence of humankind would then lie in the fact that a social system can reflect upon itself only within its own frame of reference. The existence of God was the traditional solution to this paradox; otherwise, people could not judge themselves objectively, because they are and remain themselves even in the act of judgment. Science offered to replace God but, human-made itself, cannot claim and maintain the same kind of legitimacy.

If metaphysical solutions are unacceptable, then paradox itself must be accepted. As Hofstadter (1980) pointed out in *Gödel, Escher, Bach,* mathematicians, painters, and musicians were always aware of this paradox, and instead of being threatened by it, they toyed with many variations on the theme immortalized by Escher: a person who looks at himself reflected in a mirror that he himself holds and so on and so on . . . no resolutions, only further reflections. The catastrophists in social science were traditionally worried about this, too: will these reflections never come to an end? Sure they will, says Ashmore in his brilliant self-reflective thesis (1989): the commonsense, aesthetic criteria and the diminished "meaning added" set the limit every time one tries.

Thus, paradoxes can be seen as a property of life itself (an existential perspective), a perspective taken by an observer of autopoietic systems (a cybernetic perspective which can take both metaphysical and metaphorical shape), or as a phenomenon taking place within language (a postmodern perspective).

Jean-François Lyotard (1979) pointed out that logic is illogical because it permits the appearance of paradoxes. *Paralogy* was traditionally a name ascribed to defective logic, but Lyotard perceives it as the most useful of all inventions—an opportunity for renewal within the language. Language, through the appearance of paradoxes, is forced to change its rules; but because at the same time it permitted those paradoxes to appear in the first place, the challenge and the change take place within the same system. Many attempts have shown clearly that language cannot be changed from outside, neither by order nor by force. Equally many have proved that changes in language cannot be prevented, either, no matter how many ministries of language the purists want to establish.

But a change within a language does not take place without a battle. On the contrary, it seems that change within a language must consist in a battle against rules and principles that are taken for granted. As Thurman

Arnold put it, "[i]t seems to be the eternal paradox of the human mind that principles and faiths which are so essential to its comfort and to the orderly organization and transmission of ideas should at the same time always stand as the greatest obstacle to discovery" (1935, 24).

The image of human beings as rational decision makers controlling the environment requires a linear vision of the world, in which conflict and ambiguity are temporary aberrations to be removed by the next rational action. Much can be said about the practical advantages of such a vision of the world; as usual, however, focusing on certain aspects forces us to gloss over others. In this case, the inherent paradoxicality of human and social life is the victim.

In organization studies, as Van de Ven and Scott Poole (1988) pointed out, a quest for coherent and consistent theory led to the neglect of the organizational paradoxes. The observed paradoxes, for example, in field studies, were taken to be cases of "anomalous communication" (Manning 1992). And yet this anomalous communication lies at the heart of modern institutions as we know them. "Having determined what action to take by logic of appropriateness, in our culture we justify the action (appropriately) by a logic of consequentiality," observed March and Olsen (1989, 162) with unerring acuteness. When facing action, we judge its kind and context from the perspective of our own identity and accordingly choose an appropriate action from the accessible repertoire. When questioned, we justify the action in terms of rationality (logic of consequentiality): motivated by personal gains (premises that all can accept), we chose the best way of achieving them (steps that can be followed by all) and arrived at the best possible result (conclusions and evaluations that must be universally accepted; Pitkin 1972). In other words, the two rhetorics—or two kinds of logic, according to March and Olsen—of reflective account and of justificatory account are usually at odds.

Usually, but not always: there are contexts when the two can be safely separated. Also, the organizational narrative smoothly accommodates both of them by the device of direct or indirect speech. In the earlier mentioned study by Jansson (1992), a decision about what kind of energy should be provided for a town was reached by the logic of appropriateness and both justified and questioned within the logic of consequentiality: the decision makers claimed that their decision was based on calculation of comparative costs, whereas a "serious counter-calculation" was demanded from the critics of the decision.

Such tension, say March and Olsen, is typical of political institutions, and therefore, I may add, it is not surprising that we find it in public administration organizations as well. "It can be seen as resulting in a kind of healthy charade of hypocrisy in which reasons and actions are not tightly linked but place pressure on each other in a way that strengthens each" (1989, 162).

Consequently, an important organizational paradox that should be preserved and not purged is that interruptions and "frictions" both hamper and assist change and renewal, as illustrated by the stories and the series. To recognize this, it is necessary and sufficient to abandon the idea of planned change as the smooth journey of an idea launched by the leaders. "The resistance to change" presented conventionally as an obstacle and interpreted as psychological backwardness (usually attributed to people at the lower levels of the hierarchy) becomes, in political terms, the right to question the ideas that are presented as unavoidable. The result may be a displacement (a translation for one's own purposes) or a rejection. But neither diminishes the value of interruptions in the accomplishment of change. The paradoxical observation that one and the same event both obstructs and promotes change is in fact only a variation on a more basic observation, namely, that change and stability are an integral part of all social institutions, or that reforms can be usefully portrayed as routines (Brunsson and Olsen 1993).

## *Programmatic Paradoxes*

The sociologists of science tend to turn the issue on its paradoxical head. They aspire to a *reflective* attitude, which can be expressed as a conviction that "irrational commitment is often needed in order to set in motion rational courses of economic action" (Ashmore, Mulkay, and Pinch 1989; see also Brunsson 1985). However, there are two clearly different ideas ("programs") about how to make use of this paradox. Ashmore, Mulkay, and Pinch studied health economics in England and sketched two "programs" they found in the field, a strong one and a weak one.

One could claim that "the modern project" in Sweden, which was supposed to set life and the world to rights (Hirdman 1989), was an expression of such a "strong program." In fact, the strong program can be seen behind any reformist project in the public sector. Paradoxes shock nobody; they are perceived as a "challenge" or even as an impetus to rational action. Jean Lipman-Blumen and Susan Schram described U.S. agriculture as "obsessed with paradoxes" and concluded that "these paradoxes continue to fuel a demand for intensified priority setting in the agricultural research

| Strong Program | Weak Program |
| --- | --- |
| Radical, total change of existing practices | Small, step-by-step changes that take into consideration existing practices |
| Economic thinking necessary for everybody in organization | Economics and economists as useful expert technicians |
| Systematic research | Quick and dirty studies |
| Testing and experimenting | Learning by doing |
| Distinct successes and failures which can be evaluated impartially | Successes and failures difficult to differentiate as evaluation is a part of implementation |
| One rational way of talking and acting (calculating rational actors) | Many ways of talking and acting, each with its own rationality |
| Politics as unfortunate distortion of rational action | Politics as the necessary form of mediation, negotiation, and persuasion between groups with different rational expectations |

and extension system, the critical underpinnings of agricultural productivity" (1984, I-8). A summary of a report from the Ministry of Civil Affairs in Sweden was entitled "Municipal Autonomy and Equal Municipalities: A Problem Which Exists to Be Solved."

The present book can be seen as belonging to (giving expression to) the "weak program," but it is abundantly clear that its existence depends on the existence of the strong program (it needs something to differ from). Both programs exist and probably will continue to exist, together with many nonprogrammatic attitudes. They are separate voices with their own rationalities. What is more, we all espouse them at various times and in differing conditions. Any kind of practical action requires what Luhmann (1991) calls deparadoxification.[4]

## Paradoxes and Narratives
### Deparadoxification and the Tragedy of Action

The urge to "dissolve" paradoxes does not come only from the aesthetic unpleasantness of encountering a logical error. No matter how reflective our attitude toward paradoxes may be, in the role of actors we necessarily engage in the more or less creative process of "deparadoxification" (*Entparadoxierung*, Luhmann 1991; Gumbrecht 1991). Complaining that "the paradoxification of civilization did nothing to civilize the paradoxes" (1991,

60), Luhmann criticizes the postmodernists, declaring that their call for a celebration of the paradox is like encouraging us to look straight in the face of one of the Gorgons—which, as we know, would turn us into stone.[5] Reflectivity paralyzes. I agree with both those who want to celebrate the paradoxes and those who demand their removal. This metaparadox can actually be solved with the help of the first of the two deparadoxification strategies described by Gumbrecht (1991), that is, temporization. I will agree first with one, then with the other view, promising a reconciliation in the future.

*Temporization,* as Gumbrecht points out, really amounts to *narrativization.* The conflicting elements are detached from one another in time and the conflict resolved in the future. The story of the new budget and accounting routine in Big City can be told as follows: "We came up with a new proposal, which we then tried to legitimate by relating it to existing routines, hoping in time to achieve a practice that combines novelty and tradition in a way satisfactory to everybody."

The best example of temporization, says Gumbrecht, is the Hegelian dialectic. Arnold claimed that "[t]his technique is as old as the parables of the New Testament. It is only its dialectical formulation that is modern" (1935, 30). He noted also that such a temporized series of observations is at odds with conventional science, understood as a logically formulated set of principles valid at all times. And he added, very much in the same spirit as the one imbuing this book, that "[i]f this point of view must have a name we prefer to call it an anthropological approach towards social ideas."

Arnold also stressed the need to dramatize the reconciling narrative. In a letter (quoted by Samuels 1979), he thus presented his dramatistic theory of society:

> A workable philosophy [of action], it seems to me, is necessarily a maze of contradictions so hung together that the contradictions either are not apparent or else are reconciled by a mystical ritual . . . the unity and the rhythm of institution requires people dancing in different directions and alternatively coming together and apart. (Arnold 1937, as quoted in Samuels 1979, 1001)

Contemporary organization theorists also noted some other possibilities for deparadoxification lying hidden in a narrative. Conflicting issues can be decoupled not only over time but also in space (March 1988; Manning

1992). "This committee deals with the technical problems, and that committee deals with the psychosocial aspects of the proposed change." The antitheses are simultaneously present, but not in the same place. In this context, Brunsson (1989) spoke of four strategies, all variations of temporization and spatialization: decoupling over time, between issues, between types of relevant environment, and between suborganizational units.

Sometimes, however, neither temporization nor spatialization works. The promise of a synthesis in the future is not convincing; the committees meet in the corridor by mistake, and no longer stick to the issues in their domains. Decentralization is perceived[6] by the people subjected to it as centrally ordered, a paradox that to them is a source of frustration and a cause of apathy. The deparadoxification strategy used in this context consists of explaining different perceptions by the different levels of observation, where the first-level observer is always blind to his or her own position and role in the system. It should be added that even this strategy fits perfectly well the possibilities of the narrative, as defined throughout his book. It is a matter of actorial shifting operations (Latour 1988b), whereby the reader or listener can see the world through the eyes of one or another first-level observer but, by virtue of being a second-level observer, can also understand the limitations of that "native" point of view.

In a political context, a mediator can be called in and can claim the position of second-level observer (a consultant might be able to see not only the points of view of management and the unions but also—seeing from outside the difference in their positions in the system—may understand the reason why they are as they are). In a hierarchical context, the higher level claims the position of a second-level observer ("Down at the local office, you cannot see the whole picture, and so you fail to observe that what the management is doing is actually decentralization!").

Those two variations of deparadoxification by way of relativization are well known in organizational life. It is therefore equally well known that they do not always work. Management and the workers are locked into a stalemate, in which two points of view cannot be reconciled as neither of the parties wants to acknowledge the relativity of their position.

Herein lies the tragic aspect of paradoxicality, says Gumbrecht (1991), and he goes on to define it as a situation in which an actor, in the role of first-level observer, perceives another actor as ambiguous ("What is management *really* trying to achieve?"). It breaks the unity and causes a rupture, sometimes just an "interruption," sometimes quite literally the breakdown of a person.

Again, there is nothing peculiar about this—"it is impossible to imagine a reality constructed without paradoxes," as Gumbrecht puts it (1991, 487). And while it is easy to agree with Luhmann that the contemplation of paradoxes excludes action, it is impossible not to notice that the two deparadoxification strategies described by Gumbrecht frequently fail to work, and existence—individual and organizational—reveals its tragic side. In Luhmann's (1986a) terms, the possibilities of further communication (that is, "jumping over" an unsolvable paradox) may not always be seen as close at hand. The communication breaks down, as in failed peace negotiations.

In life as in art, the reaction to all this seems to be an oscillation between the levels of observation. One way to metaphorically "see" a blind spot is by way of self-reflection. True, this is like meeting a Gorgon face-to-face, but perhaps we do not turn to stone at the first encounter but become more "resistant" (which means "thinglike"). After all, even with Medusa removed from the world, the two other sisters will remain forever.

Many of the officials I talked to seemed to have mastered the art of oscillation between action and reflection, between observation on the first level (an actor acting) and observation on the second level (an observer observing the actors acting, including themselves). This is no promise of yet another optimistic solution; it is simply a repetition of Gumbrecht's observation that, outside Greek tragedy, "there is no general rule which posits that in certain conditions an experience of a paradox *must* lead to rupture" (1991, 492).

Gumbrecht reconciled Luhmann's caution and Lyotard's enthusiasm in the face of paradox. As a rupture of individual experience in a real-life tragedy, the paradox reveals a culture's failure to solve its problems (which is why the same tragedies onstage are so instructive, without being threatening). As an object of reflective observation, the paradox indicates the possibility for a culture to surpass itself, to create new solutions, and to build new institutions. The increased visibility of paradoxes signals an epistemological crisis within a tradition (MacIntyre 1988), which in organizational context usually takes the form of a legitimacy crisis or an identity crisis.

In other words, the direct experience of paradox is threatening to individuals and institutions, but becomes a topic for reflection when the experience is indirect as in a stage play or a TV series. May we extend it to a case of organized reflection, let us say, of a book like this one, and see that

it also opens the possibilities for institutional renewal? Ruptures in unity
are culture's windows on chaos—both chaos-without-culture and chaos-
as-prelude-to-cultural-renewal.

## Observers of Institutions

Paradox can thus be seen as an opportunity for the renewal of language
and the transformation of institutions. And as Bruner (1990) points out,
the force of the narrative is that it can accommodate paradox: it serves
the purpose of social negotiations by putting the exceptional alongside the
conventional and rupture alongside unity, and by offering a variety of alternative linear plots. Paradox destroys the rational decision model, but only
makes the narrative more interesting. Paradox is an enemy of the paradigmatic mode of knowing, but at home with the narrative one.

Thus, if we "catch" an actor out in a contradiction—even a collective actor, such as the public administration—it does not mean that we are
showing the superiority of the logo-scientific mode over the narrative. It
may just be that we have failed to observe how temporization has been
employed, perhaps because it was done tacitly. Perhaps we forgot to "rela-
tivize" (that is, to relate ourselves to the actor's standpoint), or perhaps, in
Latour's words, we glossed over an actor's meaning and imposed our categories instead of deploying the actor's own (Latour 1993a, 140). If an actor
does not regard something as a contradiction and we do, it is then our task
to see how this is possible, rather than solving our own paradox by "pull-
ing rank" and appointing ourselves as observers of the "second level." It is
a sobering thought—and one that we should constantly remind ourselves
of—that in connection to our own practice, which is research, we generally
remain blind to our own role and position. And this applies not only to us
as individual researchers, but also and above all to the disciplines we represent and obey. In the ironic eye of that arch-pragmatist Thurman W.
Arnold, we are at the core of the business of deparadoxification. This is
what he wrote in *Symbols of Government*:

> To accomplish this task of keeping alive faith that institutions
> are somehow rational, the study of government is divided into
> three separate sciences in order to conceal the fact that the sym-
> bols . . . are contradictory. Law proves that good government is
> achieved by constantly refining and restating rules. Economics
> convinces us that everything will work out all right if we only
> leave it alone. Sociology, a loose and cloudy way of thinking,
> provides us a shelf on which we may put the humanitarian ide-

als which run counter to the eternal rule-making of the law and the eternal automatism of economics. This makes the intellectuals happy because they can toss facts inconvenient to one science over to another science for cataloguing and classification. Unthinking people are comforted by the belief that somewhere in books which they never have time to read there is an absolute proof of the rationality of their symbols. (1935, 18)

When the unthinking people—intellectuals included—start thinking, they notice the paradox, and this can lead to frustration or to a new attempt at deparadoxification and thus at innovation. Blurring the genres in the social sciences (Geertz 1980a) is one possible way of going beyond the disciplinary division of labor in academia. This is certainly an innovative move, although it causes frustration among young novices in the social sciences, who like to know what is what and to take notes about it.

This chapter started and now ends by stating that one of the central paradoxes in the important cultural narratives is the simultaneous presence of convention and exception, of tradition and change. On a personal level, "the Self . . . stands both as a guardian of permanence and as a barometer responding to the local cultural weather"; on a societal level, "the culture . . . provides us with guides and stratagems for finding a niche between stability and change" (Bruner 1990, 110). Therefore, "the viability of a culture inheres in its capacity for resolving conflicts, for explicating differences and renegotiating communal meanings" (47). Bakhtin was thinking along these lines when he pointed out the dangers of a monologic discourse, in which some kind of authoritarianism—political, literary, scientific—smooths out tension and conflict. In his view, all knowledge development emerges from a "sharpened dialogic relationship" between concepts and meanings that already exist (Kelly 1992).

# Changing Devices

## Trans-Formation of Genres
### *Narration as the Constitutive Action Mode*

Traditionally the description of social life starts by specification of its basic
units, individual actors, and continues by following the interactions that
develop between them (economic transactions, for example); these ulti-
mately stabilize to become structures, which in turn act as constraints on
subsequent interactions (note that this rendition of social developments
follows the rules of a conventional narrative). However, the very notion of
"basic units" is now being criticized. An emerging notion of the "relational
self" (Gergen 1991) postulates *relationships* as the basic topics or foci
of analysis, rather than "units" existing in "reality." A given (or rather a
selected) net of relationships can be regarded as *producing* both identities
("actors") and institutions ("structures").

Paraphrasing the terminology in Callon (1986) and Latour (1986),
I made action nets the basic focus of analysis.[1] This view denies the conventional hierarchy of "levels of analysis," with their labels "individual," "group," "organization," "society." Action nets are neither people nor
groups; they may be large (across several organization fields) or small (a
project); the focus of analysis can be a combination or collection of such
nets (an organization field). It is from the action net that we deduce which
actors are involved, not the other way around. This means, for example,
that the net will continue to exist even when the actors are exchanged for
others, or the original actors change their identity (they may become machines), although it always means the change in the character of the net as
well; that the changing net may press for a change in the identity of the
actors (as we have seen in this book), that the actors may be of mixed status
(humans and nonhumans; Latour 1992a, 1992b)—a fact we would miss
if we looked exclusively at human actors and their interactions. The adoption of this view means that the old debate about which comes first—
agency or structure—is resolved, or rather it is dissolved by the fact that
priority is given to actions that, when repeated, produce and reproduce
themselves, the individual identities, and the institutions of a given field.

The identities and institutions in turn both enable and constrain the actions that produced them in the first place. The narrative acquires a circular quality, which solves many problems but also creates some new ones. For the moment, let us stay with the action nets that produce a given organization field.

Action nets are labeled, delimited, and given meaning by the production and reception of speech acts—in other words, in conversations. The reader who is going to protest at this point that actions in the physical sense are at the core of organizing is referred once again to chapter 1 above, where it was established that behaviors become actions through interpretation, and to chapter 3, where I argued that the word is always material. Talk must equip physical movements with meaning so that they will be recognized as actions: there is a difference between "banging your fingers against a moving surface" and "typing." At the same time, things and machines accompany and make possible all we say; the action of producing utterances is a physical act.

The most frequent but not the only form of speech act is the *narrative,* as I have been claiming throughout this book. Following Gumbrecht (1992), one could also mention *descriptions* or portions of logo-scientific knowledge ("this box measures three feet by three feet") and *argumentation,* or normative speech acts ("you ought to save money"), where some actors tell others what they ought to do. Description and argumentation can be seen as genres conventionally ascribed to social science. Without any intention of denying their existence or importance, I focus instead on narrative as *the constitutive action mode,* a type of action constituting actors, fields, and action nets. Description and argumentation are usually dragged into this operation in a subordinate manner ("On a fine summer morning, my husband and I finally measured the box: it was three feet by three feet, as I always said" and "He tells everybody to save, but his own department overspends"). In other words, narrative is but one communication form used in conversations, but it is the one that constitutes relationships.

Thus, we can conceive an organization field as delineated by its typical *genres* (combinations of characters, modes of narration, and rhetorical conventions) which consequently limit the possible repertoire and the plots. The concept of "repertoire" is the same as what Warren, Rose, and Bergunder (1974) call the institutional thought structure. Past and present actions are interpreted and classified at a given time with the use of an often implicit code, which represents a genre (Lejeune 1989). Actors create their identities by trying to fit into a plot and expect others to comply (Davies and Harré 1991). Constant improvisation, however, causes plots to undergo changes; competitive plots lead to conflicts, expectations are frustrated or surpassed—all this feeds rejuvenation and increases the vitality of the genre or genres involved, while also increasing the probability of their "demise."

The very attempt to define a genre, as Lejeune (1989) points out, is doubly paradoxical. To begin with, it can only be done by exploring the gray zones and borderline cases. Genres blur as soon as you look at them at close range. What is more, the analysis of a genre is one of its main constitutive forces. As social scientists, we busy ourselves constructing the institutions we describe.

Neither paradoxicality nor the presence of conflict debilitates a field; on the contrary, they enhance its controlling power. MacIntyre made a similar claim, describing the medieval period as a time when—as he put it—all the institutions we now take for granted were waiting to be invented. Centralized equitable justice (modern law), universities (localized centers of learning), the modern city—these institutions all existed, but as potential plots in some people's heads. Against this there was a solid background or stage set of a local rural community that put customs before anything else, local power elites, and the global power of the church.

> The resources available for this task are slender: feudal institutions, monastic discipline, the Latin language, ideas once Roman of order and of law, and the new culture of the twelfth-century renascence: how is so little culture going to be able to control so much behavior and invent so many institutions?
>
> Part of the answer is: by generating just the right kind of tension or even conflict, creative rather than destructive, on the whole and in the long run, between secular and sacred, local and national, Latin and vernacular, rural and urban. (MacIntyre 1981/1990, 171)

MacIntyre describes an organization field that creates itself from scratch and keeps its vitality by maintaining a proper level of conflict and tension (see also 1988, 383). It is a beautiful picture, but it suggests perpetuum mobile, that very medieval dream of constantly renewed energy. This is in fact a typical accusation levied against new institutionalism, which seems to play the role of *laudator temporis acti,* the apologist of indestructible organization fields.

This is, of course, only one possible interpretation. How we interpret institutionalism certainly also depends on what is chosen as an instance of an institutional approach. Let us take the example of Warren, Rose, and Bergunder's seminal study (1974); it certainly shows how fiercely the field protects itself from genuine innovators. But the authors' interpretation is far from apologetic. Without indulging in ideological recitations, the authors nevertheless manage to transmit a powerful message on behalf of the alleged beneficiary of the city reform described in the study, namely, the low-income citizens. And, true enough, in the quoted case the field "wins"; the reform succeeds on its own terms, which means that everything remains as it was. It is certainly correct to say that most reforms are undertaken in the interest of preserving the status quo, as was also obvious in the examples described in this book. It does not mean, however, that the results of a study must be laudatory of such status quo. Institutionalist authors such as Warren, Rose, and Bergunder succeed in unmasking the complexity of social change without moralizing or avoiding the adoption of a moral stance.

One can also see Warren, Rose, and Bergunder as victims of the very paradox they are describing. Their study must have been as revolutionary in terms of the adopted paradigm as the defeated Oakland Economic Development Council, Inc., which they studied; hence the relatively scant attention paid to their work, which is brilliant. Scott and Meyer (1991) claim that an *Administrative Science Quarterly* article by Warren (1967) concentrating on horizontal relations within interorganizational field rather than on the vertical relations to the institutionalized thought structure overshadowed the study. The field won.

But a field might also "lose," or even be destroyed, for example, if some totalitarian intervention removes the salutary conflict and tension, or if these are allowed to grow to the size of a civil war. Can a field ever change? Does the Swedish public administration stand a sporting chance, to use one of its own favorite metaphors? Can a change be accomplished if those responsible for change are also responsible for the state that led to the demand for change? Can a deconstruction be accomplished with the same conceptual tools that were used for construction? "The master's tools will never dismantle the master's house," warns the African-American feminist Audre Lorde.

This is a pessimistic view. But it can also be pointed out that some change of identity is necessary, because the founts of societal legitimation are drying up. There is also a certain willingness to change—if simply out of a feeling for adventure and variety. As for the material to work upon, what is seen as the administration's main weakness—a pride in tradition—may turn out to be its main asset. That is, if its sense of tradition is "adequate," which can be understood as having "a grasp of those future possibilities which the past has made available to the present. Living traditions, just because they continue a not-yet-completed narrative, comfort a future whose determinate and determinable character, so far as it possesses any, derives from the past" (MacIntyre 1981/1990, 223).

The paradox of lifting oneself up by one's bootstraps was, interestingly enough, a popular image in the narratives of the field. There seemed to be a profound if puzzled sense that in the memory of the past lies a possibility of overcoming the troublesome present to the advantage of the future, which, however, will treat that very past with not more than a touch of nostalgia. Will they pull it off? The narrative approach has no means of knowing, and no ambitions to know the future. It only helps us to understand what mechanisms are at work.

## A Postmodern Identity: An Oxymoron or a Quest?

I have claimed here that one of the major problems in searching or questing for a new organizational identity is the general turbulence in organization fields: institutions are undergoing transformations. I have also postulated that individual identity is a modern institution; should it not follow that the institution of individual identity is undergoing a transformation as well?

The defenders of modernity will come up with a negative answer (see, e.g., that indefatigable defender of modernity, Marshall Berman 1992). Another negative answer can be grounded not in the faith that modernism will "win" but in a claim that all phenomena described as "postmodern" belong in fact to modernity. Indeed, the description of modern identity in Berger, Berger, and Kellner (1974) is very close to what has been regarded as an emergent postmodern identity. These authors cite four aspects peculiar to modern identity: its *openness* (life as a project), *differentiation* (because of the individual's immersion in plural and unstable life-worlds, reality loses substance and acquires complexity), *reflectivity* (necessarily resulting from the first two), and *individuality* (the individual as the final test of existence and reality). For Berger, Berger, and Kellner (1974), identity is still related to subjectivity, and although strongly influenced by institutions is not itself an institution. As Gergen points out, "[t]he major difference between the kind of fragmentation said to characterize mod-

ernist writing and that found in the postmodern lies . . . in the modernist
lament of loss. For the modernist, one *should* possess a unified identity"
(1991, 277).

What are the claims of those who see institutional transformations taking place? The radical claim problematizes the notion of identity, calling it
a myth, an illusion, and declaring that "in postmodern culture, the subject
has disintegrated into a flux of euphoric intensities, fragmented and discon-
nected" (Kellner 1992, 144) and that it has resulted in "postmodern selves
who are allegedly devoid of the expressive energies and individualities characteristic of modernism" (p. 146). Gergen goes on to say that "[f]or the
postmodernist the supposition of a unified identity ceases to be compelling.
There is little lament, anxiety or dread at aimless fragmentation, which
simply becomes a way of life without strongly negative connotations"
(1991, 272).

Let us therefore take a look at this postmodern "identity" and search,
as before, for analogies between personal and organizational identities.
Kellner (1992) emphasizes the central role played by the mass media in the
structuring of contemporary identity. Television everywhere and news-
papers specifically in Scandinavia (where every household subscribes to at
least one daily) assume some of the traditional socializing functions of
myth and ritual: integrating individuals into the social order, celebrating prevalent values, offering role models. In times when the lack of public
participation is often mourned, it is important to note that television not
only competes with politics in offering sports or other entertainment; it
also offers central politics being played out in front of the cameras instead
of local meetings with little drama in them.

The main characters in the TV genres considered typical for postmodernity (Kellner cites "Miami Vice") have multiple identities and multiple
pasts which may or may not influence the present; added to which the nature of influence is changeable as well. "In each case, their identity is fragmented and unstable, different and distinctive in each character, yet always
subject to dramatic change" (Kellner 1992, 151). If we look for analogies
in the organization world, we are immediately reminded of the large corporations, which humbly abandon their established role in order to engage
in a quest for the good of the community; here, "ecological conversion" is
the most popular type of dramatic change. In both personal and organizational identities, speed and mobility are values that have replaced resistance
to change and the need for consistency. New institutions emerge, dedicated
to helping the establishment of new identities. "In contemporary society,

an abundance of communities and identities are presented. . . . One does not have to be born a Scandinavian, a Swede or a European—there are instructions and special courses on how to become any of these" (Frykman 1993, 156; my translation).

These changes and adaptations in identities also alter the role of the public. The social environment is no longer prepared to accept the "adult personality" as formed once and for all; it appreciates chameleonic changes. This view is based on a shared assumption that identity is constructed and not given, that it is a matter of choice and style rather than genotype or soul. Redefined as a matter of choice and style, individual identity moves from the "serious" arena of life to "leisure"; it becomes a game, a play celebrated by organizations with even louder fanfares than by individuals (even if, as in the case of clothing maker Bennetton, the playfulness is supposed to signal simultaneously a very serious involvement in the matters of the world).

Thus, both societal arenas and organization fields are full of players rather than actors in the literal sense of the word: postmodern identities are constituted theatrically through role-playing and image construction. There are no referees in this game, Rorty (1992b) reminds us, because nobody knows the rules in advance. It is the admiration and applause of other players that decide the "winners." Language and pictures are of the utmost importance in the play.

In this context, it is important to repeat what was said in chapter 5 above, that fashions have great influence on the way identities are constructed and changed. Fashion, that distinctively paradoxical phenomenon, promotes both conformity and freedom, creativity and reification—all of which were already needed for a modern identity. It is the device that changes more than the material: multiplicity and constant change—which to the moderns were the main discovery as well as the main source of anxiety—acquire a taken-for-granted place in postmodern identity formation. As Kellner (1992) and Rorty (1992b) both point out, there is a continuity between modernism and postmodernism that some radical postmodernists deny.

Another interesting reconciliation of modern and postmodern claims is suggested in Marcus (1992), where it is pointed out, for example, that the "homeless mind" (Berger, Berger, and Kellner 1974) was a description of identity from the period of modernization (a process) rather than of modernity (a state). "We have never been modern," says Latour (1993b) provocatively. The only commentary that needs to be added to the perceptive description of identity in a period of modernization provided by Berger, Berger, and Kellner is that what these writers thought was transitional and moving toward resolution in fact stayed with us for good.

Marcus adds that the problem of collective and individual identities now stands at the center of the globalization-localization processes and of the studies devoted to these processes (1992). This means that the fate of the organizations I studied is neither exceptional nor lonely, and their quest for identity does not have to be equated with plunging into the unknown, with a frightening relativism. It is a quest in which their own active role gives them a chance to influence the rules of the game as much as the other players. What they cannot count upon, though, is the arrival of a referee who will tell everybody what the new rules are (although, undoubtedly, many will try).

## Translations in Theoretical Fields
### The Paradoxes of Institutionalism

My reason for attempting to join a narrative approach to the new institutionalism is, I hope, clear by now: the two can help each other by achieving greater metaphorical clarity. On the one hand, there is a need to explain how narratives emerge and how they become dominant or vanish. Institutional theory is able to do this, although, in all fairness, it should be added that the narrative paradigm did not need new institutionalism for this; there was an adequate institutional theory of literature already in existence (see, e.g., Zeraffa 1973). On the other hand, the new institutionalism, in order to live up to its mission of explaining the social character of the organizational world, needs to reflect on its own metaphors.

The issue at stake is much more than some kind of metaphorical purism. It is possible, within the model of translation advocated in this book, to translate the physical metaphors of new institutionalism into literary categories as well as the other way around, each time producing some sort of a creative displacement. I would even risk suggesting that the theory of literature would gain more "meaning added" from physical metaphors than the theory of organized action, simply because of the distance, and therefore new insights, achieved. In our case, however, the replacement of physical by cultural metaphors removes the assumption of stability that sneaked into the new institutionalism.

Let us focus on the notion of *institutional isomorphism* as explicated in DiMaggio and Powell (1983). This idea assumes the homogenization of an organization field brought about by coercive pressures, mimetic processes, and normative pressures. Later comments by Powell (1991), written in reply to various criticisms, address the issue of the sources of heterogeneity, albeit only as a kind of error variance.[2]

This problem is not troublesome anymore once the metaphors are exchanged. In the narrative version of organization fields, the sources of homogeneity and heterogeneity are one and the same. The result may veer to one or another side temporarily and locally; what is more, because no "thermostats" are fitted, the imbalance can lead to an extinction of a culture or to its horrible dominance over others. No predictions of the kind "If A, then B" can (or need) be made, but an understanding of the dynamics can be attempted.

In these terms, coercive pressures or attempts to use power to establish the superiority of one genre over another invariably produce *counternarratives* and *subversive genres*. In truly paradoxical mode, we could claim that the Académie Française promoted freedom of expression in French art; that the increasing control of positivism revealed the strength of symbolist approaches; and that the bureaucratic orders of central administrations produce bursts of creative avoidance activities.

Mimetic processes become much more complex when interpreted in terms of *fashion* (a social phenomenon) rather than of imitation (a cognitive process). The concept of fashion combines the will to be like everybody else with the will to be original by the single act of following a fashion. The municipalities espousing yet more reforms and changes are afraid of being left alone ("What if everybody else reforms?") and are proud of being in the avant-garde ("We were there before anybody else").

Finally, normative (professional) pressures may be the most ambiguous of all. They were described in DiMaggio and Powell (1983) as, on the one hand, idealistic and at variance with social realities and, on the other, as hierarchical and authoritarian and thus akin to coercive pressures. The narrative version of institutionalism needs no more than to corroborate this ambiguity. All the actors in the stories, serials, and themes were exposed to pressures from their professional environments—the simultaneous pressure to keep to tradition and to rebel against it, to create new traditions and to follow the conventional way of doing things.

An example from my own organization field. At a plenary session of a disciplinary conference, one of the senior participants delivers at the invitation of the authors a public review of a book of readings on the topic central to the conference. The review, critical in tone, concentrates on the fact that the authors made an intentional attempt to institutionalize their own efforts by establishing (or rather creating) historical precedents, by relating their book to all existing trends within the discipline, and by including a self-reflection exercise of the self-congratulatory type. As the presentation proceeds, the reactions of the authors (delighted) and the audience (partly rebellious and partly approving) indicate that the reviewer is in fact doing what the authors intended: institutionalizing their work by examining historical precedents (albeit critically), relating their book to existing trends (albeit to claim disruptions), and replacing congratulatory self-reflection with a critical reflection of a higher legitimating value. The review, after its oral presentation, was immediately conscripted for publication.

In the field of public administration, examples abound. In the study reported here, they can be found in literally every story, theme, or serial. In "The Story of a New Budget," the innovators proceed with two parallel systems, one old and one new, and alternate between excursions into creativity and retreats into tradition. In "The Story of the Tax Reform," the government tries to change the material and the device at the same time, and then retreats as the crop of unexpected consequences grows too confusing. In "Company-ization," all techniques are adopted in turn and with different results. The rhetorical feat reported in "The Identity Quest" shows how an organization, as a professional agent, changes the script by changing its performance but plays within the established repertoire.

In all these attempts, there is an interplay between intentionality and field forces that is hardly visible in the "institutional isomorphism" version of events. Narratives can be and are consciously constructed, but it does not mean that the intentions of the readers will ever approximate the intentions of the authors and that a text can be intentionally created as an exemplar, a beginning of a new genre ordered by fiat. Once a pattern begins to emerge, actors try to appropriate it, give it a name, translate it for their own needs, construct their identity around it—*authorize* it, as it were. Once again, the reaction of the readers—or the spectators—may be accepting or not. The conference audience could have decided that the lecture hall was too stuffy (it was) and nobody would have heard the review; and the "rhetorical feat" could be flooded (actually, is flooded) by "rhetorical flops" as in the counterexample.

All these, however, would not be given proper attention within the "institutional isomorphism" view. "Looking at the system from the outside" is a metaphorical, paradoxical attempt in Escherian spirit, as Luhmann repeatedly states in his writing. Thus, it does not make sense, from this imaginary travel to outside, to make "predictions" or to form "recommendations for action" which can be used "inside." "It is not the task of an external observation to de-paradoxize the system and describe it in a way which is suitable for multi-level logical analysis" (Luhmann 1986a, 179). What our imaginary "vision from outside" says is that the system survives thanks to its fictions, its illusions of selection, rational choice, intentionality—complexly combined with the knowledge of closeness, repetition, and self-reflection. Arnold (1935) understood it very well, but stopped short of entering into a paralogical reasoning, and thus did not know what to do with his paradoxical insight.

Pointing out the "iron cage" of institutions, DiMaggio and Powell fail to see what Luhmann has been emphasizing all along: of course, it is an iron cage, but it "functions" quite well, as long as people inside believe that they are free. "The autopoiesis does not stop in face of logical contradictions: it jumps, provided that possibilities of further communication are close enough at hand" (Luhmann 1986a, 180). It would be unfair to claim that DiMaggio and Powell are unaware of this paradox, but they try to deparadoxify their theory; a quite unnecessary feat, as a theory describing paradoxes does not entail being paradoxical itself. Neither does it have to exclude paradoxes at all costs: in general, it does not have to imitate the system it describes. Such an "anthropological approach toward social ideas," as Arnold (1935, 30) called it, is not supposed to lead to "a logically formulated set of principles" which the new institutionalists try to develop. Neither should it demand that the system it observes stop producing such principles: "It is the system under examination which can no more help producing principles than a hen can keep from laying eggs" (Arnold 1935, 30)

It is interesting to contrast the new institutionalism as represented by DiMaggio and Powell with other approaches to organizations that came to paradoxical insights. As mentioned above, Arnold depicted the social system[3] as consisting, on the one hand, of ideologies, norms, and values—religion and science included—and, on the other, of unruly practice. The two diverge or even contradict each other most of the time, with such exceptions as wars and other emergencies, when the normative subsystem dominates the other part, achieving a high level of functioning, deadly to those involved. Arnold realized well that it is impossible to describe either the functioning of practice or the paradoxical relationship between the two in the language of the normative system ("scientific logic"). This was, however, the very task of a scientist! The reader feels sympathy seeing Arnold torn between his knowledge and the demands of the professional knowledge that he represents, and this sympathy softens their disappointment at the way out that is finally proposed: that the world of practice must conquer the world of norms. Such a solution goes, of course, against the grain of his whole work.

This dilemma was neatly resolved in the works of the later authors who exploited the paradigm shift of the 1970s, which allowed for "descriptive," hermeneutical knowledge with no normative ambitions. Once the researchers gave up the ambition to shape reality, they could lean back and report what they saw. And what they saw was paradoxical. In the meantime, the works of biologists such as Maturana and Varela and of philosopher-sociologist Niklas Luhmann legitimated this observation. Thus, Weick (1979) described the world of organizations as very similar to that observed by Arnold, and added the mechanism of "loose coupling," which permitted different and even contradictory subsystems to coexist peacefully under the same label and under the same organizational roof. Brunsson (1985, 1989), inspired by Arnold and by such early new institutionalist works as Meyer and Rowan (1977), which spoke about rationalist decision façades and action-oriented practices, postulated hypocrisy as a joining mechanism; also, March and Olsen (1989) spoke of "healthy hypocrisy," describing the tension between logic of appropriateness (which rules action) and logic of consequentiality (which rules justification).

DiMaggio and Powell steer away from all these solutions and return to Arnold's dilemma, doing precisely what in his opinion did not make sense: formulating their observations about the paradoxical nature of the system in a language of one of the subsystems, the one that forbids paradoxicality. One can defend Arnold's solution by pointing out that although he also proposed "resolving" the paradox once and for all (an operation different from deparadoxification, which must be constantly repeated), at least he did so by leaning toward the subsystem that tolerates paradoxes. Not so the new institutionalists. Although DiMaggio and Powell are the most representative example, the same could be said of Zucker (1987), Meyer, Boli, and Thomas (1987), and others. March and Olsen (1989) do both: when speaking about political institutions ("the field"), they point out their paradoxicality and existing tensions. When speaking of research perspectives, they begin by characterizing institutionalism against those perspectives it opposes: contextualism (or, rather, structuralism), reductionism, utilitarianism, instrumentalism, and functionalism. Throughout their book, however, they lean back—explicitly toward the first two, implicitly toward all of them. Healthy hypocrisy or lack of self-reflection? A paradox in text—by design or by default? wonders the reader.

Maybe this need to formalize and formulate predictions is connected with the trap of institution maintenance that lies in wait for every institutionalist. Genres and other social institutions presuppose permanence (an institution is a practice that lasts) and difference (an institution must be different and differentiable from other institutions)—a statement apparently in perfect congruence with the stationary assumptions of the new institutionalism. As long as a genre or an institution is used properly—for classification—this is exactly the way it works. "Any public tends to classify what it receives and to receive it through a classification of everything that it has received before" (Lejeune 1989, 147). This is what the concept of the "institutional thought structure" is all about. Thus, neo-institutionalism, intent on questioning the utilitarist paradigm, carefully preserves reductionism and functionalism. Thus, the phenomenon that is in the focus of reflection—the unproblematic use of classificatory devices—recurs within the reflection itself.

"To elaborate 'a theory of genres' is to try to formulate a synthesis in the absolute by making use of concepts that make sense only in the historical field" (Lejeune 1989, 152). What Lejeune says about Frye's (1957) attempt at creating "the theory of genres" can be applied to attempts of DiMaggio and Powell as well.[4] First, their practice (as illustrated by the second part of their original paper, 1983) does not follow the interesting principles that have been set at the beginning. Second, as Frye introduces the universal of the "myth" borrowed from psychoanalysis, so DiMaggio and Powell introduce "isomorphism" borrowed from biology. Both are static concepts, useful in a desired synthesis ("grand theory") but bothersome when applied to analysis ("local stories"). Third, everything that is inconsistent with the model is classified as failure, exception, or an irrelevant case (Frye 1957; Powell 1991).

What institutionalists refused to do was to place themselves and their analysis in the closed system they depicted. The narrative addition makes self-reflection easier, in view of the observation that theoretical narratives are produced within the same institutional thought structure as the narratives of the field. Otherwise, the theoreticians are doomed to including a blind spot in their theory, which covers their own position in it.

## Institutional Sitz-im-Leben

Lack of self-reflection is not a trait characteristic of the new institutionalism only; the "old" institutionalists similarly took for granted one institution, namely, social science research. Even sociologists of knowledge such as Berger and Luckmann assumed that their task is to study everybody else; sociology itself can be studied only by philosophy (Berger and Luckmann 1966). One could argue, however, that the "old" institutionalism was born in harmony with its institutional environment, in the sense that its ideas blended well into the mainstream of its time. Not so the new institutionalism, which is somewhat in opposition to the present mainstream in social sciences, and which seems to try to appease the institutional core by sacrificing its traditional methods, close to anthropology, for more modern statistical analyses. The result, however, seems not so much paradoxical as confused. Several studies reported in Powell and DiMaggio report straightforward statistical analyses; surely it is the task of an institutionalist to explore how statistics are built and used, and not to take them as "facts,"[5] "revealing regularities"? Many contributions contain predictions and formalizations: How can this be reconciled with the basically constructivist assumptions behind the institutionalist ideas? Why should one attempt to formalize a world under construction?

All these contradictions may be connected with a paradox that seems to be inherent in institutionalism, at least in its constructivist version (Sismondo 1993 uses Berger and Luckmann 1966 as an example). On the one hand, the *construction* of institutions implies and demands a proactive vision of human actors, busying themselves with plotting, performing, accounting for what they do, and thus producing reality as they know it. On the other hand, the notion of institutions suggests *accretion,* a passive process not under anyone's control, just happening.

For Sismondo, this is a historical accident, a somewhat unreflective combination of two different thought traditions, which is obviously wrong, but there is no point in insisting that it be corrected. For me, it opens a vast area of possibilities, because and not in spite of its lack of coherence. Is not a fuller, richer picture of knowledge and reality being created by this emphasis on a combination of plots and intentions, which produces unintentional but powerful changes? According to this reading, even institutionalism and the rational model can complement each other. The rational model promotes change, promotes the illusion of controllability, which, according to Luhmann (1986a), is so important to keep a system going. The institutional response is that the change happens only within the frames permitted by the institutional thought structure, and observations confirm this view insofar as it concerns planned change. But changes are many, and the truly radical ones are by definition unpredictable, although it could be claimed that the probability of such radical changes would be smaller if all planned change ceased to exist. Thus, even for the analysts situated within the institutionalist-constructivist core, there is always the possibility of alternating between the observer and the actor alternative, this time as observers of and actors in social science.

The consequences of this somewhat uncomfortable seat-in-scientific-life are discussed further in chapter 10. I would like to end this chapter by stating that my intention is neither to correct new institutionalism nor to prove the superiority of the approach advocated here (indeed, it would be both presumptuous and impossible to attempt such a feat). My intention has been to propose a variation on the institutionalist perspective, as already suggested in the chapter title. To make this clearer, I shall borrow DiMaggio and Powell's (1991) instructive comparison of the "old" and "new" institutionalism and extend it by a "narrative" one, as shown in the table below.

|  | Old | New | Narrative |
|---|---|---|---|
| Conflict of interest | Central | Peripheral | An important type of plot |
| Source of inertia | Vested interests | Legitimacy imperative | The "natural attitude" (Schütz), taken-for-grantedness of everyday world |
| Structural emphasis | Informal structure | Symbolic role of formal structure | Language structures, narrative structures |
| Organization embedded in | Local community | Field, sector, or society | Field, but also "institutional thought world" (Warren, Rose, and Bergunder) |
| Nature of embeddedness | Co-optation | Constitutive | Constitutive |
| Locus of institutionalization | Organization | Field or society | Action nets |
| Organizational dynamics | Change | Stability | Change/stability paradox (Brunsson and Olsen) |
| Basis of critique of utilitarianism | Theory of interest aggregation | Theory of action | Theory of action as a search for meaning |

|                                  | Old                        | New                                     | Narrative                                                                                              |
| -------------------------------- | -------------------------- | --------------------------------------- | ------------------------------------------------------------------------------------------------------ |
| Evidence for critique of utilitarianism | Unanticipated consequences | Unreflective activity                   | "Evidence" not appropriate expression; the role of ethics and aesthetics in shaping action            |
| Key forms of cognition           | Values, norms, attitudes   | Classifications, routines, scripts, schema | Narratives                                                                                          |
| Cognitive basis of order         | Commitment                 | Habit, practical action                 | The accessible repertoire of textual strategies                                                        |
| Goals                            | Displaced                  | Ambiguous                               | Devices organizing narrative                                                                           |

The third column contains a variation on the second that, among other things, includes what could be seen as an attempt to capture that "which has been lost in the shift from the old to the new institutionalism" (DiMaggio and Powell 1991, 27), especially what could be seen in the impressive work of Warren, Rose, and Bergunder (1974), where even the notion of "narratives from the field" is used. This is the role of emotions and aesthetic experience, not as complementary processes but as inseparable aspects of any act of cognition; the role of texts in the organizational action supposedly dedicated entirely to practical results; and the central role of communication in the condition of postmodernity. No doubt, many further versions and especially improvements of the present one are possible. What seems most important just now is to indicate the need for such variations and reformulations of the institutional theory.

# TEN

# Constructing Narratives

## Whose Voice Is Heard?

The analysis adopted in this study has consisted of the interpretation of various texts and voices. The best way of explaining what an interpretation means to me is to call it a conversation between various texts that, in complete contravention of the ideal speech conditions, I force to speak to each other on my conditions, with myself drawing the conclusions and having the last word. This raises at least two objections: one is my expected commitment to the voices[1] from the field, and another is the danger of over-interpretation.

### Whose Polyphony? The Paradox of Applied Relativism

The problem of voices in field studies perhaps came into the sharpest focus in anthropology. "The gap between engaging others where they are and representing them where they aren't, always immense but not much noticed, has suddenly become extremely visible" (Geertz 1988, 130). After decades of all-knowing anthropologists who explained "native ways of being" to the "more developed civilization," a wave of political and ethical doubts pervaded the discipline. One of the most loquacious representatives of reflective anthropology was Stephen Tyler (1986), who opted for a different, polyphonic ethnography, in which people could speak in their own voices. That led to much discussion about whether it was in fact possible. Another member of the same group, George Marcus, writing in 1992, renamed postmodern ethnography as "modernist" (in a tribute to the 1920s movement) and claimed that in spite of many obvious problems, one must try to approach at least a semblance of polyphony.

There are many ways of interpreting this debate, even if it is limited to the three authors mentioned above (whose voices are rather central to it). It is possible to see Geertz as accusing Tyler and Marcus of propagating "ventriloquism" and "dispersed authorship," and the other two as cherishing "postmodern" or "modernist alternative" illusions of a completely new and liberating antirhetoric. It is equally possible to see all three of them agreeing that, old illusions gone, it is important to "deepen the burden of authorship," which includes crossing the border between fact and fiction. The nuances of their debate, however, belong to another context. Let us limit ourselves to those parts that can be regarded as relevant to organization studies.

Lejeune points out that the notion of the "ethnological gap" arose in the first place in relation to cultures where speech goes "before writing" (Lejeune 1989). This gap seemed enormous, and the optimists looked forward to diminishing it by increasing literacy. This achieved, the gap changed into a gap of "different languages," aggravated by political and moral animosities toward Western dominance. Lejeune takes up yet another case, that of representing those who, for instance, read but do not write, such as the working class. He shows many interesting examples of workers who became writers, thus ceasing to be workers and keeping the gap intact. Writers belong among the intellectuals, no matter where they come from, whom they pose as, or what social group they are writing about.

This argument can apply to some, but not many, organization studies. The majority of organization studies have a managerial tilt, and this represents yet another complication. Our "voices from the field" are completely literate, and in more or less the same language; in fact, our "representations" are often in competition with theirs (at least, mine were). Do we silence them by speaking for them? Do we represent them more fully than anybody else, considering that the "otherness" is minimal? In his corporate ethnography, Kunda (1991) portrayed a woman who taught "organizational culture" in a corporation he was studying, and who had earlier obtained a Ph.D. in anthropology with a dissertation on this very subject. Who *was* he when studying her—"his sister's keeper" or a doppelgänger? No wonder Leach (1985) warned anthropologists to stay away from their own cultures in order to avoid this claustrophobic spiral.

The choice seems to lie between the devil and the deep blue sea: either to lose oneself in the Other and end up doing narcissistic exercises or to cultivate estrangement and retain the gap.[2] An application of self-reflection reveals that the researchers manage to combine them both. Ashmore, Mulkay, and Pinch pursued the matter by interrogating a voice from the field, a "Mrs. Jones" who had this to say about the "weak program" and its polyphonic ambitions:

> "I'm no more than a textual device of their making. I'm entirely under their control . . . I'm an illusion of multivocality . . . behind which the [social scientists] continue to assume their own

privileged knowledge of the social world. So I think we need one more paradox: that social scientists can only claim to speak on our behalf by refusing to let us speak for ourselves. I think we'll call this the 'paradox of applied social science.'" (1989, 208)

What is to be done? Apologizing to Mrs. Jones is one possibility. But within the narrative approach we have something that is not a solution but a justification of the "paradox of applied social science." Mrs. Jones is indeed a textual device. This device has a long and honorable tradition in the novel. It is worth recalling that Tyler and Marcus took inspiration from Bakhtin when they spoke of their polyphony. And Bakhtin had in mind not a polyphony in which many people are speaking, but something called *heteroglossia*, that is, "variegated speech" or, in Russian, *raznorechje*. This is an authorial strategy consisting of the fact that the *author speaks different languages* (dialects, slangs, and so on) in the text. There is no need for the illusion that "those people" talk for themselves; indeed they do not. But the author pays them a compliment by making the reader clearly aware of the fact that there *are* different languages being spoken within one and the same linguistic tradition, making the otherness of the Other clear (instead of pretending that the Other is some kind of a clone of the author: "They are really like us, only underdeveloped").

Such a textual device helps to create a dialogic relationship with the world, the best we can hope for, said Bakhtin, who a good sixty years ago postulated a common road for literature and the social sciences (a poetics for sociology; Bakhtin/Medvedev 1928), while also regarding their joint task as very different from what the natural sciences set out to do:

> The entire methodological apparatus of the mathematical and natural sciences is directed toward mastery over *mute objects, brute things,* that do not reveal themselves in words, that do not *comment on themselves.* . . .
>
> In the humanities . . . there arises the specific task of establishing, transmitting and interpreting the words of others.
>
> The word can be perceived purely as an object (something that is, in its essence, a thing). In such a word-object even meaning becomes a thing: there can be no dialogic approach to such a word of the kind immanent to any deep and actual understanding. (Bakhtin 1981, 351)

Reifying the word so that, like a mute object, it cannot talk back to us any longer is only one possibility and not the most attractive. The interesting possibilities appear when the authors are prepared to get into a dialogue with what they hear as being said to them, no matter whether they hear correctly or not:

> dialogizing opens up fresh aspects in the word which, since they were revealed by dialogic means, become more immediate to perception. Every step forward in our knowledge of the word is preceded by *a sharpened dialogic relationship to the word*— that in turn uncovers fresh aspects within the word. (352)

Sociologists of science and technology claim that rather than muting the world, we should give voice even to nonhumans[3] (Callon 1986; Latour 1992a, 1992b, 1994; Woolgar 1988). But theirs is no romantic version of "giving voice to the Other" with a radical tint. In the opinion of those authors, we can still become at best the spokespersons for the others, *translating* their speech by saying something that we think they mean (as in the case of Mrs. Jones). Voices are irreducible to one another, apart from that translation procedure which is a socially accepted reduction procedure and is known as representation (Latour 1988a).

Thus, we end up with a dialogue in which the goal of representation (in the political sense of the word) must live side by side with the awareness that we are performing an act of ventriloquism. This amounts to giving up the ambition of speaking on behalf of the Other in any literal sense, the ambition to be "a tribune for the unheard, a representer of the unseen, a kenner of the misconstrued" (Geertz 1988, 133). In response to Mrs. Jones's critique, one can point out that, as any iconic representation or representations tested by correspondence are impossible, all that remains is political representation, often unasked for, always faulty by displacement, and always fictive. It might be suggested that the fictiveness of our polyphony, once revealed, relieves us of the criticism of silencing the voices. We do most harm when we impose our interpretations on what we claim are "authentic voices from the field." If rendering these voices to a wide audience is our goal, the way to go about it is to silence our own voices and to engage in the political activity of creating speaking platforms for those who are not heard.

Once it is clear to both authors and readers that our dialogue is fictive, we can go further and admit that it can never be a democratic dialogue on equal grounds. The author always has an initial advantage over the "other" voices. But this does not mean that we cannot quarrel with these voices if necessary: glossing over paradoxes, otherness, and conflict serves no one.

Nor does it mean that the author always wins: a reader might decide otherwise, handing the laurel to the author's creation. Which brings us to the
other point: the dangers of overinterpretation, or who has the last word?

### Whose Interpretation? The Paradox of Applied Pragmatism

To interpret means to react to the text of the world or to the world of a
text by producing other texts. . . . The problem is not to challenge the
old idea that the world is a text which can be interpreted, but rather
to decide whether it has a fixed meaning, many possible meanings, or
none at all.

Umberto Eco, The Limits of Interpretation

The fact that research amounts to text analysis is never as clear as when
one returns from the field (Van Maanen 1988). Participant observation,
surveys, sustained contacts, or superficial interviews—all produce an ava-
lanche of texts: field notes, interview transcripts, documents, letters, stories, tables. They do not all assume narrative form, but the division is less
important than ever here: they all have to be interpreted. In discussing
problems connected with interpretation, I use stories only as examples of
texts; the kind of text whose interpretation has, historically, captured more
attention than any other kind. Further, "interpretation" is taken here in
the sense of all inquiry, of recontextualization, and not as a contrast to
explanation (Rorty 1991).

The question is thus, one meaning, many meanings, or no meaning at
all? In response to the recent wave of reader-oriented theories of interpretation, Eco (1992) pointed out that interpretations are indefinite but not
infinite. They are negotiations between the intention of the reader (*intentio
lectoris*) and the intention of the text (*intentio operis*), as the good old
hermeneutical circle tells us. They can end with a first-level reading (typical
for a semantic reader) or an overinterpretation (a tendency of a semiotic
reader). Most of the readers live someplace between those two extremes,
and different readers have different interpretation habits.

Rorty (1992a) had difficulty in accepting this apparently pragmatic
interpretation model, precisely because of his pragmatist position. Despite
all repudiations, there is a clear hierarchy between Eco's two extreme readers: the semiotic reader is a clever one (presumably a researcher), whereas
the semantic reader is a dupe (presumably an unreflective practitioner).
Also, the difference proposed by Eco between an "interpretation" (which
respects *intentio operis*) and "use" (for example, lighting the cigarette with
a text, but more generally just a disrespectful reading) is something that

Rorty could not accept. For him, all readings are "uses." If a classification of uses—that is, readings—is required, Rorty suggested a distinction between a *methodical* reading, one that is controlled by the reader and the purpose at hand, and an *inspired* reading, which changes the reader and the purpose as much as it changes the text.

For me, these issues have more significance than simply being a part of an altercation between two theoreticians who otherwise stand very close to each other. To understand this wider significance, one has to assume that in undertaking organization research we are joining a conversation on this topic that is not limited to organizational researchers.[4] The picture of our discipline presented by Astley and Zammuto (1992) as a soliloquy in many voices, paints our future in lonely colors. It seems both exciting and gratifying (as well as frustrating and difficult) to try to speak to the Other, and among many Others, practitioners are one possible partner in such a conversation.

I do not intend to say, naively, that practitioners read or ought to read everything we write: there are clearly issues of a self-reflective nature that are not of much interest to outsiders. Nor do I intend to announce condescendingly that we have to "adapt to practitioners' needs," by which is usually meant that we have to operate at the level of *Reader's Digest*. I claim that practitioners are educated enough to understand what we write; they rarely read us because they do not find our texts interesting. I would also postulate that there is no such thing as "practitioners' needs," at least not as a fixed entity.

So let me introduce a practitioner's voice into this debate (as a textual device, of course; see below). Such a voice, were it to speak as one, could be persuaded to Eco's line of reasoning concerning the distinction between interpretation and use, but would join Rorty in disliking the implied idea of a stupid and a sophisticated reader. Thus, we have a disagreement between a practitioner, a pragmaticist, and a pragmatist. Further, each of the voices suggests a road ending in a paradox.

The practitioner opts for first-level reading, but also for equating the lay reading with an analytic reading. When this requirement is fulfilled, the researcher who chooses to be a faithful reader is rewarded by the practitioner with a "We knew that all along."

The "pragmaticist," in agreement with Eco, opts for two levels of reading, one bowing to "common sense," the other much wider but not unlimited. The practitioner is satisfied, having received a respectful nod for the first-level reading and a whiff of intellectual sophistication. There is, however, a lot of explaining to be done about how to establish the divisions between a "first-level" and a "second-level" reading, and between an "open text" and an "overinterpretation." Who has the right to issue these labels?

Finally, following the pragmatist ("I will read as I please, that is, with my own purpose at hand; and it is my highest ambition that my purpose and I myself will change with this reading"), one is assured of consistency and coherence but accused of radicalism and, even worse, of relativism. "Science is methodical reading; inspirational readings are for poets!" say the practitioner and the pragmaticist in unison.

All these options are known to organization researchers and practiced by them. As before, I do not offer any resolution of paradoxes inherent in all of them. I postulate a conscious reflection on the fact that all options have their rewards and their price. The price to be paid may seem less costly if it is clear that there is no perfect solution or costless alternative. Why not admit what is well known: that it is impossible to please all audiences at once, and that it is impossible to control the reactions of any chosen audience?

This reasoning concerns the impossibility of carrying through the *intentio auctoris*, of foreseeing and successfully manipulating an audience. But is there no *intentio operis*? Can readers interpret as they please?

As the examples from practice show, there was nothing in the texts that was not put there by the readers. What is a "reasonable interpretation" and what is an "overinterpretation" is negotiated not so much between the text and the reader as among the readers. In that sense, *intentio operis* seems an excellent device, to be treated pragmatically. It is impossible, however, to establish the *intentio operis* of a given text once and for all. Intentions are being read into the text each time a reader interprets it. Again, this does not mean there is an unlimited variety of idiosyncratic interpretations. In a given time and place, there will be *dominant* and *marginal readings* of the same text (DeVault 1990), which makes the notion of *interpretive communities* very useful (Fish 1989).

Such a dominant reading of the public administration in Sweden results in its being constantly reproached and chided for its inconsistencies and ambiguities. Over and over again, diligent researchers drafted a straight line to progress for the public-sector organizations. Life was supposed to follow science. My marginal reading ended with a plea for the reverse—for science to follow life. Instead of denouncing paradoxes and straightening them out, we can start cashing in on them, in theory as well as practice.

## Writing Ergonographies
### *What Is in the Name?*

*Ergonography* is obviously a neologism, chosen not for its beauty but from a need for something different enough to be noticeable. The reason I am attempting to launch a new term is partly political—to distinguish a genre that is typical for the kind of studies I undertake—and partly etymological, since other possible candidates have an etymological past that makes them less suitable.

What I mean is something like "ethnographies of organizations," but I do not wish to employ this term. I retain the *graphon* (Greek) element: it is clear that our business is to write, but it is not clear what. The prefix *ethno-* has a somewhat complicated history. In ethnology, it means (by use, not by definition) studying what people do *outside* organizations. While it is possible that this connotation might wither away in time, our problem here is simply that the word *ethnography* seems to suggest the opposite of what the organization researchers are actually studying. *Etho-*, as in ethology, which Rom Harré (Harré and Secord 1972; Harré 1979) has suggested, shares its name with animal studies, and although there is nothing to prevent us extending the constructionist approach to animal studies, it evokes associations somewhat remote from a narrative approach.

*Ergon* is a Greek word meaning "work," but it is akin to *organon*, "instrument." We are writing narratives on work organizations—ergonographies. The unexpected coupling of *ergon* and *graphon* warns the reader against association with ergonomics, which adopted a physicalist approach to work.

How, then, are ergonographies written? Many styles and textual strategies are available. I will take up those that are usual and those considered attractive.

### *Are Ergonographies Fictions?*

The adoption of a narrative approach naturally leads to a redefinition of what research produces. What may be disconcerting is the closeness between business administration and literary theory that results from the approach. For example, let us look at the budget bill in chapter 6. What are the possible similarities and differences between an ergonographic description of the Swedish public sector and a fiction about Hollywood's history?

The first conventional difference, of course, is the one between fact and fiction. Yet it is well known that Fitzgerald's book is based on firsthand participant observation, while mine is only secondhand, so to speak. In fact, as Watts (1990) pointed out, many "works of fiction" are based on sound ethnologic studies. And, as Geertz puts it, "the resistance to the notion that ethnographic writing requires the employment of stories, pictures, symbols and metaphors is due to the confusion between the imagined and the imaginary, the fictive and the false, 'making things out' and 'making them up'" (1988, 140).

The second difference that might be expected would concern style. But in fact both accounts are written in a conventional realistic mode, with dialogues to increase the credibility. Scientific realism, says Latour (1988b), differs from fictional realism by the textual strategy of inviting the reader to inspect the source of facts (my alleged study of budgeting processes, Czarniawska-Joerges 1992b, which probably contains other references of this kind, the final loop in the chain consisting of interview transcriptions or other "hard data"). In terms of the frequency of occurrence, this is correct, although the same strategy has been faked in fiction, the most remarkable example being Jean d'Ormesson's *The Glory of the Empire (Le Gloire de L'Empire)*, complete with footnotes, page references, and all.

The third possible difference, the one I have tried to avoid in this text, is that fiction works are more commonly "authored" whereas scientific texts are "written." The removal of this difference does not have to lead to tedious self-presentations or explicit self-reflection. Even self-explanatory texts use a variety of authorial textual strategies (Eco 1979), of which the impression of "automatic writing" is perhaps the least attractive.

To sum up: there is no clear difference between fact and fiction. There are varieties of realism, and there are many textual strategies available to an alert author. Does it mean that we should all become novelists?

## *The Researcher's Identity as a Writer*

An organization researcher is in many respects more like a literary critic than a novelist. The organizations that the researchers describe are only in a certain sense products of their minds (in the sense that they are responsible for their own texts); the organizations are originally written by organizational actors. These last, like the literary authors, have quite a lot to say about the critics' opinions of their products. Organization researchers thus live forever on shaky ground, insofar as they mediate between the "organizational authors" and the academic theorists. Accordingly, I propose a role somewhere between those of the novelist and the literary critic: a semiotic writer, let us say. And as it is not the difference between fact and fiction that distinguishes us from the novelists and critics, it must be the kind of texts we analyze and the kind of texts we write.

Practitioners and consultants are busy writing texts and authoring works. The researchers' role is to interpret these texts (although this requires the creation of yet another text). They build worlds; we inspect the construction (although this requires the construction of yet another world).

Our task is, in fact, a double one. First we must allow space for a conventional narrative, which plays an important role in organizations. What Lejeune said about autobiography in general applies to organizational autobiographical acts in particular:

> Any original inquiry into the structure of the narrative awakens the mistrust of the reader, who perceives something contrived, whereas the use of traditional narrative gives him [or her] the impression that it is a personal experience. Studies of the modern novel are useless . . . life continues to resemble Balzac. (1989, 71)

In other words, there are many and serious demands for realism in our stories from the field. Stern underlines the difference between "realism" as a philosophical orientation or orientation toward life and "realism" in literature. Stern's scrutiny of literature and literary critique reveals at least three ways of understanding this second kind of realism: as "a way of depicting, describing a situation in a faithful, accurate, 'life-like' manner; or richly, abundantly, colourfully; or again mechanically, photographically, imitatively" (1973, 40).

It is against the third and for the second interpretation of realism that my present appeal is made. A realist study does not have to denote naive simplicity of a straight chronological "report." Lejeune goes on to say:

> the method traditionally used in chronological narrative, like dramatic anticipation, explanatory flashback, or recapitulative sequences; these breaches of chronological order, after all, indeed show that this order is unnatural, since we are incessantly obliged to violate it in order to understand the *meaning* of a life story. Up to and including chronological order, it is *meaning* finally that organizes the narrative. (1989, 72)

As an example, Lejeune refers to Sartre's *Les Mots,* in which meaning is favored at the expense of chronology, but where temporality is one of the central themes. I do not want to focus on Sartre's work here, or to stretch the metaphor of autobiography beyond sensible limits. But I have mentioned Lejeune's analysis to demonstrate that such a feat is possible: the device of *dialectical narrative* refuses the commonsensical notion of a past separate from the present (the past exists only as the present of the narrator, and constitutes part of another shifting operation), and rejects the notion of mechanical causality (*post hoc, ergo propter hoc*) that is typical of a simple narrative.

The dialectical narrative is only one possible device, one that is perhaps inaccessible to us humble ergonographers. But there are many others: *dialogical narrative* in the sense proposed by Bakhtin (a text that interrogates the world), or *interruptive narrative* as in the ethnomethodological version proposed by Silverman and Torode (a world that interrogates a text, or maybe just a text that interrogates another text). Different as these narratives are, they all share two traits. They set out to preserve the "naive" narrative of the field, real or imaginary, but they also claim the right to problematize and to ironize, which requires an examination of one's own text, a self-reflection. I am well aware that I am proposing the authorial equivalent of a conjuring trick, but I can add that it is easier done than said.

# Notes

## Chapter One
## (pages 11–29)

1. This feat was, of course, never accomplished, although it was seriously attempted. The best example of lingering ambiguity is the famous—and infamous—psychological notion of "attitude," which, by insisting on preserving the mechanical together with the intentional, promised much and gave little.

2. For a more systematic critique, see my "Changing Times and Accounts," 1996.

3. I am not suggesting that the two kinds of conversation should be distinguished except for some specific purpose. Even if the "positioning" (Davies and Harré 1991) that takes place in imaginary conversations does not encounter the usual resistance from other actors, sooner or later it is tried out in "real" conversations, and the difference vanishes.

4. Maybe this is why the predictability of serials gives such comfort to viewers (see chapter 7).

5. Unpredictability is far from total: there are predictabilities that we ourselves create (as in timetables); there is predictability in statistical regularities; there is knowledge of causal regularities in nature and social life.

6. A process that has its counterpart in organizational socialization.

7. An interesting tautology, as Bruner points out; *narrative* probably comes from the Latin *gnarus,* "knowing."

8. Indeed, Fisher (1987) goes to great lengths to construct such criteria for narrative, and thus to defend it from this particular criticism.

9. Here, once again, one is reminded of the ethnomethodological redefinition of rationality as a rhetoric to account for social actions (Garfinkel 1967).

10. This should not be taken for moralizing; the authors' interests mentioned here lie in improving the discourse of morality, not in telling people or nations what they should do with their lives.

11. I mean his interpretation of the Gulf War, 1991; see also Mitchell's comparison between CNN's narration of the Gulf War and Oliver Stone's story of Kennedy's assassination (Mitchell 1992).

12. For a more thorough presentation and classification of organizational culture literature, see Alvesson and Berg (1992).

## Chapter Two
### (pages 30–53)

1. On the treatment of Burke's work in the social sciences, see Overington 1977a, 1977b.

2. MacIntyre gives examples from Japanese Noh plays and English medieval morality plays. *Commedia dell'arte* is another example (Czarniawska-Joerges and Jacobsson 1995).

3. In Giddens's, not Burke's, meaning of the term.

4. Note the wealth of possibilities that arises here for a creative narrative that can explain the deviations away.

5. The argument is, of course, much more complicated than this. On "Essentialist Self" and "Conceptual Self," see Bruner 1990.

6. See also Gergen (1991) for a review of modern thinking from David Hume to Erik Erikson in the same vein.

7. Excessively conscious commitment may be regarded as artificial or manipulative.

8. Each member of the audience is also a narrator, of course.

9. Needless to say, this distinction is as impossible to maintain in autobiography as anywhere else, but it is the claim that distinguishes a genre, not the complications of employing it in practice.

10. For genre as a literary institution and especially on autobiography as genre, I rely mainly on two contemporary classics on this theme: Elisabeth Bruss (1976) and Philippe Lejeune (1989).

11. Here again I am quoting a fiction writer, which shows how genres become blurred in practice. Vidal uses the form of autobiography to achieve an effect of historical realism.

## Chapter Three
### (pages 54–72)

1. The situation is different in anthropology, where Marcus and Fischer (1986) described in great detail the ambitions and needs of interpretive anthropology, which originated to a large extent in Geertz's seminal *The Interpretation of Cultures* (1973).

2. Especially in cognitive organization theory, however, there is an attempt to coopt interpretation for paradigmatic uses (for an overview, see Schneider and Angelmar 1993).

3. The term coined to denote a technique made famous by Garfinkel (1967) and consisting in disrupting the social order by refusing to cooperate.

4. "A visit to the Other" is an expression of my student Kjell Tryggestad (1995).

5. I write more on the use of anthropological methods in organization studies in *Exploring Complex Organizations* (1992a).

6. This fashion of comic self-description and the attitude of irreverence, as one of the reviewers put it, is well rooted in anthropology. See, e.g., the hilarious tale of recounting *Hamlet* in another culture, Bohannan 1966.

7. *Vnenahodimost* in Russian, it is sometimes translated as "exotopy" or "extopy."

8. In *Music for Chameleons* (1981).

9. Model Reader, like Model Author (the one who appears in a text) is a textual strategy created by the author, not a concrete person or persons.

10. As the present text is very much under the influence of Rorty's pragmatist ideas, I must add that Rorty sees certain complications in Eco's postulate (see chapter 10). Similarly, Tyler (1986) parodies (with no relation to Eco's text) the two models by contrasting a reader immune to any nuance in the text and a paranoid reader who thinks the author is either a dupe (a structuralist reader) or a charlatan (a power analyst).

### Chapter Four
### (pages 75–99)

1. I am evoking here a version of Swedish history as created for the requirements of the welfare state (Löfgren 1993). Other versions also exist, e.g., monarchist Sweden, recently dusted off after decades of disregard.

2. The fourth is, of course, the trade unions.

3. I will use these acronyms to indicate the source of an utterance in quotations from the interviews.

4. In cognitive psychology, such knowledge about how people behave in certain circumstances is termed "scripts" (Mandler 1984). I do not employ this concept since it is not specific enough: stories and serials also have their "scripts."

### Chapter Five
### (pages 100–21)

1. Sveriges Allmännyttiga Bostads Organisation: Swedish Association of Municipal Housing Companies.

2. That is how things appeared at the time. In a subsequent decision, the National Judicial Board for Public Lands and Funds has refused to exempt the company from stamp duty. An appeal was pending at the time of this writing.

3. I implied—somewhat meanly—that this was not just coincidence, but my interlocutor loyally denied this.

4. In the insurance operations, computers are "for men"; studies in Europe have shown, however, that although men continue to dominate the manufacture of hard- and software, women are the major users of computers at work.

5. This led to a debate on questions of privacy, a topic that is omitted from this analysis.

6. TV serials (no doubt, in their reception as well as in the production) appear to be subject to special national "biases." British serials describe oppression and the difficult sides of life; U.S. serials deal with glamor and success; Latin America specializes in family sagas; and Australian serials represent the "triumph of mediocrity" (Alexander 1991).

7. Of course, it is very well known even in private business.

8. A postmodernist, radical solution which is not tackled here. The combination of innovation and repetition is still within the modernist aesthetic. The "post-postmodern sensibility" (Eco 1990) where TV serials replace Greek tragedies in our culture is still a consideration for the future, albeit an interesting one.

9. The noun *kvinnor* (women) is used only in programmatic utterances, even by women themselves. The world of organizations is populated by "girls" (*tjejer*) interspersed by "ladies" (*damer*), a linguistic habit that I think captures very well the situation of women in organizations.

## Chapter Six
### (pages 122–41)

1. It should be added, however, that the bulk of public operations in Sweden (in terms of both taxation and spending) resides in the municipalities.

2. Fitzgerald notes also that this role was very much resented by the "true" writers, an observation that is probably autobiographical. The 1993 Robert Altman movie *The Player* sharpens this picture to a caricature, while Joel Coen's *Barton Fink* tells the story of Hollywood in the 1930s in a Kafkaesque mood.

3. A functional interpretation would have it that Sweden, like many democracies, has problems in differentiating the programs of the various parties in the eyes of the electorate, hence the drama. The public expression of emotions, however, is at odds with cultural norms, which is what made the narrator uneasy.

4. This was the budget bill in the year preceding the case described above. The budget bill announces the amount of the state contribution (until recently, specifically destined) to municipal finances (a relatively small contribution, as each municipality is an independent taxation unit). The important role of the bill consists in indicating priorities and preferences.

5. The irony of this statement lies in the fact that both the National Audit Bureau and the Government Administration Office are the agencies whose only task is to supervise and give advice to other state agencies. But even more ironic is the fact that this criticism, which comes from the NSIB, is an exact copy of what social insurance offices say about this very board.

6. In personifying organizations, I follow the custom of my interlocutors. When I tried to prompt them into a more differentiated picture ("who in the association?"), they often refused to follow my lead. In time I learned that such personi-

fication fulfills an important role: it makes it possible to distinguish between inter-actions with specific individuals and a principal reaction to "the organization's" sayings and doings. Another indication that the organization-as-person conception has many pragmatic uses.

7. This may be wishful thinking. During the second of those conferences, I presented my study, trying to achieve maximum provocation. At the end of my speech, the person highest in the hierarchy among those present reinterpreted my talk in terms of the conventional frame, leaving me speechless and the world of insurance intact.

8. The authors are using the Peircean differentiation between two modes of signification: symbols (conventional associations) and indexes (factual con-nections) (see, e.g., Hernadi 1987). In doing so, they deviate from the more com-monsensical understanding used in symbolist analyses, where "symbols" are seen as signs standing for something else.

### Chapter Seven
### (pages 142–66)

1. This is connected with the belief that skillful rhetoric is a sign of dishon-esty. Roger Brown (1969, 340) speaks ironically of "tweed rhetoric," observing that "one can be quiet, modest, tweedy, and yet a villain." The equivalent in Sweden would be a "wooden clogs rhetoric" (alluding to the shoe style of the 1960s).

2. See Czarniawska-Joerges 1990 for a discussion of the Swedish predilec-tion for sporting and hunting metaphors.

3. This does not imply that I agree with the argumentation. My analysis is confined to the form.

4. The first of these is granted to everybody who is a Swedish citizen, the second only to the employed. The text does not mention the fact that neither of these is in the hands of the social insurance system any longer. Their fate is another interesting story.

### Chapter Eight
### (pages 167–78)

1. That is, he supplies generic terms whereas I provide organizational ex-amples.

2. Although Burke would rather speak of "action" and "knowledge."

3. Although it is being claimed increasingly often that images take over the role of words, see, e.g., Godzich 1991; one language is encroaching upon the other.

4. Luhmann's translators sometimes call it "deparadoxization" (e.g., Luh-mann 1986a). I was advised against this neologism by my language consultants, Nancy Adler and Professor Donald Fanger.

5. The only sister Gorgon who made a real career is Medusa; Stheno and Euryale are usually forgotten. The reason for that is simply pragmatic and very

relevant in the context of this book: Medusa was the only one of them who was mortal, and therefore vulnerable to human action.

6. "A paradox is of course always a problem of an observer" (Luhmann 1991, 62).

## Chapter Nine
### (pages 179–94)

1. They prefer to speak about "actants"—a semiotic term that encompasses an action and the agency to which it is attributed; an attractive alternative but difficult to incorporate into the organizational discourse.

2. The introduction to Powell and DiMaggio (1991) takes a more generous view of those matters, but it is also rather abstract, in contrast to the very specific original wording.

3. I am using the vocabulary of systems theory because it is convenient for making this kind of comparison. Obviously, however, Arnold did not use it in 1935.

4. An analogy that can only be taken as a compliment, I hope.

5. "Facts, as telescopes and wigs for gentlemen, were a seventeenth century invention" (MacIntyre 1988, 357).

## Chapter Ten
### (pages 195–205)

1. "Voice" is a metaphor that has replaced "perspective" in ethnographic parlance, in an act of rebellion against the visual, structuralist tone of the latter; see, e.g., Marcus 1992.

2. A typical ornamental antithesis; there are, of course, other ways. Lejeune (1989) recommends video recording, which, considering the ever-increasing role of pictures (Godzich 1991), seems to be a promising way (with its own complications, of course). As far as I know, only Gibson Burrell, Marta Calás, and Brian Rusted use it in organization theory.

3. Rorty (1991) explains convincingly why the Diltheyan difference between "nature" and "history," "explanation" and "understanding" is untenable.

4. This brings us to the issue of incompatible discourses. Although there is no room here to go into this fully, the obvious comment must be made that between the exaggerated hopes and exaggerated desperation associated with our communication with the Other, there is an insatiable curiosity that compels us at least to try.

# References

Abelson, Robert P. 1986. Beliefs are like possessions. *Journal for the Theory of Social Behaviour* 16 (3): 223–50.

Ahrne, Göran. 1989. *Byråkratin och statens inre gränser.* Stockholm: Rabén & Sjögren.

Albert, Stuart, and David A. Whetten. 1985. Organizational identity. In Larry L. Cummings and Barry M. Staw, eds., *Research in organizational behavior,* vol. 7, 263–95. Greenwich, Conn.: JAI Press.

Alexander, John. 1991. *Televersions. Narrative structure in television.* Warren Farm, Pyrford: InterMedia Publications.

Alvarez, José Luis, and Carmen Merchán Cantos. 1992. The role of narrative fiction in the development of imagination for action. *International Studies of Management & Organization* 22 (3): 27–45.

Alvesson, Mats, and Per-Olof Berg. 1992. *Corporate culture and organizational symbolism.* Berlin: De Gruyter.

Alvesson, Mats, and Ivar Björkman. 1992. *Organisatorisk identitet.* Lund: Studentlitteratur.

Anderson, Walter E. 1990. *Reality isn't what it used to be.* San Francisco: Harper & Row.

Anton, Thomas J. 1967. Roles and symbols in state expenditures. *Midwest Journal of Political Science* 11 (Feb.): 27–43.

Antonio, Robert J. 1979. The contradiction of domination and production in bureaucracy: The contribution of organizational efficiency to the decline of the Roman Empire. *American Sociological Review* 44 (December): 895–912.

Arnold, Thurman W. 1935. *The symbols of government.* New Haven, Conn.: Yale University Press.

———. 1937. *The folklore of capitalism.* New Haven, Conn.: Yale University Press.

Åsard, Erik. 1980. Employee participation in Sweden 1971–1979. *Economic and Industrial Democracy* 1 (3): 371–93.

Ashfort, Blake, and Fred Mael. 1989. Social identity theory and the organization. *Academy of Management Review* 14: 20–39.

Ashmore, Malcolm. 1989. *The reflexive thesis: Wrighting sociology of scientific knowledge.* Chicago: University of Chicago Press.

Ashmore, Malcolm, Michael Mulkay, and Trevor Pinch. 1989. *Health efficiency: A sociology of health economics.* Milton Keynes: Open University Press.

Astley, Graham W., and Raymond F. Zammuto. 1992. Organization science, managers, and language games. *Organization Science* 3 (4): 443–60.

Bakhtin, Mikhail / P. N. Medvedev. 1928/1985. *The formal method in literary scholarship: A critical introduction to sociological poetics.* Cambridge: Harvard University Press.

———. 1981. *The dialogic imagination.* Austin, Tex.: University of Texas Press.

Baldwin, John D. 1986. *George Herbert Mead: A unifying theory for sociology.* Beverly Hills, Calif.: Sage.

Barley, Nigel. 1983. *The innocent anthropologist: Notes from a mud hut.* London: Penguin.

———. 1986. *A plague of caterpillars: A return to the African bush.* London: Penguin.

———. 1988. *Not a hazardous sport.* London: Penguin.

———. 1989. *Native land.* London: Penguin.

Barthes, Roland. 1966/1977. Introduction to the structural analysis of narratives. In Stephen Heath, trans., *Image—Music—Text,* 79–124. Glasgow: William Collins.

———. 1975. *S/Z.* New York: Hill & Wang.

———. 1979. From work to text. In Josue V. Harari, ed., *Textual strategies,* 73–82. Ithaca, N.Y.: Cornell University Press.

Baudrillard, Jean. 1987. *L'autre par lui-même.* Paris: Éditions Galilée.

———. 1991. *La guerre du Golfe n'a pas lieu.* Paris: Éditions Galilée.

Becker, Howard S. 1970. *Sociological work.* Chicago: Aldine.

Berg, Per-Olof. 1989. Postmodern management? From facts to fiction in theory and practice. *Scandinavian Journal of Management* 5 (3): 201–17.

Berger, Peter, and Thomas Luckmann. 1966. *The social construction of reality.* New York: Doubleday.

Berger, Peter, Brigitta Berger, and Hanfried Kellner. 1974. *The homeless mind.* London: Penguin.

Berman, Marshall. 1992. Why modernism still matters. In Scott Lash and Jonathan Friedman, eds., *Modernity and identity,* 33–58. Oxford: Blackwell.

Bernstein, Richard J. 1983. *Beyond objectivism and relativism.* Oxford: Blackwell.

Blumer, Herbert. 1969. *Symbolic interactionism.* Englewood Cliffs, N.J.: Prentice-Hall.

———. 1973. Fashion: From class differentiation to collective selection. In G. Wills and D. Midgley, eds., *Fashion marketing.* London: Allen & Unwin.

Boden, Deirdre. 1994. *The business of talk: Organizations in action.* Cambridge: Polity Press.

Bohannan, Laura. 1966. Shakespeare in the bush. *Natural History Magazine* (Aug./Sept.): 28–33.

Boje, David. 1991. The story-telling organization: A study of story performance in an office-supply firm. *Administrative Science Quarterly* 36: 106–26.

Boland, Richard J. Jr. 1989. Beyond the objectivist and the subjectivist: Learning to read accounting as text. *Accounting, Organizations and Society* 14 (5/6): 591–604.

———. 1994. Identity, economy and morality in "The Rise of Silas Lapham." In

B. Czarniawska-Joerges and P. Guillet de Monthoux, eds., *Good novels, better management*, 115–37. Reading, U.K.: Harwood Academic Publishers.

Boland, Richard J. Jr., and W. F. Day. 1989. The experience of system design: A hermeneutic of organizational action. *Scandinavian Journal of Management* 5 (2): 87–104.

Boland, Richard J. Jr., and Ramkrishnan V. Tankasi. 1995. Perspective making and perspective taking in communities of knowing. *Organization Science* 6 (3): 350–72.

Bradbury, Malcolm. 1992. Closer to chaos: American fiction in the 1980s. *Times Literary Supplement* 22: 17.

Brown, Richard H. 1977. *A poetic for sociology: Toward a logic of discovery for the human science*. New York: Cambridge University Press.

———. 1980. The position of narrative in contemporary society. *New Literary History* 11 (3): 545–50.

———. 1987. *Society as text: Essays on rhetoric, reason and reality*. Chicago: University of Chicago Press.

———. 1989. *Social science as civic discourse: Essays on the invention, legitimation and uses of social theory*. Chicago: University of Chicago Press.

Brown, Roger W. 1969. *Words and things*. New York: Free Press.

Bruner, Jerome. 1986. *Actual minds, possible worlds*. Cambridge: Harvard University Press.

———. 1990. *Acts of meaning*. Cambridge: Harvard University Press.

Brunsson, Nils. 1985. *The irrational organization*. London: Wiley.

———. 1986. Politik och handling. In Nils Brunsson, ed., *Politik och ekonomi*. Lund: Doxa.

———. 1989. *The organization of hypocrisy: Talk, action and decision in organizations*. London: Wiley.

———. 1994. Politicization and "company-ization"—on institutional affiliation and confusion in the organizational world. *Management Accounting Research* 5: 323–35.

Brunsson Nils, and Sten Jönsson. 1979. *Beslut och handling: Om politikers inflytande på politiken*. Stockholm: LiberFörlag.

Brunsson, Nils, and Johan Olsen, eds. 1993. *The reforming organization*. London: Routledge.

Bruss, Elisabeth W. 1976. *Autobiographical acts: The changing situation of a literary genre*. Baltimore: Johns Hopkins University Press.

———. 1982. *Beautiful theories*. Baltimore: John Hopkins University Press.

Bulmer, Martin. 1984. *The Chicago school of sociology*. Chicago: University of Chicago Press.

Burke, Kenneth. 1945/1969. *A grammar of motives*. Berkeley, Calif.: University of California Press.

Burrell, Gibson, and Gareth Morgan. 1979. *Sociological paradigms and organizational analysis*. Aldershot, U.K.: Gower.

Calás, Marta, and Linda Smircich. 1991. Voicing seduction to silence leadership. *Organization Studies* 12 (4): 567–601.

Callon, Michel. 1986. Some elements of a sociology of translation: Domestication of the scallops and the fishermen of St Brieuc's Bay. In J. Law, ed., *Power, action and belief,* 196–229. London: Routledge and Kegan Paul.

Callon, Michel, and Bruno Latour. 1981. Unscrewing the big Leviathan: How actors macro-structure reality and how sociologists help them to do so. In Karen Knorr Cetina and Aaron V. Cicourel, eds., *Advances in social theory and methodology,* 277–303. London: Routledge and Kegan Paul.

Castaneda, Carlos. 1968/1986. *The teachings of Don Juan: A Yaqui way of knowledge.* Harmondsworth, U.K.: Penguin.

Chandler, Alfred D. 1977. *The visible hand.* Cambridge: Harvard University Press.

———. 1990. *Scale and scope.* Cambridge: Harvard University Press.

Cicourel, Aaron V. 1974. *Cognitive sociology: Language and meaning in social interaction.* New York: Free Press.

Clark, Burton R. 1972. The organizational saga in higher education. *Administrative Science Quarterly* 17: 178–84.

Clegg, Stewart. 1987. The language of power and the power of language. *Organization Studies* 8 (1): 61–70.

Collins, Harry M. 1985. *Changing order: Replication and induction in scientific practice.* London: Sage.

Czarniawska-Joerges, Barbara. 1988. *Ideological control in nonideological organizations.* New York: Praeger.

———. 1989. *Economic decline and organizational control.* New York: Praeger.

———. 1990. Merchants of meaning: Management consulting in the Swedish public sector. In Barry A. Turner, ed., *Organizational symbolism,* 139–49. Berlin: De Gruyter.

———. 1992a. *Exploring complex organizations.* Newbury Park, Calif.: Sage.

———. 1992b. *Styrningens paradoxer: Scener ur den offentliga verksamheten.* Stockholm: Norstedts.

———. 1994. Gender, power, organizations. In John Hassard and Martin Parker, eds., *The new organization theory revisited,* 227–47. London: Routledge.

Czarniawska, Barbara. 1996. Changing times and accounts. In Rolland Munro and Jan Mouritsen, eds., *Accountability, power and ethos,* 307–28. London: Chapman & Hall.

Czarniawska-Joerges, Barbara, and Pierre Guillet de Monthoux, eds. 1994. *Good novels, better management: Reading realities in fiction.* Reading, U.K.: Harwood Academic Press.

Czarniawska-Joerges, Barbara, and Bengt Jacobsson. 1989. Budget in cold climate. *Accounting, Organizations and Society* 14 (1/2): 29–39.

———. 1995. Politics as *commedia dell'arte. Organization Studies* 16 (3): 375–94.

Czarniawska, Barbara, and Bernward Joerges. 1995. Winds of change. In Samuel Bacharach and Pasquale Gagliardi, eds., *Research in the sociology of organizations,* 171–209. Greenwich, Conn.: JAI Press.

Davies, Bronwyn, and Rom Harré. 1991. Positioning: The discoursive production of selves. *Journal for the Theory of Social Behaviour* 20 (1): 43–63.

Democracy and Power in Sweden (*Demokrati och makt i Sverige. Maktutredningens huvudrapport*). SOU 1990: 44.

DeMott, B. 1989. Reading fiction to the bottom line. *Harvard Business Review* (May/June): 128–34.

DeVault, Marjorie L. 1990. Novel readings: The social organization of interpretation. *American Journal of Sociology* 95 (4): 887–921.

Diener, Paul, Donald Nonini, and Eugene E. Robkin. 1980. Ecology and evolution in cultural anthropology. *Man* 15: 1–31.

DiMaggio, Paul. 1983. State expansion in organizational fields. In Richard H. Hall and Robert E. Quinn, eds., *Organizational theory and public policy*, 147–61. Beverly Hills, Calif: Sage.

DiMaggio, Paul J., and Walter W. Powell. 1983. The iron cage revisited: Institutional isomorphism and collective rationality in organizational fields. *American Sociological Review* 48: 147–60.

———. 1991. Introduction. In Walter W. Powell, and Paul J. DiMaggio, eds., *The new institutionalism in organizational analysis*, 1–38. Chicago: University of Chicago Press.

Douglas, Mary. 1986. The social preconditions of radical scepticism. In J. Law, ed., *Power, action and belief*, 68–87. London: Routledge and Kegan Paul.

———. 1987. *How institutions think*. London: Routledge and Kegan Paul.

———. 1992. Thought style exemplified: The idea of the self. In *Risk and blame*. London: Routledge.

Downs, George W., and Patrick D. Larkey. 1986. *The search for government efficiency: From hubris to helplessness*. Philadelphia: Temple University Press.

Dutton, Jane E., and Janet M. Dukerich. 1991. Keeping an eye on the mirror: Image and identity in organizational adaptation. *Academy of Management Journal* 34 (3): 517–54.

Eco, Umberto. 1979/1983. *The role of the reader: Explorations in the semiotics of texts*. London: Hutchinson.

———. 1989. *The open work*. Cambridge: Harvard University Press.

———. 1990. *The limits of interpretation*. Bloomington and Indianapolis: Indiana University Press.

———. 1992. *Interpretation and overinterpretation*. Cambridge: Cambridge University Press.

Edelman, Murray. 1964. *The symbolic uses of politics*. Urbana, Ill.: University of Illinois Press.

———. 1977. *Political language: Words that succeed and policies that fail*. New York: Free Press of Glencoe.

———. 1988. *Constructing the political spectacle*. Chicago: University of Chicago Press.

Fish, Stanley. 1989. *Doing what comes naturally: Change, rhetoric, and the practice of theory in literary and legal studies*. Durham, N.C.: Duke University Press.

Fisher, Walter R. 1984. Narration as a human communication paradigm: The case of public moral argument. *Communication Monographs* 51: 1–22.

———. 1987. *Human communication as narration: Toward a philosophy of reason, value, and action.* Columbia, S.C.: University of South Carolina Press.

Fiske, John. 1987. *Television culture.* London: Routledge.

Forester, John. 1992. Critical ethnography: On fieldwork in a Habermasian way. In Mats Alvesson and Hugh Willmott, eds.,*Critical management studies,* 46–65. London: Sage.

Frost, Peter J., V. F. Mitchell, and Walter S. Nord. 1978. *Organizational reality: Reports from the firing line.* Santa Monica, Calif.: Goodyear.

Frost, Peter J., Larry F. Moore, Meryl Reis Louis, Craig C. Lundberg, and Joanne Martin, eds., 1985. *Organizational culture.* Newbury Park, Calif.: Sage.

———. 1991. *Reframing organizational culture.* Newbury Park, Calif.: Sage.

Frye, Northrop. 1957/1990. *The anatomy of criticism.* London: Penguin.

Frykman, Jonas. 1993. Nationella ord och handlingar. In Billy Ehn, Jonas Frykman, and Orvar Löfgren, *Försvenskningen av Sverige,* 120–210. Stockholm: Natur och Kultur.

Fukuyama, Francis. 1992. *The end of history and the last man.* London: Hamish Hamilton.

Fuller, Steve. 1996. Talking metaphysical turkey about epistemological chicken and the poop on pidgins. In David Stump and Peter Galison, eds., *Disunity and context: Philosophies of science studies.* Stanford: Stanford University Press.

Fussell, Paul. 1975. *The great war and modern memory.* Oxford: Oxford University Press.

Gabriel, Yiannis. 1995. The unmanaged organization: Stories, fantasies and subjectivity. *Organization Studies* 16 (3): 477–501.

Gagliardi, Pasquale, ed. 1990. *The symbolics of corporate artifacts.* Berlin: De Gruyter.

Garfinkel, Harold. 1967. *Studies in ethnomethodology.* Englewood Cliffs, N.J.: Prentice-Hall.

Geertz, Clifford. 1973. *The interpretation of cultures.* New York: Basic Books.

———. 1980a. Blurred genres: The refiguration of social thought. *American Scholar* 29 (2): 165–79.

———. 1980b. *Negara: The theatre state in nineteenth century Bali.* Princeton, N.J.: Princeton University Press.

———. 1988. *Works and lives: The anthropologist as author.* Stanford: Stanford University Press.

Gergen, Kenneth J. 1991. *The saturated self: Dilemmas of identity in contemporary life.* New York: Basic Books.

Giddens, Anthony. 1991. *Modernity and self-identity: Self and society in the late modern age.* Cambridge: Polity Press.

Ginzburg, Carlo. 1966. *I Benandanti: Stregoneria e culti agrari tra Cinquecento e Seicento.* Torino: Einaudi.

Ginzburg, Carlo. 1976. *Il formaggio e i vermi: I cosmo di un mugnaro del'500.* Torino: Einaudi.

————. 1995. *Storia notturna: Una decifrazione del sabba.* Torino: Einaudi.

Godzich, Wlad. 1991. Vom Paradox der Sprache zur Dissonanz des Bildes. In Hans Ulrich Gumbrecht and K. Ludwig Pfeiffer, eds., *Paradoxien, Dissonanzen, Zusammenbrüche. Situationen offener Epistemologie,* 747–58. Frankfurt: Suhrkamp.

Goffman, Erving. 1959. *The presentation of self in everyday life.* New York: Doubleday.

————. 1974. *Frame analysis.* Boston: Northeastern University Press.

————. 1981. *Forms of talk.* Oxford: Basil Blackwell.

Goodman, Nelson. 1978. *Ways of worldmaking.* Indianapolis: Hackett.

Gould, Stephen Jay. 1995. Ladders and cones: Constraining evolution by canonical icons. In Robert B. Silvers, ed., *Hidden histories of science,* 37–68. New York: New York Review of Books.

Guillet de Monthoux, Pierre. 1991. Modernism and the dominating firm—on the managerial mentality of the Swedish model. *Scandinavian Journal of Management* 7 (1): 27–40.

Gumbrecht, Hans Ulrich. 1991. Inszenierte Zusammenbrüche oder: Tragödie und Paradox. In Hans Ulrich Gumbrecht and K. Ludwig Pfeiffer, eds., *Paradoxien, Dissonanzen, Zusammenbrüche. Situationen offener Epistemologie,* 471–94. Frankfurt: Suhrkamp.

————. 1992. *Making sense in life and literature.* Minneapolis: University of Minnesota Press.

Gustavsen, Bjørn. 1985. Workplace reform and democratic dialogue. *Economic and Industrial Democracy* 6 (4): 461–79.

Habermas, Jürgen. 1974. *Theory and practice.* London: Heineman.

————. 1984. *The theory of communicative action.* Boston: Beacon Press.

Harari, Josue V. 1979. Critical factions/Critical fictions. In Josue V. Harari, ed., *Textual strategies: Perspectives in post-structuralist criticism,* 17–72. Ithaca, N.Y.: Methuen.

Harré, Rom. 1979. *Social being.* Oxford: Basil Blackwell.

————. 1982. Theoretical preliminaries to the study of action. In Mario von Cranach and Rom Harré, eds., *The analysis of action,* 5–34. Cambridge: Cambridge University Press.

Harré, Rom, and Paul F. Secord. 1972. *The explanation of social behaviour.* Oxford: Basil Blackwell.

Hatch, Mary Jo. 1993. Personal communication, 3 October.

Hernadi, Paul. 1987. Literary interpretation and the rhetoric of the human sciences. In John S. Nelson, Allan Megill, and D. N. McCloskey, eds., *The rhetoric of the human sciences,* 263–75. Madison, Wis.: University of Wisconsin Press.

Hernes, Gudmund. 1978. *Forhandlingsøkonomi og blandingsadministrasjon.* Bergen: Universitetetsförlag.

Hinnings, Bob, and Royston Greenwood. 1988. The normative prescription in organizations. In Lynne G. Zucker, ed., *Institutional patterns and organizations: Culture and environment.* Cambridge, Mass.: Ballinger.

Hirdman, Yvonne. 1989. *Att lägga livet till rätta.* Stockholm: Carlsson.

Hofstadter, Douglas. 1980. *Gödel, Escher, Bach: An eternal golden braid.* New York: Vintage Books.

Hofstede, Geert. 1967. *The game of budget control.* Assen, Neth.: Van Gorcum.

———. 1987. The cultural context of accounting. In B. E. Cushing, ed., *Accounting and culture.* Sarasota, Fla.: American Accounting Association.

Holzner, Burkhard. 1968. *Reality construction in society.* Cambridge, Mass.: Schenkman.

Jacobsson, Bengt. 1990. Automats, combats and rain dances: Images of budgeting in public organizations. In Claes Gustafsson and Lars Hassel, eds., *Accounting and organizational action,* 93–110. Åbo: Åbo Academy Press.

Jansson, David. 1989. The pragmatic uses of what is taken from granted: Project leaders' applications of investment calculus. *International Studies of Management & Organization* 19 (3): 49–63.

———. 1992. *Spelet kring investeringskalkyler.* Stockholm: Nordstedts.

Jones, Michael Owen, Michael Dane Moore, and Richard Christopher Snyder, eds. 1988. *Inside organizations: Understanding the human dimension.* Newbury Park, Calif.: Sage.

Kellner, Douglas. 1992. Popular culture and the construction of postmodern identities. In Scott Lash and Jonathan Friedman, eds., *Modernity and identity,* 141–77. Oxford: Blackwell.

Kelly, Aileen. 1992. Revealing Bakhtin. *New York Review of Books,* 24 September, 44–48.

———. 1993. Bakhtin the "outsider": A reply to Fred Davis. *New York Review of Books,* 10 June, 61–62.

Knorr Cetina, Karin. 1981. *The manufacture of knowledge.* Oxford: Pergamon.

———. 1994. Primitive classification and postmodernity: Towards a sociological notion of fiction. *Theory, Culture and Society* 11: 1–22.

Kostera, Monika. 1995. The modern crusade: The missionaries of management come to Europe. *Management Learning* 26: 331–52.

Kuhn, Thomas. 1964/1996. *The structure of scientific revolutions.* Chicago: University of Chicago Press.

Kunda, Gideon. 1991. *Engineering culture: Control and commitment in a high-tech organization.* Philadelphia: Temple University Press.

Kundera, Milan. 1988. *The art of the novel.* London: Faber and Faber.

Latour, Bruno. 1986. The powers of association. In J. Law, ed., *Power, action and belief,* 261–77. London: Routledge and Kegan Paul.

———. 1988a. *The pasteurization of France.* Cambridge: Harvard University Press.

———. 1988b. A relativistic account of Einstein's relativity. *Social Studies of Science* 18: 3–44.

———. 1992a. Technology is society made durable. In J. Law, ed., *A sociology of monsters: Essays on power, technology and domination,* 103–31. London: Routledge.

———. 1992b. The next turn after the social turn. In E. McMullin, ed., *The social dimensions of science,* 272–92. Notre Dame, Ind.: University of Notre Dame Press.

———. 1993a. Pasteur on lactic acid yeast: A partial semiotic analysis. *Configu-rations* 1 (1): 129–46.

———. 1993b. *We have never been modern.* Cambridge: Harvard University Press.

———. 1994. On technical mediation. *Common Knowledge* 3 (2): 29–64.

Laufer, Romain, and Catherine Paradeise. 1990. *Marketing democracy: Public opinion and media formation in democratic societies.* London: Transaction Publishers.

Leach, Edmund R. 1985. Observers who are part of the system. *The Times Higher Education Supplement,* 29 November, 14–18.

Leidner, Robin. 1993. Fast food, fast talk: Service work and the routinization of everyday life. Berkeley, Calif.: University of California Press.

Lejeune, Philippe. 1989. *On autobiography.* Minneapolis: University of Minnesota Press.

Lewontin, Richard C. 1995. Genes, environments and organisms. In Robert B. Silvers, ed., *Hidden histories of science,* 115–40. New York: New York Review of Books.

Lincoln, Yvonne S. 1985. The substance of the emergent paradigm: Implications for researchers. In Y. S. Lincoln, ed., *Organizational theory and inquiry: The paradigm revolution,* 137–57. Beverly Hills, Calif.: Sage.

Lindner, Rolf. 1996. *The reportage of urban culture. Robert Park and the Chicago School.* Cambridge: Cambridge University Press.

Lindsey, Stephen, Robert Grafton Small, and Paul Jefcutt, eds. 1995. *Understanding management.* London: Sage.

Lipman-Blumen, Jean, and Susan Schram. 1984. *The paradox of success: The impact of priority setting in agricultural research and extension.* Washington, D.C.: U.S. Department of Agriculture, January.

Lodge, David. 1988. *Nice work.* London: Penguin.

Löfgren, Orvar. 1993. Materializing the nation in Sweden and America. *Ethnos* 3–4: 161–96.

Luhmann, Niklas. 1986a. The autopoiesis of social systems. In Felix Geyer and Johnnes van der Zeuwen, eds., *Sociocybernetic paradoxes: Observation, control and evolution of self-steering systems,* 172–92. London: Sage.

———. 1986b. Das Problem der Epochenbildung und die Evolutionstheorie. In Hans Ulrich Gumbrecht and Ursula Link-Heer, eds., *Epochenswellen und Epochenstrukturen im Diskurs der Literatur-und Sprachhistorie,* 11–33. Frankfurt: Suhrkamp.

———. 1991. Sthenographie und Euryalistik. In Hans Ulrich Gumbrecht and K. Ludwig Pfeiffer, eds., *Paradoxien, Dissonanzen, Zusammenbrüche. Situationen offener Epistemologie,* 58–82. Frankfurt: Suhrkamp.

Lymann, Stanford M., and Marvin B. Scott. 1975. *The drama of social reality.* New York: Oxford University Press.

Lyotard, Jean-François. 1979/1986. *The postmodern condition: A report on knowledge.* Manchester: Manchester University Press.

MacIntyre, Alasdair. 1981/1990. *After virtue.* London: Duckworth Press.

———. 1988. *Whose justice? Which rationality?* Notre Dame, Ind.: University of Notre Dame Press.

MacKay, Donald M. 1964. Communication and meaning—a functional approach. In F. S. C. Northrop and Helen H. Livingston, eds., *Cross-cultural understanding: Epistemology in anthropology,* 162–79. New York: Harper and Row.

Mandler, Jean Matter. 1984. *Stories, scripts and scenes: Aspects of schema theory.* London: Lawrence Erlbaum.

Manning, Peter K. 1979. Metaphors of the field: Varieties of organizational discourse. *Administrative Science Quarterly* 24: 660–71.

———. 1992. *Organizational communication.* New York: Aldine de Gruyter.

March, James G. 1988. *Decisions and organizations.* Oxford: Blackwell.

March, James G., and Johan Olsen. 1989. *Rediscovering institutions: The organizational basis of politics.* New York: Free Press.

Marcus, George E. 1992. Past, present and emergent identities: Requirements for ethnographies of late twentieth-century modernity world-wide. In Scott Lash and Jonathan Friedman, eds., *Modernity and identity,* 309–30. Oxford: Blackwell.

Marcus, George E., and Michael M. Fischer. 1986. *Anthropology as cultural critique: An experimental moment in the human sciences.* Chicago: University of Chicago Press.

Martin, Joanne. 1982. Stories and scripts in organizational settings. In A. H. Hastrof and A. M. Isen, eds., *Cognitive social psychology,* 165–94. New York: North Holland-Elsevier.

Martin, Joanne, Mary Jo Hatch, and Sim B. Sitkin. 1983. The uniqueness paradox in organizational stories. *Administrative Science Quarterly* 28: 438–53.

McCloskey, D. N. 1986. *The rhetoric of economics.* Madison, Wis.: University of Wisconsin Press.

———. 1990. *If you're so smart: The narrative of economic expertise.* Chicago: University of Chicago Press.

Merelman, Richard M. 1969. The dramaturgy of politics. *Sociological Quarterly* 10: 216–41.

Merleau-Ponty, Maurice. 1964. *Signs.* Evanston, Ill.: Northwestern University Press.

Merton, Robert. 1965/1993. *On the shoulders of giants.* Chicago: University of Chicago Press.

Meyer, John W. 1986. Myths of socialization and of personality. In T. C. Heller, M. Sosna, and D. E. Wellbery, eds., *Reconstructing individualism: Autonomy, individuality and the self in Western thought,* 208–21. Stanford, Calif.: Stanford University Press.

Meyer, John W., John Boli, and George M. Thomas. 1987. Ontology and rationalization in the Western cultural account. In G. M. Thomas et al., eds., *Institutional structure: Constituting state, society and the individual,* 12–37. Beverly Hills, Calif.: Sage.

Meyer, John W., and Brian Rowan. 1977. Institutionalized organizations: Formal structure as myth and ceremony. *American Journal of Sociology* 83 (2): 340–63.

Mitchell, W. J. T. 1992. Culture wars. *London Review of Books* (23 Apr.): 7–10.

Mitroff, Ian, and Ralph Kilmann. 1975. Stories managers tell: A new tool for organizational problem solving. *Management Review* 64: 13–28.

Morgan, Gareth. 1986. *Images of organization.* London: Sage.

Oakeshott, Michael. 1959/1991. The voice of poetry in the conversation of mankind. In *Rationalism in politics and other essays,* 488–541. Indianapolis: Liberty Press.

Olsen, Johan P. 1970. Local budgeting, decision-making or a ritual act? *Scandinavian Political Studies* 5 (3): 85–118.

Olsen, Johan P., Paul G. Roness, and Harald Soetren. 1989. Styring gjennom institusjonsutforming. In J. P. Olsen, ed., *Petroleum og politikk.* Bergen: TANO.

Olson, Mancur. 1990. *How bright are the northern lights? Some questions about Sweden.* Lund: Lund University Press.

Overington, Michael A. 1977a. Kenneth Burke and the method of dramatism. *Theory and Society* 4: 131–56.

———. 1977b. Kenneth Burke as social theorist. *Sociological Inquiry* 47 (2): 133–41.

Park, Robert E. 1951. *Human communities.* Glencoe: Free Press.

Park, Robert E., and Ernest W. Burghess. 1921. *Introduction to the science of sociology.* Chicago: University of Chicago Press.

Peirce, Charles. 1940. *The philosophy of Peirce: Selected writings,* ed. Justus Buchler. New York: Harcourt, Brace.

Perrow, Charles. 1991. A society of organizations. *Theory and Society* 20: 725–62.

Pestoff, Victor A. 1991. *The demise of the Swedish model and the resurgence of organized business as a major political actor,* 2. Stockholm: Stockholm University Studies in Action and Enterprise.

Péteri, György. 1993. The politics of statistical information and economic research in communist Hungary. *Contemporary European History* 2 (2): 149–67.

Pinch, Trevor. 1986. *Confronting nature.* Dordrecht: Reidel.

Pitkin, Fenichel Hanna. 1972. *Wittgenstein and justice.* Berkeley, Calif.: University of California Press.

———. 1984. *Fortune is a woman: Gender and politics in the thought of Niccoló Macchiavelli.* Berkeley, Calif.: University of California Press.

Polanyi, Karl. 1944/1957. *The Great Transformation: The political and economic origins of our time.* Boston: Beacon Press.

Polanyi, Michael. 1958/1983. *Personal knowledge.* London: Routledge and Kegan Paul.

Polkinghorne, Donald. 1987. *Narrative knowing and the human sciences.* Albany, N.Y.: State University of New York Press.

Pondy, Louis, et al., eds. 1983. *Organizational symbolism.* Greenwich, Conn.: JAI Press.

Powell, Walter W. 1991. Expanding the scope of institutional analysis. In Walter W. Powell and Paul J. DiMaggio, eds., *The new institutionalism in organizational analysis,* 183–203. Chicago: University of Chicago Press.

Powell, Walter W., and Paul J. DiMaggio, eds. 1991. *The new institutionalism in organizational analysis.* Chicago: University of Chicago Press.

Putnam, Linda L., and Michael Pacanowsky, eds. 1983. *Communication and organizations: An interpretive approach.* London: Sage.

Ricoeur, Paul. 1981. The model of the text: Meaningful action considered as text. In John B. Thompson, ed. and trans., *Hermeneutics and the human sciences,* 197–221. Cambridge: Cambridge University Press.

Rombach, Björn. 1990. "I like budget for the same reason that I drink beer—I feel I need it, but I like the effect as well." In Claes Gustafsson and Lars Hassel, eds., *Accounting and organizational action,* 71–92. Åbo: Åbo Academy Press.

Rorty, Richard. 1980. *Philosophy and the mirror of nature.* Oxford: Basil Blackwell.

———. 1982. *Consequences of pragmatism.* Minneapolis: University of Minnesota Press.

———. 1987. Scientific rationality as solidarity. In J. Nelson, A. Megill, and D. N. McCloskey, eds., *The rhetoric of the human sciences,* 38–52. Madison, Wis.: University of Wisconsin Press.

———. 1989. *Contingency, irony and solidarity.* New York: Cambridge University Press.

———. 1991. Inquiry as recontextualization: An anti-dualist account of interpretation. In *Objectivity, relativism and truth: Philosophical papers,* vol. 1, 93–110. New York: Cambridge University Press.

———. 1992a. The pragmatist's progress. In Stefan Collini, ed., *Interpretation and overinterpretation,* 89–108. Cambridge: Cambridge University Press.

———. 1992b. Cosmopolitanism without emancipation: A response to Lyotard. In Scott Lash and Jonathan Friedman, eds., *Modernity and identity,* 59–72. Oxford: Blackwell.

Sacks, Harvey. 1992. *Lectures on conversation.* Oxford: Blackwell.

Sahlin-Andersson, Kerstin. 1989. *Oklarhetens strategi: Organisering av projektsamarbete.* Lund: Studentlitteratur.

Sahlins, Marshall. 1985. *Islands of history.* Chicago: University of Chicago Press.

———. 1995. *How "natives" think, about Captain Cook, for example.* Chicago: University of Chicago Press.

Samuels, Warren J. 1979. Legal realism and the burden of symbolism: The correspondence of Thurman Arnold. *Law & Society Review* 13 (4): 997–1011.

Sanday, Peggy Reeves. 1979. The ethnographic paradigm(s). *Administrative Science Quarterly* 24 (4): 527–38.

Saussure, Ferdinand de. 1983. *Course in general linguistics.* London: Duckworth.

Schneider, Susan C., and Reinhard Angelmar. 1993. Cognition in organizational analysis: Who is minding the store? *Organization Studies* 14 (3): 347–74.

Schütz, Alfred. 1953/1971. Don Quixote and the problem of reality. In A. Schütz, *Collected papers II: Studies in social theory,* 135–58. The Hague: Martinus Nijhoff.

———. 1973. On multiple realities. *Collected papers I: The problem of social reality,* 207–59. The Hague: Martinus Nijhoff.

Sclavi, Marianella. 1989. *Ad una panna da terra.* Milan: Feltrinelli.

Scott, Richard W., and John W. Meyer. 1991. The organization of societal sectors:

Propositions and early evidence. In Walter M. Powell and Paul J. DiMaggio, eds., *The new institutionalism in organizational analysis,* 108–40. Chicago: University of Chicago Press.

Sellerberg, Ann-Mari. 1987. *Avstånd och attraktion.* Stockholm: Carlssons.

Selznick, Phillip. 1949. *TVA and the grass roots.* Berkeley, Calif.: University of California Press.

Silver, Maury, and John Sabini. 1985. Feelings and constructions in making a self. In Kenneth J. Gergen and Keith E. Davis, eds., *The social construction of the person,* 191–201. New York: Springer Verlag.

Silverman, David. 1970. *Towards the new theory of organizations.* London: Heinemann.

Silverman, David, and Jill Jones. 1976. *Organizational work.* London: Collier Macmillan.

Silverman, David, and Brian Torode. 1980. *The material word: Some theories of language and its limits.* London: Routledge and Kegan Paul.

Simmel, Georg. 1904/1973. Fashion. In G. Wills and D. Midgley, eds., *Fashion marketing,* 171–91. London: Allen & Unwin.

Sims, David, Yiannis Gabriel, and Stephen Fineman. 1993. *Organizing and organizations: An introduction.* London: Sage.

Sismondo, Sergio. 1993. Some social constructions. *Social Studies of Science* 23: 515–53.

Snehota, Ivan. 1990. *Notes on theory of business enterprise.* Uppsala, Sweden: Department of Business Administration.

Solow, Robert M. 1988. Comments from inside economics. In A. Klamer, D. N. McCloskey, and R. M. Solow, eds., *The consequences of economic rhetoric,* 31–37. New York: Cambridge University Press.

Starbuck, William H. 1983. Organizations as action generators. *American Sociological Review* 48: 91–102.

Stein, Maurice R. 1960. *The eclipse of community.* Princeton, N.J.: Princeton University Press.

Stern, J. P. 1973. *On realism.* London: Routledge and Kegan Paul.

Thomas, William Isaac, and Florian Znaniecki. 1918/1920. *The Polish peasant in Europe and America.* New York: Knopf.

Thompson, G. 1991. Is accounting rhetorical? Methodology, Luca Pacioli and printing. *Accounting, Organizations and Society* 16 (5/6): 572–99.

Toulmin, Stephen. 1984. The evolution of Margaret Mead. *New York Review of Books,* 6 December, 3–9.

Traveek, Sharon. 1992. Border crossings: Narrative strategies in science studies and among physicists in Tsukuba Science City, Japan. In Andrew Pickering, ed., *Science as practice and culture,* 429–66. Chicago: University of Chicago Press.

Tryggestad, Kjell. 1995. *Teknologistrategier og postModerne Kapitalisme—Introduksjon av computerbasert produksjonsteknikk.* Lund: Lund University Press.

Turner, Barry A., ed. 1990. *Organisational symbolism.* Berlin: De Gruyter.

Tyler, Stephen. 1986. Post-modern ethnography: From document of the occult to occult document. In J. Clifford and G. Marcus, eds., *Writing culture: The poetics and politics of ethnography,* 122–40. Berkeley, Calif.: University of California Press.

Van de Ven, Andrew H., and Marshall Scott Poole. 1988. Paradoxical requirements for a theory of change. In Robert E. Quinn and Kim S. Cameron, eds., *Paradox and transformation: Toward a theory of change in organization and management,* 19–64. Cambridge, Mass.: Ballinger Publishing.

Van Maanen, John. 1982. Fieldwork on the beat. In John Van Maanen, J. Dabber, and R. Faulkner, eds., *Varieties of qualitative research.* Beverly Hills, Calif.: Sage.

————. 1988. *Tales of the field.* Chicago: University of Chicago Press.

Waldo, Dwight. 1968. *The novelist on organization and administration.* Berkeley, Calif.: Institute of Government Studies.

Warren, Roland L. 1967. The interorganizational field as a focus for investigation. *Administrative Science Quarterly* 12: 396–419.

Warren, Roland L., Stephen M. Rose, and Ann F. Bergunder. 1974. *The structure of urban reform: Community Decision Organizations in stability and change.* Lexington, Mass.: D.C. Heath.

Watts, Cedric. 1990. *Literature and money.* Hemel Hempstead, U.K.: Harvester/Wheatsheaf.

*Webster's New Collegiate Dictionary.* 1981. 8th ed. Springfield, Mass.: G. & C. Merriam Company.

Weick, Karl E. 1979. *The social psychology of organizing.* Reading, Mass.: Addison-Wesley.

Whyte, William Foote. 1943. *Street corner society.* Chicago: University of Chicago Press.

Whyte, William Hollingsworth Jr. 1956. *The organization man.* New York: Simon & Schuster.

Woolgar, Steve, ed. 1988. *Knowledge and reflexivity.* London: Sage.

Yin, Robert K. 1984. *Case study method.* Beverly Hills, Calif.: Sage.

Zeraffa, M. 1973. The novel as literary form and as social institution. In Elisabeth Burns and Thomas Burns, eds., *Sociology of literature and drama,* 35–55. Harmondsworth, U.K.: Penguin.

Zucker, Lynne G. 1987. Institutional theories of organizations. *Annual Review of Sociology* 13: 443–64.

# Index

Abelson, Robert P., 55, 213
accountability, 13, 45–46
accounts, 41, 46, 65, 67, 100, 155, 171, 192, 203
accretion, 192
action nets, 66, 67, 77, 78, 92, 109, 143, 153, 159, 179–80
actorial shifting operations, 51, 175
Ahrne, Göran, 94, 213
Albert, Stuart, 43, 213
Alexander, John, 118, 120, 210, 213
Altman, Robert, 210
Alvarez, José Luis, 27, 213
Alvesson, Mats, 43, 207, 213, 218
ambiguity, 134, 158, 171, 187
Anderson, Walter E., 35, 213
Angelmar, Reinhard, 208, 224
Anton, Thomas J., 122, 130, 213
Antonio, Robert J., 162, 213
Arnold, Thurman W., 164, 171, 174, 177, 189–90, 211, 213, 224
Åsard, Erik, 77, 213
Ashfort, Blake, 44, 213
Ashmore, Malcolm, 170, 172, 196, 213
ASIO. See Association of Social Insurance Offices
Association of Social Insurance Offices, 78, 111, 113, 133, 142, 143, 153, 154, 159
Astley, Graham W., 200, 213
Authors, 50–52, 123, 127, 134–35, 154–55, 157–58, 160, 188, 195–99, 203–205
autobiographical acts, 50, 53, 142, 153–54
autobiography, 17, 29, 30, 40, 48–49, 50, 52–53, 142, 153–54, 158, 160, 204–205
autonomy (as an aspect of modern identity), 47, 143
autopoietic systems, 97, 170

backstage, 34
Bakhtin, Mikhail M., 23, 46, 47, 62, 163, 178, 197, 198, 205, 214, 220, 223
Baldwin, John D., 44, 214
Balzac, Honoré de, 119–20, 204

Barley, Nigel, 60, 61, 214
Barthes, Roland, 11, 57, 127, 214
Baudrillard, Jean, 26, 57, 58, 214
Becker, Howard S., 13, 214
Berg, Per-Olof, 162, 207, 213, 214
Berger, Brigitta, 183, 185, 186, 214
Berger, Peter, 13, 43, 55, 63, 183, 185, 186, 192, 214
Bergunder, Ann F., 67–68, 81, 94, 98, 180, 182, 193–94, 226
Berman, Marshall, 22, 183, 214
Bernstein, Richard J., 58, 214
Björkman, Ivar, 43, 213
Blumer, Herbert, 13, 116–17, 214
Boden, Deirdre, 140, 214
Bohannan, Laura, 209, 214
Boje, David, 28, 214
Boland, Richard J. Jr., 27, 28, 122, 140, 214
Boli, John, 42, 46, 159, 190, 222
Borges, Jorge Luis, 98
Bradbury, Malcolm, 26, 215
Brown, Richard H., 7, 23–26, 45, 48, 215
Brown, Roger W., 211, 215
Bruner, Jerome, 6, 18–20, 44, 46, 50, 53, 55, 177–78, 194, 207, 208, 215
Brunsson, Nils, 93, 97, 109, 112, 114, 129, 131, 169, 172, 175, 190, 193, 215
Bruss, Elisabeth W., 7, 17, 49–50, 52–53, 208, 215
budget bill, 122–27
budgetary processes, 122–40
Bulmer, Martin, 7, 215
bureaucratic rhetoric, 151
Burghess, Ernest W., 223
Burke, Kenneth, 30–32, 35, 43, 57, 97, 167–69, 208, 211, 215, 223
Burrell, Gibson, 28, 54, 212, 215
Buzzatti, Dino, 98

Calás, Marta, 47, 212, 215
Callon, Michel, 127, 179, 198, 216
canonical tradition, 68

Capote, Truman, 62
case studies, 26, 27, 64, 65
Castaneda, Carlos, 60, 216
catharsis, 36, 120
Chandler, Alfred D., 64, 216
characters, 32, 37, 40, 50–52, 123, 131,
    142, 153, 155, 157, 180, 184
Chicago School, 7
Cicourel, Aaron V., 13, 216
Clark, Burton R., 27, 216
Clegg, Stewart, 58, 216
Clifford, James, 216, 226
climax, 120
Cohen, Joel, 110
coherence (of an identity narrative), 48, 52
Collins, Harry M., 65, 216
commitment (in an identity narrative), 48
company-ization, 71, 79, 100–109, 117,
    121, 159, 168, 188
computerization, 109–17, 121, 158
congeries, 144, 148
constellation, 66
construction of meaning, 55, 63, 65, 92
constructivist views, 24, 39–41, 44, 55, 66,
    131, 153, 169, 192, 202
continuity (in an identity narrative), 48, 52
control philosophy, 38–41, 130, 159
conversations, 13, 14, 42, 44–45, 53, 63,
    66, 69–71, 96, 108, 136, 153, 159, 180,
    195, 200
Cortazar, Julio, 98
County Social Insurance Offices, 78, 133,
    136,153
critical reader. See semiotic reader
CSIO. See County Social Insurance Offices
Czarniawska-Joerges, Barbara, 27, 29, 35,
    41, 58, 66, 116, 117, 122, 132, 136,
    203, 216

d'Ormesson, Jean, 203
Dada, 22
Darwin, Charles, 3, 4
Davies, Bronwyn, 14, 30, 44, 181, 207,
    217
Day, W. F., 140, 215
demise of the narrative, 25, 26, 181
demise of the Swedish Model, 75
demonization, 115
DeMott, B., 27, 217
deparadoxification, 31, 37, 98, 173–90

DeVault, Marjorie L., 201, 217
device, 6, 47, 49–50, 59, 71, 78, 93, 96,
    118, 120, 167, 169, 171, 179, 185, 188,
    191, 194, 196, 197. See also material
dialectical narrative, 205
dialogical: approach, 197; narrative, 205;
    relationship, 178; self, 46
Diener, Paul, 97, 217
differentiation, 183
diffusion, 95
DiMaggio, Paul J., 6 43, 77, 159, 186,
    187, 189–94, 212, 217, 223, 225
Douglas, Mary, 42, 46, 68, 162, 217
Downs, G. W., 76, 217
drama, 29–38, 93, 97–98, 117, 120, 121,
    140, 150, 168
dramatism, 30
dramatistic: method, 30–31, 35, 40, 130,
    167; model (pentad), 32, 53
dramatization, 34
Dukerich, Janet M., 43, 217
Dutton, Jane E., 43, 217

Eco, Umberto, 51, 70, 118–20, 134–35,
    199–200, 203, 209–10, 217, 224
economic decline, 35, 37
Edelman, Murray, 36, 122, 131, 217
efficiency (as an aspect of modern iden-
    tity), 47, 143
Emerson, Caryl, 223
enacted narratives, 13, 15, 122
enthymeme, 148
epistemological crisis, 176
ergonography, 202–206
Escher, M. C., 98–99, 170, 188
ethnomethodology, 13, 69, 140, 205
ethos, 144, 145, 148
expert rhetoric, 148
explanation, 18–20, 141, 168, 199. See
    also interpretation
extopy. See outsidedness
extralinguistic reality, 20

fashion: 101, 116–17, 148, 161, 167, 185,
    187; leaders, 117
feminine narrative, 120
Feyerabend, Paul, 26
Fineman, Stephen, 27, 225
Fischer, Michael M., 62, 208, 222

Fish, Stanley, 201, 217
Fisher, Walter R., 6, 21–25, 28, 30, 152, 153, 207, 218
Fiske, John, 120
Fitzgerald, Scott F., 123, 203
Flaubert, Gustave, 95
flexibility (as an aspect of modern identity), 47, 143
Forester, John, 28, 218
Freud, Sigmund, 30
friction, 79–82, 94–98, 172
frontstage, 34
Frost, Peter, 27, 28, 218, 223
Frye, Northrop, 191, 218
Frykman, Jonas, 185, 218
Fukuyama, Francis, 14, 218
Fuller, Steve, 62, 218
Fussell, Paul, 121, 218

Gabriel, Yiannis, 27, 28, 218, 225
Gagliardi, Pasquale, 28, 216, 218
Garfinkel, Harold, 13, 207, 208, 218
garfinkeling, 59
Geertz, Clifford, 5, 7, 15, 31, 51, 54, 61, 178, 195, 198, 203, 218
genre, 16, 17, 29, 31, 40, 43, 48–50, 120, 178–81, 184, 187–88, 191, 202
Gergen, Kenneth J., 44, 45, 48, 141, 179, 183, 184, 194, 208, 218, 225
Giddens, Anthony, 25, 46 218
Ginzburg, Carlo, 65, 218, 219
Godzich, Wlad, 211, 212, 219
Goffman, Erving, 30, 31, 35, 56, 219
Goodman, Nelson, 24, 68, 219
Gorgons, the, 174, 176
Gould, Stephen Jay, 4, 219
Greenwood, Royston, 117, 219
Guillet de Monthoux, Pierre, 27, 29, 161, 216, 219
Gumbrecht, Hans Ulrich, 22, 173, 174, 175, 176, 180, 219, 221
Gustavsen, Bjørn, 23, 219

Habermas, Jürgen, 23, 45, 219
Harari, Josue V., 11, 50, 219
Harré, Rom, 12, 13, 14, 30, 44, 181, 202, 207, 217, 219
Hatch, Mary Jo, 27, 152, 219, 222
Hedberg, Bo, 3

Heller, Joseph, 2
hermeneutics, 12, 141
Hernadi, Paul, 211, 219
Hernes, Gudmund, 163, 219
*heteroglossia* (variegated speech), 197
high modernity, 46
Hinings, Bob, 117, 219
Hirdman, Yvonne, 172, 219
historical ethnographies, 65
Hofstadter, Douglas, 170, 220
Hofstede, Geert, 122, 128, 220
Holzner, Burkhard, 55, 220
*Homo narrans,* 21
*Homo oeconomicus,* 137
human action, 12–14, 141

ideal speech situation, 23
ideas in residence, 95
identification, 36, 62, 120
identity, 32, 40, 43–44, 77, 105, 106, 108, 142, 158–59, 171, 179, 182–88, 203; crisis, 142, 176; as a modern institution, 30–39, 142, 183; as a narrative, 46–47, 49
illusion of controllability, 38–40
individuality, 183
inherited devices, 3
institutional: isomorphism, 186–88; order, 43, 48; thought structure, 67–68, 98, 126, 152, 163, 180, 191–92
institutionalism, 6, 7, 67–68, 71, 87, 140, 163, 181, 182, 186–87, 189–92
institutionalization, 138, 188
institutions, 5, 24, 31, 40, 42–46, 49–50, 92, 109, 143, 161, 164, 172, 174, 176–77, 179, 180–81, 183–84, 189, 191, 192
interpretation, 18, 20, 71, 96, 124, 127, 133–35, 138–39, 163, 180, 195, 198–201, 204. *See also* explanation
interpretive approaches, 26, 28, 54–55, 57, 62–64, 71
*interrogatio,* 149
interruption, 59, 96–98, 118, 120, 172, 175
interruptive narrative, 205
irony, 26, 58, 144

Jacobsson, Bengt, 122, 132, 136, 208, 216, 220

Jansson, David, 141, 171, 220
Joerges, Bernward, 116, 216
Jones, Jill, 13, 140, 225
Jones, Michael Owen, 28, 220
Jönsson, Sten, 129, 215

Kafka, Franz, 2
Kavolis, Vytautas, 48
Kellner, Douglas, 184, 185, 220
Kellner, Hanfried, 183, 185, 186, 214
Kelly, Aileen, 62, 178, 220
Kilmann, Ralph, 27, 223
Knorr Cetina, Karen, 65, 216, 220
Kostera, Monika, 15, 220
Kuhn, Thomas, 54, 220
Kunda, Gideon, 196, 220
Kundera, Milan, 16, 34, 95, 96, 220

language: 57, 69, 123, 134, 137–38, 148,
    152, 164, 181, 185, 189–90, 193,
    196–97; of bureaucracy, 144; of experts,
    144; of the market, 147
Larkey, Patrick D., 76, 217
late modernism, 23
Latour, Bruno, 2, 5, 13, 51, 55, 65, 70,
    95–96, 109, 127, 175, 177, 179, 185,
    198, 203, 216, 220, 221
Laufer, Romain, 137–38, 221
Leach, Edmund R., 4, 221
Leidner, Robin, 26, 221
Lejeune, Philippe, 48, 53, 180, 181, 191,
    208, 212, 221
Lewontin, Richard C., 3, 221
Lincoln, Yvonne S., 28, 221
Lindner, Rolf, 7, 221
Lipman-Blumen, Jean, 172, 221
Lodge, David, 5, 221
logic of appropriateness, 190
logic of consequentiality, 190
logic of inquiry, 54, 169
logo-scientific mode of knowing, 18, 20–
    21, 26–27, 177, 180. See also paradig-
    matic mode
logos, 144–45, 151
Luckmann, Thomas, 13, 43, 55, 63, 192,
    214
Luhmann, Niklas, 26, 37, 94, 97, 98, 116,
    168–69, 173–74, 176, 189–90, 192,
    211, 212, 221

Lymann, Stanford M., 30, 221
Lynch, David, 107
Lyotard, Jean-François, 5, 14, 17–18, 25–
    26, 161, 162, 170, 176, 221
Löfgren, Orvar, 209, 218, 221

MacIntyre, Alasdair, 6, 11–12, 15–16, 21–
    25, 32–34, 39–40, 42, 48, 68, 160, 176,
    181, 183, 208, 212, 221
MacKay, Donald M., 61, 222
Mael, Fred, 44, 213
Mandler, Jean Matter, 18, 77, 209, 222
Manning, Peter K., 95, 171, 174, 222
March, James G., 6, 42, 46, 94, 159, 171,
    174, 190, 222
Marcus, George E., 62, 185, 186, 195,
    197, 208, 212, 216, 222, 226
Martin, Joanne, 27, 218, 222
material, 47, 66, 68, 69, 78, 95, 116, 118,
    143, 167, 183, 185, 188. See also device
Maturana, Humberto, 190
McCloskey, D. N., 7, 122, 140, 144, 219,
    222, 224, 225
Mead, George Herbert, 30, 44, 216
Mead, Margaret, 60, 225
meaning, 134, 168, 180, 197, 199, 205
Merchán Cantos, Carmen, 27, 213
Merelman, Richard M., 36, 120, 222
Merleau-Ponty, Maurice, 168, 222
Merton, Robert, 95, 222
metaaccounts, 62
*Metamorphoses*, 1
metanarratives, 14, 15, 18, 25, 162
metaphors: 1, 122, 127, 130, 138–40, 144,
    145, 148 176, 186–88, 203; of the field,
    95; of identity, 157; of the organization
    as superperson, 41–42, 46, 142
Meyer, John W., 6, 42, 46, 48, 143, 159,
    182, 190, 222, 224
Mitchell, V. F., 27, 218
Mitchell, W. J. T., 34, 222, 223
Mitroff, Ian, 27, 223
Model Author, 209
Model Reader, 70, 209
modern: identity, 31, 42, 48, 143, 183,
    185; institutions, 40, 46, 171, 181; proj-
    ect, 39, 161–62, 172
modernist: aesthetics, 118; ethnography,
    195; lament, 184; rhetoric, 141; world
    view, 152

modernity, 17, 33, 46, 161, 183
Moore, Michael Dane, 28, 220
moral discourse, 25, 85, 164
moral philosophy, 11
Morgan, Gareth, 28, 41, 54, 122, 215, 223
Morson, Gary Saul, 223
muddling through, 121
Mulkay, Michael, 172, 196, 213
multiple realities, 30, 163
multivocality. See polyphony

naive reader. See semantic reader
narration as the constitutive action mode,
    179–80
narrative: approaches, 5, 6, 11, 24–25,
    160, 163, 183, 186; fidelity, 22; of iden-
    tity, 14; institutionalism, 194; knowl-
    edge, 34, 55, 167; mode of communicat-
    ing, 21; mode of knowing, 17, 18, 19,
    24, 27; paradigm, 30, 152–53, 186;
    presentation, 19; probability, 22; ratio-
    nality, 22
narrativization, 174
Narrators, 50–52, 153, 158, 205
National Social Insurance Board, 75, 78,
    88–90, 110–14, 132, 151, 153, 155,
    157–59
Nonini, Donald, 97, 217
Nord, Walter S., 27, 218
novel, 16, 29, 50, 70, 118, 120, 197, 204
NSI. See National Social Insurance Board

Oakeshott, Michael, 7, 71, 223
observant participation, 66
officialese, 144, 148, 152
Olsen, Johan P., 6, 42, 46, 122, 128, 159,
    171, 172, 190, 193, 215, 222, 223
Olson, Mancur, 161, 223
open text (work), 13, 132, 134, 139, 201
organization fields, 66–67, 77, 79, 158,
    159, 165, 179, 180–87
organizational: autobiographical acts, 40,
    52, 204; communication, 28; control,
    35; drama, 36; fashion, 100; genres,
    135; identities, 46, 52, 184; identity
    crisis, 41; narratives, 26–27, 58, 142,
    171; symbolism, 28; texts, 72, 139
Orwell, George, 56
outsidedness, 62

Overington, Michael A., 168, 208, 223
overinterpretation, 195, 199–201
Ovid, 1
oxymoron, 183

Pacanovsky, Michael, 28, 54, 224
Pacioli, Luca, 138, 225
Paradeise, Catherine, 137–38, 221
paradigmatic mode of knowing, 18, 22,
    55, 167, 177
paradox: 31–32, 39, 87, 92–94, 97–99,
    105, 109, 117, 131, 152, 156, 162, 167–
    93, 197, 200–202; of applied pragma-
    tism, 199; of applied relativism, 195
paradoxicality, 31, 98, 171, 175, 181,
    190
paralogy, 31, 167–70
Park, Robert E., 7, 223
participant observation, 66
pathos, 144
Peirce, Charles, 57, 223
periodization, 115, 116
Perrow, Charles, 1, 12, 223
personification, 36, 120
Pestoff, Victor A., 162, 223
Péteri, György, 138, 223
phenomenology, 13, 140
pidgin, 62
Pilhes, René-Victor, 2
Pinch, Trevor, 65, 172, 196, 213, 223
Pitkin, Fenichel Hanna, 48, 171, 223
plot, 18, 32, 43–44, 78, 86, 97 177, 180,
    181, 192, 193
poetics, 23, 134, 135, 197
Polanyi, Karl, 223
Polanyi, Michael, 223
political rhetoric, 144, 148, 151
Polkinghorne, Donald, 6, 18–19, 223
polyphony, 96, 163, 195–98
Pondy, Louis, 28, 223
positioning, 14, 44, 53, 108
postmodern: condition, 23, 34, 117, 135,
    161–62, 184, 194; identity, 183–85
Powell, Walter W., 6, 43, 159, 186–94,
    212, 217, 223, 225
power, 24, 61, 67, 93, 94, 111, 112, 115,
    125, 135, 162, 181, 187
pragmatic counting, 137. See also symbolic
    counting
pragmatism, 13, 169, 177, 199–201

prospective studies, 65
Putnam, Linda L., 28, 54, 224


quest, 15, 16, 142, 160–63, 171, 183–84, 186


reflectivity, 183
relational self, 179
retrospective studies, 65
return of the narrative, 25
Reytersvärd, Oskar, 99
rhetoric, 29, 45, 135, 138–39, 141, 144–59, 171, 180, 188
Ricoeur, Paul, 12, 141, 224
rituals of reason, 122
Robkin, Eugene E., 97, 217
Rogers, Everett, 95
Roman virtues, 48
romanticist rhetoric, 141
Rombach, Björn, 122, 224
Roness, Paul G., 159, 223
Rorty, Richard, 4, 14, 22, 23, 41, 44, 45, 56, 57, 58, 59, 64, 72, 169, 185, 199–200, 209, 212, 224
Rose, Stephen M., 67–68, 81, 94, 98, 180, 182, 193–94, 226
routines, 75, 78, 92, 95, 98, 129, 150, 172, 174, 194
Rowan, Brian, 190, 222
Rusted, Brian, 212


Sabini, John, 45, 225
Sacks, Harvey, 13, 224
Sahlin-Andersson, Kerstin, 159, 224
Sahlins, Marshall, 65, 224
SALA. See Swedish Association of Local Authorities
Samuels, Warren J., 174, 224
Sanday, Peggy Reeves, 60, 224
Sartre, Jean-Paul, 205
Saussure, Ferdinand de, 57, 168, 224
scene-act ratio, 35, 37, 39, 43, 130–31
Schneider, Susan C., 208, 224
Schram, Susan, 172, 221
Schütz, Alfred, 12, 13, 22, 30, 45, 55, 193, 224
Sclavi, Marianella, 62, 224
Scott, Marvin B., 30, 221

Scott, Richard W., 182, 224
Scott Poole, Marshall, 171, 226
screenplay, 122, 123
Secord, Paul F., 202, 219
self: 57, 178; conceptual, 208; essentialist, 40, 43, 208; image, 138; —, reflection, 170, 176, 188–91, 196, 200, 203, 205; —, respect (as an aspect of modern identity), 47, 143; as an institutionalized myth, 45; as narrator, 50; as socially constructed, 45
Sellerberg, Ann-Mari, 117, 225
Selznick, Phillip, 225
semiotic (critical) reader, 34, 70, 119, 199
semantic (naive) reader, 70, 119, 199
semantic and semiotic readings, 72
semiotics, 141
sequentiality, 19
serials, 78–79, 100–21, 167, 168, 187
Silver, Maury, 45, 225
Silverman, David, 13, 58, 59, 96, 140, 205, 225
Simmel, Georg, 116, 225
Sims, David, 27, 225
Sismondo, Sergio, 192, 225
Sitkin, Sim B., 27, 222
Smircich, Linda, 47, 215
Snehota, Ivan, 67, 225
Snyder, Richard Christopher, 28, 220
Soetren, Harald, 159, 223
Solow, Robert M., 140, 225
spatialization, 175
sports metaphor, 145, 182
stage directions, 122, 131
stage-set, 35, 38–40, 75, 128, 142, 181
Starbuck, William H., 41, 225
Stein, Maurice R., 7, 225
Stern, J. P., 204, 225
stock of characters, 32–33, 153
stories, 78, 79, 92, 93, 117, 122, 140, 167, 187, 191, 199, 203, 204
strong program, 172, 173
Study of Power and Democracy in Sweden, the, 76
suspense, 36, 119, 120, 136, 144
Svevo, Italo, 2
Swedish Association of Local Authorities, 78, 81, 83–87, 98, 102–103, 126, 142–43, 155
Swedish Model, 76, 142, 161
Swedish public sector, 75–164, 167

symbolic counting, 137. *See also* pragmatic counting
symbolic interactionism, 13
symbolic realism 23
symbolist analysis, 122, 187
symmetrical anthropology, 5

tacit knowledge, 24
tales from the field, 63, 76
tales of the field, 63, 78
Tankasi, Ramkrishnan V., 27, 215
Taylorism, 3
temporary and localized agreements, 56
temporization, 174, 175
textual strategies, 50, 68, 153, 194, 202, 203
theater metaphor, 30–31, 117, 131, 167–68
theme, 78–79, 117, 167, 187
Thomas, George M., 42, 46, 159, 190, 222
Thomas, William Isaac, 7, 225
Thompson, G., 138, 225
thought worlds, 68, 193
Torode, Brian, 13, 58, 59, 96, 140, 205, 225
Toulmin, Stephen, 60, 225
translation, 95, 96, 186, 198
Traveek, Sharon, 65, 225
traveling ideas, 95
Tryggestad, Kjell, 208, 225
Turner, Barry A., 28, 225
Tyler, Stephen, 96, 195, 197, 209, 225

unmasking, 34, 120, 182

Van de Ven, Andrew H., 171, 226
Van Maanen, John, 13, 26, 78, 199, 226
Varela, 190
Vico, Giambattista, 17
Vidal, Gore, 51, 208

Waldo, Dwight, 1, 27, 226
Warren, Roland L., 67–68, 81, 94, 98, 180, 182, 193–94, 226
Watts, Cedric, 203, 226
weak program, 173
Weick, Karl E., 3, 87, 124, 190, 226
Whetten, David, 43, 213
Whyte, William Foote, 7, 226
Whyte, William Hollingsworth Jr., 2, 58, 226
window studies, 64–65
Wolfe, Thomas, 26
Woolgar, Steve, 198, 226

Yin, Robert, 64, 226

Zammuto, Raymond F., 200, 213
Zeraffa, M., 186, 226
Znaniecki, Florian, 7, 225
Zucker, Lynne G., 190, 219, 226